N
W
E
S
NEW
YORK
DUTCHESS
ORANGE
PUTNAM
CO
FAIRFIELD
WESTCHESTER
ROCKLAND
Hudson River
Delaware River
PASSAIC
NEW
JERSEY
BERGEN
MORRIS
ESSEX
HUDSON
NEW YORK
BRONX
QUEENS
NASSAU
KINGS
UNION
RICHMOND
Long
SOMERSET
MIDDLESEX
MONMOUTH
Delaware River
Atlantic

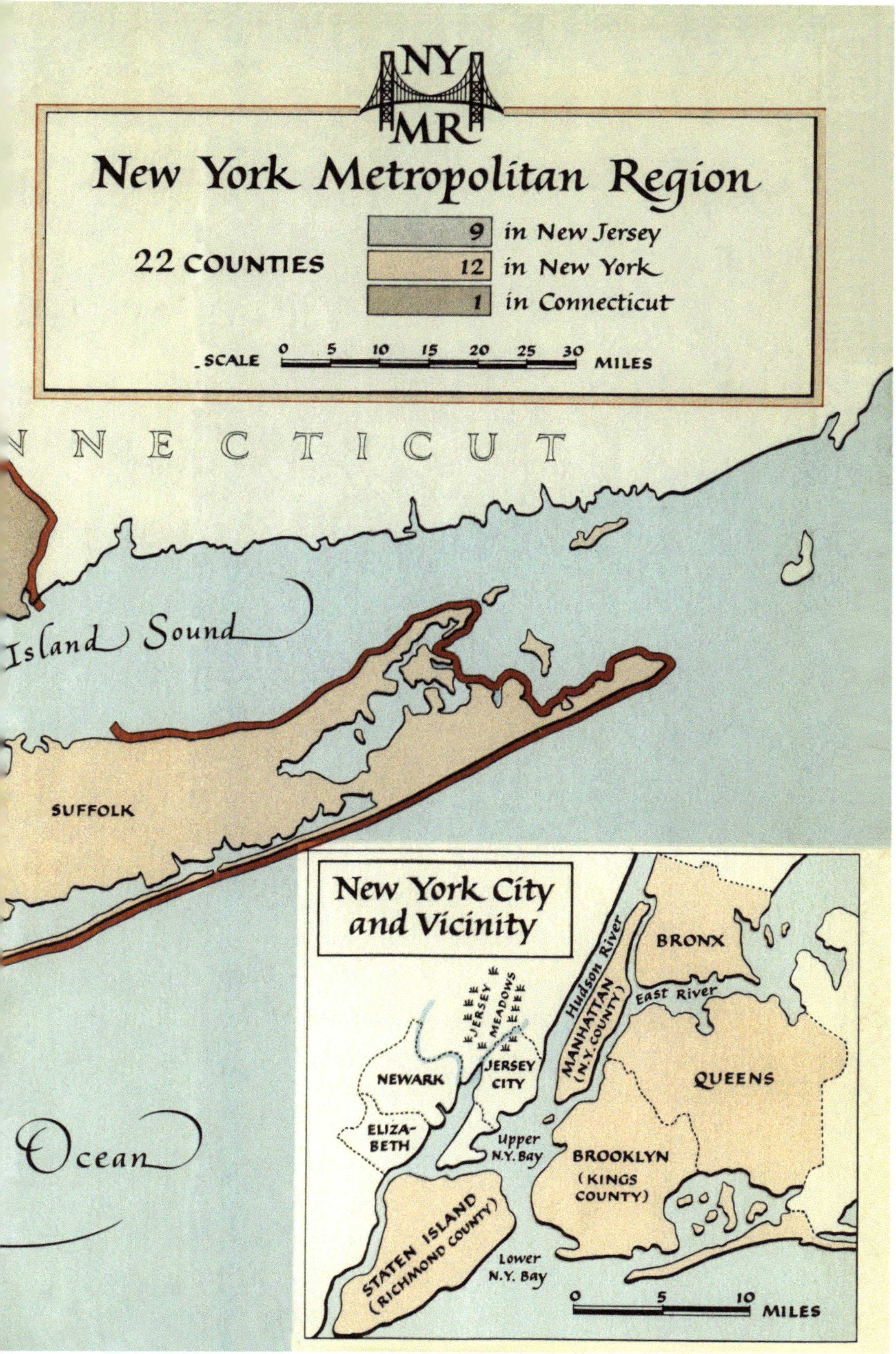
NY
MR
New York Metropolitan Region
22 COUNTIES
9 in New Jersey
12 in New York
1 in Connecticut
SCALE 0 5 10 15 20 25 30 MILES
NECTICUT
Island Sound
SUFFOLK
Ocean
New York City and Vicinity
BRONX
Hudson River
MANHATTAN (N.Y. COUNTY)
East River
JERSEY MEADOWS
JERSEY CITY
NEWARK
QUEENS
ELIZA-BETH
Upper N.Y. Bay
BROOKLYN (KINGS COUNTY)
STATEN ISLAND (RICHMOND COUNTY)
Lower N.Y. Bay
0 5 10 MILES

NEW YORK METROPOLITAN REGION STUDY

RAYMOND VERNON, DIRECTOR

A STUDY UNDERTAKEN BY THE GRADUATE SCHOOL OF PUBLIC ADMINISTRATION, HARVARD UNIVERSITY, FOR REGIONAL PLAN ASSOCIATION, INC.

Max Hall, Editorial Director

MONEY METROPOLIS

A LOCATIONAL STUDY OF FINANCIAL ACTIVITIES IN THE NEW YORK REGION

By Sidney M. Robbins
and Nestor E. Terleckyj

With the collaboration of Ira O. Scott, Jr.

HARVARD UNIVERSITY PRESS
Cambridge, Massachusetts · 1960

Endpaper map by Jeanyee Wong

Charts by H. I. Forman

Designed by Marcia R. Lambrecht

Library of Congress Catalog Card Number 60-8001
Printed in the United States of America

Foreword

This is one of a series of books on the forces that shape metropolitan areas. In particular, the series has to do with the forces that shape the largest and most complex metropolitan area in the United States, a 22-county expanse which takes in parts of three states but which, for convenience, we have termed the New York Metropolitan Region.

In 1956, the Regional Plan Association, a nonprofit research and planning agency whose purpose is to promote the coordinated development of these 22 counties, requested the Graduate School of Public Administration of Harvard University to undertake a three-year study of the Region. The challenging task was to analyze the key economic and demographic features of the Region and to project them to 1965, 1975, and 1985.

The resulting studies are reports to the Regional Plan Association. At the same time, they are designed to be of service to a much broader audience. Most Americans now live in metropolitan areas; indeed, ever-increasing proportions of the world's populations are gravitating to metropolitan clusters. Their well-being depends to a considerable extent on how these areas develop. Yet the scholar's understanding of the currents underlying the rise of such areas seems grossly inadequate.

As a study of these underlying currents, this project is neither a blueprint for action nor an analysis of metropolitan government. It has no recommendations to make about the physical structure of the Region or about the form or activities of the governmental bodies there. At the same time, it is a necessary prelude to future planning studies of the Region and to well considered recommendations for governmental action. Its end product is an analysis of the Region's probable development, assuming that the economic and demographic forces in sight follow their indicated course and assuming that the role of government is largely limited to existing policies.

The results of the Study, it is hoped, will be applied in many ways. Governments and enterprises in the Region should be in a better position to plan their future programs if they become more closely aware of the economic environment in which they may expect to operate. Other metropolitan areas, it is already evident, will benefit from the methodology and the conclusions which the Study has developed.

From the first, there has been a general recognition that the main part of the Study would have to be done by a group located within the New York Metropolitan Region and devoted exclusively to the project. Such a group was assembled in New York. The work that followed was a complex partnership. The New York staff functioned in close harness with members of the Harvard University faculty. It drew on the faculties of other universities, including Columbia University, Fordham University, Hofstra College, New York University, and Rutgers University. It obtained the help of dozens of governmental organizations in the Region, and literally hundreds of private groups and individuals. It made use of the materials which the Regional Plan Association had painstakingly pulled together in prior years.

Each book in the series has a place in the total structure of the Study; yet each is designed to be a complete work in itself. A summary report, containing the synthesis and projections of the Study, is scheduled for publication in the fall of 1960.

It is not easy to account for all the elements that went into the making of this book nor of the others in the series. The Regional Plan Association performed an indispensable function in conceiving and sponsoring the idea of a study. The Ford Foundation and the Rockefeller Brothers Fund provided the financial support for the New York Metropolitan Region Study as a whole. Supplementary funds were generously provided by Merrill Foundation for Advancement of Financial Knowledge, Inc., to support this particular volume in the series. The usual formula in such a situation obviously applies: credit for the Study's results must be shared with those who helped to bring it about, but the onus of error or omission lies with us.

Sidney M. Robbins was in charge of the study that produced this book, and was the principal author. Nestor E. Terleckyj participated fully in the preparation of the whole volume, giving special attention to the planning and execution of statistical analysis. Ira O. Scott, Jr., collaborated on numerous aspects, especially those concerned with the money market. Sandra Troy gave invaluable support in the preparation of the data.

While the several volumes in the series bear the names of their principal authors, the undertaking as a whole has been under the direction of Raymond Vernon. He is responsible for the summary report and substantial parts of other studies, and his guidance is evident throughout the series.

EDWARD S. MASON
for the Graduate School
of Public Administration,
Harvard University

Contents

Tables

APPENDIX A

APPENDIX B

APPENDIX C

Charts

Money Metropolis

I

The Rise of New York as a Money Market

New York was a world "capital" as far back as the 1690's. At that time it was the center of organized piracy, and notorious brigands roamed its streets and mingled with its inhabitants. About 150 years later, after much political and economic change, the City became a new kind of capital—this time of finance. Some historians have claimed, perhaps a bit cynically, that the piratical overtones remained, and they coined the lusty phrase "robber barons" to describe the Drews, Goulds, Fisks, and Vanderbilts of this later period. With the passing years, the "blood and thunder" faded; finance not only gained respectability but also assumed a mounting role in the economic life of the City and of the nation. As a sign of the change, Wall Street, once a nameless road fronting a wooden fence, became a national landmark and a dynamo for the nation's business.

Today, New York and finance seem to belong together. And the future role of the financial community of the New York Metropolitan Region will have a considerable influence on the development of the Region itself.

THE FINANCIAL COMMUNITY

A financial community is nothing more than the financial institutions of a given area. Most of these institutions are intermediaries; instead of acquiring tangible assets for operations, as a manufacturer or a retailer does, they "receive funds from other economic units as creditors, stockholders, or trustees and use these funds to make loans to, or to buy securities of, other economic units which they do not control. . . ."[1] Accordingly, they include commercial banks, insurance companies, securities dealers and brokers, savings institutions, finance companies, and investment companies. We also place in the financial community such supporting institutions as the clearing houses and securities exchanges.

The fact that a financial community embraces so many different components increases the complexity of identifying the forces that determine the location of financial activities. And the complexity is increased further by the multiplicity of functions which the components perform. A large commercial bank may render as many as seventy separate services, from accepting deposits to providing financial advice. Insurance companies also engage in varied activities, from providing annuities to operating large-scale housing developments. Yet there do exist common forces, determining the geographical distribution of financial institutions in the nation and the size and structure of the financial communities of large metropolitan areas.

The purpose of this book is to throw light on these forces, particularly as they have affected, and will affect, the New York Metropolitan Region.* Through the generation of payrolls and the use of space, the financial community exerts a direct impact on the Region's economic life. This impact can be gauged by one simple measure—the number of employees involved. Therefore, in analyzing the locational shifts of financial activities, we use manpower as our yardstick. Other things being equal, we will devote more attention to large users of manpower, notably the commercial banks and the life insurance companies, than to other groups of employers—such as mutual savings banks or savings and loan associ-

* The New York Metropolitan Region is mapped inside the front and back covers of the book. Five of its 22 counties are in New York City. There are also seven others in New York State (Nassau, Suffolk, Westchester, Rockland, Orange, Dutchess, and Putnam); nine in New Jersey (Hudson, Union, Essex, Passaic, Bergen, Monmouth, Middlesex, Somerset, and Morris); and one in Connecticut (Fairfield).

ations—whose contribution to the Region is quite substantial in some ways but whose employment rolls are comparatively light. On the other hand, there are some central segments of the financial community—to be discussed in this and the next chapter—whose importance in a locational sense far transcends the number of people they hire. These segments do not need much manpower but they attract other activities with great employment requirements; and thus their importance to the Region comes back, after all, to the matter of manpower.

Though our primary interest is the financial community of the New York Metropolitan Region—and its likely development during the next few decades—it is useful first of all to look at the country at large. The future of the Region's financial community is inseparable from that of the nation's, and the future of both is sufficiently linked with past developments to call for a brief sketch of the way in which the national financial community grew and of the circumstances that led to the centering of finance in New York City.

✓ Growth of the National Financial Community

Financial employment was negligible in the early American economy. A weak banking structure, dominated by state banks issuing a heterogeneous mass of currency, hampered the building of an effective credit system and held back the rise of financial institutions. As late as 1870, employment in finance accounted for little more than 0.3 per cent of the nation's jobs.

By that time, however, the situation was already changing fast. The thriving nation fostered larger and more complex business organizations. The credit needs flowing from this expansion could not be satisfied through private financing and informal arrangements. Therefore commercial banks began to enter the picture in increasing numbers. Moreover, the adoption of the National Banking Act in 1863 and subsequent monetary legislation created a stronger financial system with more uniform currency. Businessmen made greater use of check-book money and bank credit. The applications of the principles of insurance became more widely understood. In response to these developments the financial community absorbed a larger proportion of national employment of all kinds—probably around 1.4 per cent by 1910—thus manifesting a rate of employment growth several times greater than that of the rest of the economy.

The climate for the expansion of financial services continued favorable. Establishment of the Federal Reserve System in 1913 facilitated the exchange of funds among commercial banks and increased their lending power. To provide resources for meeting the needs of mushrooming populations, specialized financing agencies arose and the already established institutions broadened their activities. By 1929, employment in finance represented 3.2 per cent of the nation's total employment.

After 1929, the Great Depression slashed the percentage, hitting financial employment harder than other kinds. World War II brought a boom in most jobs but not in financial personnel. By 1944, while manufacturing employment had risen 64 per cent over 1929, insurance had grown only 5 per cent and banking had actually contracted 15 per cent. The net result was that financial employment in 1944 was only 1.8 per cent of total employment. But after the war the pattern was reversed once more; a swift rise in financial employment lifted it to 3.3 per cent in 1956.[2]

Emergence of the New York money market

All this time, as the nation's financial community grew, the financial institutions of the New York area grew as well. But their evolution took a highly specialized turn. Eventually there emerged in the New York Metropolitan Region a group of institutions and services which collectively function as the nation's principal money market, where all sorts of financial instruments, both long-term and short-term, are traded.* And because of this specialized de-

* Since our purpose is to make a locational analysis, we do not find it necessary to draw the distinction often drawn between a "money market,"

velopment, New York's financial community, unlike those of other metropolitan areas, came to serve not only its own hinterland but also the entire country.

It is important to understand how New York acquired this status, and to do so we must focus for a while on that portion of financial activities termed the money market. In a broad sense, a money market is an aggregate of interconnected markets in which funds required for varying intervals and purposes are shifted between borrowers and lenders. Responsive to changing historical pressures, the different segments of the New York money market have risen, flourished, and sometimes declined at different points in time.

In addition, there are certain other institutions in the financial community—some of great importance—which have grown over the years but have relatively weak ties with the heart of the money market. Notable among these institutions is the insurance industry. The historical forces that drew this industry to the New York area will be discussed in later chapters. The specialized parts of the money market itself are our present concern.

All kinds of money-market trading have shown an affinity for New York. Yet it was not always obvious that this would be so. When the United States began to take form as a nation, the signs pointed to Philadelphia as the country's first money market. Both politics and economics conspired to this end in those early years, but politics took the lead.[3]

The colonial environment had not been propitious for the development of a money market. Merchant houses had performed the banking functions of deposit and discount as an incidental part of their commercial activities. The so-called banks of that period had given their attention principally to mortgages on real

---

where short-term instruments are traded, and a "capital market," where long-term instruments are traded. A description of the relation between the New York financial community and the money market as we conceive it appears in Chapter 2.

estate. Joint stock companies and corporations had scarcely existed. The British authorities had frowned upon the establishment of American commerce, manufactures, and financial institutions.

The new nation, therefore, possessed little experience in the ways of finance, and its political leaders, after severing ties with Britain, could not draw much on existing arrangements. Thus, they were abruptly confronted with the responsibility of developing the institutional paraphernalia necessary to provide a flow of funds for financing the war and for the subsequent economic growth of the country. Finance became the handmaiden of politics, and pressures developed for creating a money market in the nation's political capital.

Philadelphia, the seat of the Continental Congress, became the location of the nation's first commercial bank, the Bank of Pennsylvania. That was in 1780. The services of this institution in helping to finance the war soon encouraged the Congress to give a national charter to the Bank of North America, which for a time served in effect as the nation's central bank, granting loans to the Government, holding its deposits, and acting as its fiscal agent. Hence, Philadelphia also was the logical location for the Bank of the United States, sponsored by Alexander Hamilton and chartered by Congress in 1791 as the central bank of the republic. With its prestige thus enhanced, Philadelphia became the unchallenged banking center of the country.

Early economic factors joined political ones in Philadelphia's behalf. The city at that time led the nation in both domestic and foreign trade; it was also the home of the few Americans with skill in banking methods, including Robert Morris, Nicholas Biddle, and Stephen Girard. Philadelphia's capitalists, who were the principal American holders of continental bonds, in 1791 founded the first securities exchange of the infant nation. Accordingly, Philadelphia also became the market center for securities and foreign exchange.

Despite these early advantages, Philadelphia's money-market star had hardly brightened when it began to fade. One reason was that the seat of government was transferred to Washington in 1800. But a stronger force was the economic rise of New York.[4]

Geography had bestowed upon New York a harbor better situated for transatlantic, coastal, and inland trade than any other on the northern Atlantic coast. By the turn of the century, New York's exports and imports began to exceed those of Philadelphia. The War of 1812 arrested this ascendancy, but only temporarily. After the peace, the British fortuitously settled upon New York as the best port for "dumping" the manufactures they had accumulated during the war, and the subsequent sale of surplus goods attracted customers from all over the country. When the British gave indications of turning to some other port, the City forestalled the move by enacting favorable auction legislation in 1817. In the same year, the state legislature adopted the Erie Canal bill, and the opening of this waterway in 1825 established New York as the export center for the growing trade of the West.

As a result of these and other developments, the City became an entrepôt where an enormous variety of goods from all over the world changed hands. Its citizens, in turn, prospered from the profits, commissions, freights, and other tolls. New York's population overtook that of Philadelphia during the decade between 1810 and 1820, and its capital investment in manufacturing enterprises became the largest in the country.

In Europe, great financial centers had risen on foundations of trade. New York, too, rose to prominence as a national money market after it had become the premier American commercial city. On the whole, the advance was gradual. Major segments of the market appeared and grew as economic needs encouraged their development and as the City's financial institutions learned to exploit new opportunities.

The securities markets, for example, originated in speculative trading in Government issues when the Federal refunding of state debts took place in 1790. In New York, merchants and commodity auctioneers acted as securities brokers to handle these transactions until the famous buttonwood-tree agreement of 1792 created the organized beginnings of a group of securities traders. In 1817 an exchange mechanism was formalized, modeling itself after the stock exchange at Philadelphia. In the same year New York State started the successful flotation of the Erie Canal bonds. These developments encouraged large amounts of state borrowing, attracted European capital, and created trading volumes that enabled the stock exchange in New York to surpass its prototype in Philadelphia.

Meanwhile, New York's economic growth had brought increased financing needs. Wresting domination from Philadelphia as the market for commercial credits was difficult, but gradually the basis for the shift was laid. Hamilton sponsored New York's first commercial bank, the Bank of New York, which started business in 1784. About seven years later the Bank of the United States opened a branch in New York. In 1799, Aaron Burr obtained a charter which was ostensibly for a water company but which contained provisions so flexible that it became possible to form the Bank of the Manhattan Company on Wall Street. By 1815, New York had eight banks, and the total authorized banking capital in the City had risen sixfold in fifteen years.

Moreover, though New York State was exposed to the usual corrupt banking practices of the period, its legislation was on a relatively high level. An early banking act, in 1804, required every banking corporation to have a charter, and this probably held down the growth of wildcat institutions. The Safety Fund Act, passed in 1829, acknowledged governmental responsibility for bank supervision designed to increase the safety of deposited funds.

Thus, New York was favored by economic growth, constructive legislation, and the rapid rise of specialized financial institutions. These are the locational ingredients which have been historically important in the creation of financial markets. True, the Bank of the United States, in Philadelphia, continued to exert a major influence by financing the movement of much of the country's vital cotton crop and by promoting the formation of a commercial credit market. Indeed, it was not until the national charter of the bank lapsed in 1836 that New York attained first position in commercial banking and unrivaled claim to the role of the nation's money market. But even before that time, New York's ascendancy seemed assured.

DEVELOPMENT OF THE MONEY-MARKET SEGMENTS

New York has maintained its financial leadership for a century and a quarter. Though one is tempted to ascribe this feat to the conspicuous advantages of an early start, there is more to it than that. Of great importance is the remarkable performance of the New York money market itself. Over the years it has gained experience, achieved tradition, and developed an elaborate operating mechanism that has extended its sphere of influence throughout the country and the world. Particularly outstanding has been the capacity of New York's financiers for adaptation and change. They have created new segments, such as the Federal funds market, as the need arose, and have withstood the loss of the call money market, once a major component, without any impairment of position. A glance at these historical sequences in the evolution of the New York money market reveals how one phase of its development led to another in the attainment of the City's present position. Though some of the segments are relatively small—witness the commercial paper market and the bankers' acceptances market—they have all contributed to the City's preeminence in finance.

✓ The markets for securities

To a large extent the character of the stocks and bonds in the nation's securities markets has mirrored the economic history of the United States.[5] During the colonial period there were practically no securities to be traded, for most businesses were conducted on an individual or partnership basis, not by stock companies; and American cities at that time rarely issued bonds. In the early years of the republic, United States Government obligations formed the basis of trading in the securities markets. (Later, the market in

United States Government securities became so important that it developed its own operational framework, which, because of its money-market significance, we will discuss in a separate section of this chapter.) The issuance of stock by the early banks and by the fire and marine insurance companies added a considerable volume of securities to those available for trading. When the New York stock brokers in 1817 converted their loose organization into a formal structure under the name of the New York Stock and Exchange Board, their action was a sign of the growing importance of both securities trading in general and New York in particular.

The stock market thereafter reflected the industrialization of the country. With the construction of carriage roads and canals, trading developed in the securities of turnpike and canal companies; with the rise of the locomotive, transactions in railroad shares became important; and as the use of petroleum increased, dealings in the first industrial shares, those of the oil companies, gained headway. In 1863 the New York Stock and Exchange Board assumed its present shorter title. In the fever of Civil War speculation, additional exchanges were organized in New York, one of them the forerunner of the present American Stock Exchange.

In the years that followed the Civil War, the New York Stock Exchange and its members strengthened their dominant position by adopting a vigorous program of mechanization. In 1867, the electric stock ticker was introduced. In 1878, telephone lines were strung from the Exchange floor to offices of member firms, and all through this period, telegraph lines were multiplied to connect New York with distant branch offices.

The composition of securities traded in the New York stock market continued to show the transformation of the United States economy. Railroad and petroleum shares were soon joined by public utility and other industrial issues. As the century progressed, the inflow of European capital strengthened the market for American flotations. The opening of the first transatlantic cable in 1886 broadened the market further.

Today, though only two of the nation's seventeen organized securities exchanges have New York addresses, these two—the New York Stock Exchange and the American Stock Exchange—account for roughly 90 per cent of the value of transactions effected on all exchanges.* These transactions emanate from all corners of the nation. The bulk of the business still originates in the Middle Atlantic area, but on a typically active business day a substantial volume of orders is likely to come from such widely dispersed states as Texas, California, Illinois, and Michigan. For nearly a century and a half, the New York Stock Exchange has remained the country's leading organized market place, and the American Stock Exchange, though a pygmy compared with its neighbor on Wall Street, is larger than any of the regional exchanges.

In actual volume, all the organized exchanges of the country combined handle only a portion of the trading in corporate and governmental securities. Despite the premier position of the New York Stock Exchange, the number of different issues traded in it has never been very large. The qualifications of corporate size and numbers of shareholders have helped to keep listings down. Therefore, as the corporate form of organization became more popular in the country, and public ownership of securities spread, it is likely that the volume of stocks and bonds in the over-the-counter markets, both in New York and elsewhere, expanded relative to those on the organized exchanges. The great improvement that occurred in the means of communication, particularly the telephone and teletype, has provided an additional strong push to trading activity in the over-the-counter markets. A 1949 survey showed that nearly 90 per cent of the sales of corporate bonds and 39 per cent of the sales of corporate stocks in a three-month period were consummated over the telephone and teletype wires which collectively make up the nation's over-the-counter system.

But even so, the "inside" market for these securities is believed

* In September 1959, the New York Mercantile Exchange, a commodity exchange, announced the incorporation of a new wholly owned subsidiary, the National Stock Exchange, Inc., to trade in securities. Governors of the new subsidiary indicated their intention to apply to the Securities and Exchange Commission for registration as a national securities exchange.

to be largely in the hands of New York dealer firms, which include practically all of the biggest ones in the country.

Meanwhile, it was only logical that still another phase of the securities business—that of underwriting the sale of new issues—should become centered in New York City. In the latter part of the nineteenth century, the focus of investment banking activity became the powerful new firm of Drexel, Morgan & Company, later called J. P. Morgan & Company. Increasingly, this firm and various other New York houses came to dominate the underwriting scene. Further binding the market in securities to the rest of the money market was the custom, which gained headway during the 1920's, for the big commercial banks to do a substantial amount of underwriting, often through controlled affiliates. Although the participation of commercial banks in underwriting corporate securities was terminated by the Banking Act of 1933, the practice for a number of years provided an integrating force that helped build up the strength of the New York money market.

THE COMMERCIAL PAPER MARKET

The organized sale and purchase of commercial paper emerged in the middle decades of the nineteenth century.[6] Before that time business firms did not customarily raise money by selling early-maturing negotiable notes, payable to the bearer. Such demand as they had for short-term credit was substantially met by the commercial banks. Some dealings in negotiable credit instruments did take place in a few of the more important commercial cities of the United States, but these were exceptional; and instruments of this sort usually circulated only in the immediate area where the issuing company was located.

Beginning about 1840, out-of-town banks began to buy commercial paper in New York and other cities, and this development led a number of states to pass laws restricting the amounts that banks could lend to persons living in other states. Though these laws probably hampered the practice, banks continued to make "foreign loans," providing some early evidence of the difficulty of attempting to curb economic trends through legislative edict. Because of New York's rising importance in the commercial world, special brokers came into existence in the City to serve as agents in selling the notes of their business customers to banks. By about 1850, "a regular system of street discounts" had been introduced in Wall Street, and the City became recognized as the principal market, such as it was, for commercial paper.[7]

After the Civil War, corporate issuers of commercial paper took to by-passing the banks by selling their unendorsed notes directly to dealers. The new form of negotiable instrument conformed better with existing commercial practices and enabled large borrowers to obtain more credit than could be provided by a single bank. New York business firms were among the first to offer their paper in the open market, and the metropolitan dealers paved the way for an expansion of the market. The country banker with inadequate credit facilities of his own relied upon the well-known city dealer for confirmation of the quality of the paper he bought, and this tended to concentrate the business increasingly in New York. At the same time, as the nation developed, both the issuers and the buyers of commercial paper became increasingly dispersed. The New York dealers expanded their operations from eastern centers to the Midwest and then reached out to the leading cities of the Pacific Coast.

The geographical range of borrowers in the commercial paper market eventually grew very wide. Table 1 shows, for instance, that in 1956 only 14 per cent of these borrowers were in the New York Federal Reserve District. The customers for commercial paper also are spread about the nation; estimates suggest that a high proportion of such paper eventually winds up in the portfolios of banks outside New York City, and a large part of the remainder is in the hands of nonfinancial corporations. Yet, despite the dispersion in flow of funds, the *transactions* have remained concentrated in New York.

Meanwhile, variants of the commercial paper market have appeared in the nation, have grown, and have become centered in

New York. One of these is the banking activity carried on by factoring houses, which provide funds to business concerns either by granting loans on the security of their accounts receivable or by outright purchase of such receivables. The factors, like other financial institutions, owe their concentration in New York partly to the early start that factoring got in the City. The forerunners

Table 1 Location of Firms Borrowing through Commercial Paper Market, According to Federal Reserve District, 1956

Federal Reserve District	Number of borrowers	Percentage of total number
Total, all districts	362	100
Chicago	65	18
New York	52	14
Richmond	43	12
Boston	40	11
St. Louis	27	7
Philadelphia	26	7
Atlanta	25	7
San Francisco	24	7
Minneapolis	18	5
Cleveland	17	5
Dallas	13	4
Kansas City	12	3

Source: National Credit Office.

of many factors were representatives of foreign mills who were attracted to New York because of its importance in the import trade and its role as a textile distribution center. As the factors increasingly assumed a financing function, they found it advantageous to remain near the selling agencies and banks in New York. At the same time, because of the growing role of credit in the New York money market, credit-rating firms and other service agencies began to appear in the City; and their advent contributed greatly to the effectiveness of the factoring houses and the desirability of their being in New York.[8]

THE CALL MONEY MARKET

New York's rise as a financial center attracted the deposits of out-of-town banks. At the same time, securities transactions grew fast, creating a demand for short-term credit to finance such transactions. These events laid the foundation for a call money market based on bank loans subject to immediate "call," with negotiable securities serving as collateral. Over the years, substantial funds were shipped into town for the specific purpose of lending in the call money market, and these extra funds considerably inflated the market's importance.[9]

Prior to the 1930's, call loans were recognized as a major segment of the New York money market. Then various factors inhibited their use. The volume of securities trading declined; new restrictions were placed on loans for the purchase of securities; and banks were prohibited from making call loans on behalf of others. Eventually the New York Stock Exchange discontinued the call money desk on the exchange floor where previously these loans could be impersonally negotiated. As a result, the call loan business, or what was left of it, was returned directly to the banks where it has become a minor part of their ordinary lending operations. These circumstances diminished the significance of this once integral section of the New York money market; yet they did not impair the City's position as the focal point of the United States in finance.

THE MARKET FOR BANKERS' ACCEPTANCES

Still another kind of money market, that in bankers' acceptances, developed in New York, adding to its luster as a national center.[10] Bills of this sort arose whenever a bank undertook to "accept" an instrument drawn upon it, demanding payment of some stated sum to the drawer or another party. In foreign trade, for instance, sellers commonly drew on banks designated by the buyer as a way of obtaining early payment for their goods. Since the bank's acceptance of the bill was evidence of its agreement to pay on some future designated date, the accepted bill could be sold to raise immediate cash.

Before the Civil War, the creation of foreign bills of exchange was done largely by private banks and large commission houses. At that time, most commercial banks in the United States had neither the skill nor the facilities to engage in this field. The nation's foreign trade, therefore, was largely conducted in sterling through British banks, rather than in dollars. But as the foreign activities of the United States grew and as the New York money market mounted in strength, American banks began to lend their names to such instruments and to buy them for investment purposes.

The Federal Reserve Act of 1913, reflecting the increasing interest in these instruments, permitted national banks to "accept" bills under specified conditions—conditions which were gradually relaxed as the institutions gained experience in the field. The Act also created the basis for a discount market in bankers' acceptances by allowing their rediscount and purchase by the Federal Reserve System. This authority encouraged the commercial banks to acquire bills in the open market because they could be used as collateral in borrowing from the Reserve banks. As part of the marketing picture, there arose discount houses, which, as dealers, bought, carried, and distributed bills at going money-market rates. In effect, this system enabled a bank to lend its name, rather than its funds, in the financing of trade.

The number of accepting banks grew rapidly, reaching about 500 after World War I. But many of them, located in small interior cities, lacked adequate knowledge or facilities for such operations, and the group accordingly shrank to 150 by the close of 1930. In that year, New York City's accepting banks accounted for the great bulk of the outstanding acceptances in the nation. Furthermore, every major dealer in these instruments had his main offices located in New York, though secondary centers of activity also existed in Boston, Chicago, and San Francisco. In 1931 the Senate Committee on Banking and Currency, seeking the reasons for this clustering in a few places, was told that it was due to the general concentration of financial resources and commercial activities in the large cities; as a result, unemployed funds flowed to these markets and dealers felt more secure when trading in acceptances drawn on banks located there.

Today, though acceptances arise from transactions originating in widely scattered places, New York City's banks are still the leading creators of such paper and the City's dealers dominate in its purchase and sale. The position of the New York banks is reflected in the figures in Table 2, which show that two-thirds of the value of

Table 2 Bankers' Acceptances Outstanding, by City of Accepting Bank, 1954

City	Millions of dollars	Percentage of total
Total	$873.1	100.0
New York	578.5	66.3
San Francisco	149.2	17.1
Boston	49.2	5.6
Dallas	29.8	3.4
Chicago	18.5	2.1
Philadelphia	14.9	1.7
Houston	9.0	1.0
New Orleans	6.4	0.7
Memphis	5.6	0.6
Other cities	12.0	1.4

Source: Robert Solomon and Frank M. Tamagna, "Bankers Acceptance Financing in the United States," *Federal Reserve Bulletin,* May 1955, p. 485.

outstanding acceptances at the end of 1954 had been accepted by institutions in New York City. In 1957, three-quarters of such acceptances were those of banks of the New York Federal Reserve District.[11]

THE FEDERAL FUNDS MARKET

Though the Government took active steps to encourage the organization of an acceptance market, the Federal funds market was a natural offshoot of the Federal Reserve System's essential activities.[12] Its origin reflects the versatility of the big New York City banks in introducing far-reaching innovations in the money market as the need arises.

A business reaction early in 1921 depleted the Federal Reserve balances of some of the City's banks; and despite heavy borrowing from the Federal Reserve, they were finding it difficult to keep their balances up to legal requirements. At the same time, there were other banks which had surplus reserves and few suitable investment opportunities. Accordingly, some of the leading City banks worked out an arrangement whereby the banks that were short of Federal Reserve balances could buy such balances from banks with excess reserves.

For a time the resulting market in these balances—or Federal funds—was small and rudimentary. No facilities existed for the central clearing of the transactions involved. But gradually the market grew in volume and in the number of participants.

As time went on, the typical transaction in the Federal funds market had the effect of an unsecured cash loan of overnight duration. Thereby, the borrower could adjust his reserve position without delay, because the funds he acquired could be credited at once to his account at the Federal Reserve Bank, which simply transferred the funds from one account to the other. In contrast, a borrower receiving a check drawn on a commercial bank could not normally acquire credit at the Federal Reserve Bank until the next day.

The appeal of these transactions was so great that the major dealers in bankers' acceptances now developed a technical apparatus for the Federal funds market. It was easy for these dealers to be drawn into this market, since they already did an acceptance business with the Federal Reserve. Though Federal funds represent reserve balances of member banks, the dealers could acquire title to them in various ways: by buying such funds from the commercial banks; by selling acceptances and Government securities to the Federal Reserve Bank of New York and receiving negotiable Federal funds in payment; by receiving Federal funds in payment for redeemed United States securities and interest coupons; and by still other means. As time went on, the dealers took to selling these funds to banks just as they might sell acceptances or securities. Eventually they developed a systematic procedure for collecting information and trading in funds on an organized basis. Several money brokers, as part of their call money operations, also found it helpful to serve as middlemen in the distribution of Federal funds among the banks; one of these firms was the forerunner of Garvin, Bantel & Company, which is now the leading Federal funds broker.

During the 1920's, the banks in each large financial center of the nation tended to confine their trades to their home areas, with little swapping between cities. At that time, banks outside New York did not vary among themselves in size so greatly as at present, a fact which permitted those of a given locality to accommodate one another's needs to a large extent. Moreover, during this early stage, some banks were hesitant to deal with those from other areas in these comparatively novel instruments. A certain amount of encouragement, however, was given to intercity trading in Federal funds by the fact that differentials then existed among Federal Reserve districts in the discount rates at which member banks borrowed from Federal Reserve Banks. Because of these differentials, a member bank in a district with a high discount rate could sometimes acquire reserves in the Federal funds market from a member bank in another district more cheaply than it could borrow from the Federal Reserve Bank in its own district. In the latter part of the 1920's, market activity increased between certain eastern banks and those on the West Coast; this occurred not only because of the discount rate differentials but also because the earlier closing time of the eastern banks enabled them to estimate their reserve positions and, if they had excesses, to sell them in the West.

Easy money conditions during most of the 1930's, coupled with the financial plight of many banks during the first part of this period, discouraged trading in Federal funds. And though some expansion occurred in the early 1940's, the market continued generally dull during the war years, because the banks relied on Treasury bills rather than funds to adjust their reserve positions. By the end of the decade, however, tighter money encouraged transactions in Federal funds, and the market grew substantially during the 1950's, reaching average daily volumes of over one billion dollars.

In this later period, the intercity transfer of Federal funds became much more common, with New York acting as a center for the activity. The tendency toward intercity exchanges was encouraged by shifts in the national economic patterns which led to wider differences in the size of banks as well as in the character of their loans. It was also accelerated by the fact that banks began to look on the sale of Federal funds as a means of investing secondary reserves for short periods of time, a role once occupied by the old call money market. On the buying side, banks increasingly employed funds in their operating positions. Finally, the improvement in the wire transfer facilities of the Federal Reserve System and the linking in 1950 of a number of banks in principal cities by means of a private wire hook-up permitted the more rapid transfer of funds and stimulated their use even further. Still other technical changes in Federal Reserve operating practices contributed to the wider use of Federal funds.

It is estimated that about 150 banks, including the largest ones in the United States, regularly have recourse to the Federal funds market. In addition, the market is occasionally used by an increasing number of smaller banks distributed widely over the country. The biggest institutions participate not only to adjust their own reserve positions and for investment purposes, but also to accommodate the requirements of their bank correspondents and regular customers. These large accommodating banks maintain skilled personnel with an intimate knowledge of the market and its mechanism. The other participating banks limit their activities to taking care of their own needs.

A factor having some bearing on the future of this market is the growing familiarity of corporate and state treasurers and other nonbankers with the use of Federal funds. More and more, they have discovered the advantages of making or receiving payment through Federal funds and thus avoiding the overnight lag which is involved when a payer transmits funds by ordinary check. A number of corporations have found it convenient to make short-term investments by turning over Federal funds to dealers in exchange for United States Government securities which the dealers agree to repurchase on a designated date at a specified price. In fact, Federal funds are used to settle a substantial part of all transactions in Government securities.

Despite the entrance of corporations and others into the Federal funds market, the commercial banks dominate the market. And New York City, with its big banks, its dealers, and its Federal funds brokers, remains the focal spot for these transactions. The only other local markets of any consequence, and these are relatively small, are in San Francisco and Chicago.

THE GOVERNMENT SECURITIES MARKET

As in the case of Federal funds, an organized framework to handle trading in United States Government securities appeared relatively late in the development of the New York money market.[13] Before the Civil War there were no recognized dealers in Government issues. That war generated the nation's first billion-dollar debt, leading to the appearance of an embryo Government securities market, which, however, did not attain maturity until the twentieth century. Trading in Government securities has taken place both in the New York Stock Exchange and in the over-the-counter markets, with the focus shifting from one market to the other. Since the mid-1920's the activity has been concentrated in the over-the-counter markets, and both practitioners and outside observers seem to agree that this kind of trading in Government securities is preferable to a formal institutional framework.

Today, the importance of the Government securities market to the money market as a whole is very great. Through the sale of Government securities, the United States Treasury is the largest single borrower in the money market. At the end of 1958, the marketable portion of the Treasury's outstanding public issues amounted to more than $175 billion. From the lender's point of view, Government securities are unique among investment media. Because they are not subject to credit risk and are widely dispersed among investor portfolios, they are more liquid than other kinds of assets. Therefore, in addition to serving as a permanent investment outlet, these securities are the primary means of making adjustments in portfolio composition.

The quality and short term of the Treasury bill make it the debt instrument *par excellence* for money-market institutions to meet the ebb and flow of cash. Because the market for bills is active and can absorb large transactions, the Federal Open Market Committee of the Federal Reserve System usually employs these bills to adjust the size of its portfolio as it seeks to reduce or expand the supply of funds available to the nation's economy. Thus, the Government securities market serves as a channel through which monetary policy may influence economic conditions.

The churning about caused by these buying and selling activities is centered upon seventeen dealers—five commercial banks and twelve securities houses—who make the market in Government securities. The Federal Reserve Bank of New York, which is the agent of the Federal Reserve System for carrying out open-market operations, has developed close working relations with the dealers, including frequent discussions and face-to-face meetings. Of the five commercial bank dealers, three are headquartered in New York. Of the twelve securities houses, eleven are New York firms. The numbers may change, of course, because any dealer is welcome to establish regular contact with the Federal Reserve Bank of New York. Some economic limitation exists, however, on the number of firms that can profitably share one market. Moreover, the skill and experience of the already participating dealers provide a barrier that a newcomer would have to overcome.

Over the years, the Government securities market has become extraordinarily efficient, and trading proceeds with a minimum of difficulty. A local insurance company, for instance, can sell a large block of securities to a dealer over the telephone, making the sale on the basis of an oral quotation and an oral commitment. The delivery of the securities and the payment ordinarily are made through a clearing bank designated by the dealer; the Manufacturers Trust Company serves as clearing agent for most of the dealers. If the insurance company is not located in New York, the trade may be for delivery and payment at a designated New York bank. Alternatively, both funds and securities may be transferred via the wire transfer facilities of the Federal Reserve System.

When the trading desk of the Federal Reserve Bank wishes to transact business for the System's open market account, it too begins with the New York dealers. It contacts them for offers or bids on bills, then holds their tentative orders while the rest of the market is being canvassed. In that way, the "Fed's" trading desk is assured of the best possible terms in its open market operations. The same desk also buys and sells issues for the investment accounts of United States Government agencies [14] and for foreign central banks, as well as for those few member banks in the New York Federal Reserve District which prefer not to go directly to the market.

HOW IT HAPPENED

As we review the factors which underlay the rise of New York's position as a money-market center, one of these surely was economic leadership apart from the financial community—a leadership represented by a substantial volume of trade in the area and the presence of large-scale corporate headquarters. In the early 1800's, the nation's new political center, Washington, which might have made a rival claim for leadership, did not have enough commerce and industry to support such a bid. Then, too, forceful and imaginative management was provided by New York's business community in order to get new organizations going, adapt them to changing circumstances, and develop effective arrangements under which they could operate. On top of this, pure chance and helpful legislation played their part.

It was New York's experience that whenever a major money-market segment became established, its existence contributed to the development of other segments at the same location. Two main factors, which will be elaborated in the next chapter, lay behind this phenomenon. Briefly, one of these was the urgent need for quick and effective communication among the decision-makers of the money market. The other was the hoary principle that the size of the market determined the degree of specialization—the growth of money-market segments brought the proliferation of specialists offering services which provided "external economies" to the money market as a whole. Because of the need for communication and the common use of specialists, the various segments of the money market became closely interwoven and the entire complex became a formidably entrenched entity.

2

Money Market and Financial Community

A money market exists wherever there is trading in the financial instruments used for the transfer of funds—and that means it is found in the offices, exchanges, and wire connections not only in New York, the principal center of money-market trading, but also in the country at large. The phrase "money market" is equally elastic when measured by the number of the people involved. Stretched to its utmost in the New York Metropolitan Region, the term can be made to cover the Region's entire financial community, for all financial firms are to some extent participants in the money market or at least somehow dependent upon it. At the other extreme, it can be thought of as embracing only a few thousand specialists in or near Wall Street whose buying, selling, or brokerage activities establish the day-to-day operating terms for the money-market segments described in the preceding chapter.

In our view the money market has no geographical dimensions and need be assigned no employment figure. But the group of money-market specialists just mentioned has a specific location and can be estimated numerically, the number being probably between five and ten thousand, counting the immediately supporting clerical assistants. Their presence in lower Manhattan helps to account for the clustering of some 120,000 other financial employees on the triangular tip of Manhattan south of Chambers Street, measuring only six-tenths of a square mile. The importance of the five to ten thousand is so considerable, in fact, that they can well be called the "money-market core" of the Region's financial community.

The community itself is many times that big, having about 312,000 people, more than three-fourths of them working in New York City and the rest distributed throughout the counties of the Region.* The aim of this chapter is to analyze the basic locational motivations of the financial community, with special attention to the reasons why so much of it is densely crowded together. To make the analysis, it will be necessary to divide the community by major functions, offering a chart on which the powerful money-market core occupies a prominent position. But first, in order to obtain a clear perspective of the entire financial community and to evaluate the relative importance of its major components, we divide it in a more obvious way—by categories of financial "industries."

FINANCIAL COMMUNITY: FACTS AND FIGURES

The industry categories are ranged in Table 3 in the same order in which they will be taken up for detailed discussion in our later chapters. The first category is commercial banking, which has its thickest concentrations in lower and midtown Manhattan and smaller numbers in the other parts of the Region. About equal to banking in manpower is the life and health insurance industry, consisting mainly of the life insurance companies with their populous office buildings in Manhattan and Newark and their widely scattered field offices and agents. Together these first two categories account for more than half the manpower of the financial community. They are followed in turn by property insurance (mainly fire and casualty); by the securities industry; and by credit institutions other than commercial banks.

In every one of these categories, the New York Metropolitan Region leads other metropolitan areas by a wide margin. With less than 10 per cent of the nation's population, the Region in 1956 had about 16 per cent of the nation's financial employment. In

* All these employment estimates are for 1956.

one category, the securities industry, the Region's share exceeded 30 per cent. Perhaps two-fifths of the 312,000 people in the financial community are engaged in "exporting" financial services; that is, they are serving firms and individuals outside the Region, or serving firms inside the Region which do business on a national scope. The other three-fifths are serving the "local" financial needs

Table 3 Composition of Employment in Financial Community of New York Metropolitan Region, 1956

	Number of employees (thousands)	Percentage of total
Total	311.7	100.0
Commercial banks	82.3	26.4
Life and health insurance	83.2	26.7
Property insurance	72.6	23.3
Security and commodity brokers, dealers, and exchanges	38.1	12.2
Credit institutions except commercial banks	28.3	9.1
Other financial employment	7.2	2.3

Sources: These are estimates based on third-quarter data collected by state departments of labor under unemployment insurance programs; and on U. S. Census Bureau, *County Business Patterns, First Quarter 1956.*

of the Region with its vast array of business firms and its 16,000,000 inhabitants.[1]

The Region's financial community, despite its far-reaching heavy hand in the nation's business, is not a very impressive proportion of the Region's total employment, when compared with manufacturing, retail trade, and various other segments. In 1956, the community absorbed 4.7 per cent of the estimated 6,700,000 jobs of the Region. Although this ratio of financial to total employment appears to be higher in the New York area than in most other metropolitan areas, interestingly enough it is not so high as in the Dallas and San Francisco areas.[2] Various factors could account for the greater proportionate concentration of financial employment in these two western communities—including differences in such things as the rate and character of economic growth, financial productivity, state banking and insurance laws, the extent of territory served outside the metropolitan area, and the definitions used for determining the metropolitan areas involved. But we have made no studies of Dallas and San Francisco and do not pretend to do anything more than surmise why their financial manpower is so large relative to their own economies.

In any case, financial activities of course assume greater and greater importance in their environment as one moves closer to the heart of the Region. In New York City the ratio of financial to total employment is 7 per cent; in Manhattan south of Central Park it rises to 10 per cent; and in the financial district it shoots much higher. Moreover, financial activities occupy nearly one-quarter of all the floor space in Manhattan's office buildings.[3]

Besides, the financial community takes on additional stature within the Region when one considers that it is a major customer of other industries. It buys large amounts of printing and advertising, requires the services of lawyers and accountants, and pays a shattering telephone bill. According to one estimate, the nation's financial institutions spend about twice as much on advertising, professional services, and utilities as they do on real estate and rentals.[4]

But none of these measures can fully express the critical role of the financial community in the Region. For example, it is impossible to measure the influence of Wall Street in attracting central offices of corporations to New York City. The things that go to make up New York's role as America's "first city" are closely interrelated. Foreign trade, central offices, business services, tourism, and culture intertwine with banks and securities exchanges to create a complex too involved for definition. Some elements in the mass are inert; they do not move unless dragged by others. But there are also elements which are not passive at all, and which in moving could start the ponderous whole to disintegrating and relocating. Some of those elements are in the financial community.

FINANCIAL COMMUNITY BY FUNCTIONS

Enough has now been said about the general composition and role of the Region's 312,000 financial employees to permit us to change the approach and depict the financial community on a functional basis. Chart 1 is an attempt to do this. It divides the community into a core and two rings, and in so doing cuts across industry lines and even company lines. For example, the same commercial bank may be represented in every part of the diagram.

At the top of the chart is the money-market core of the financial community, which was mentioned at the beginning of the chapter. Here are the Wall Street trading units, containing the money-market specialists and their immediate staffs. These specialists trade in United States Government securities, various types of other securities, Federal funds, commercial paper, and bankers' acceptances. Though a very large number of American individuals and institutions, both inside and outside the nation's financial industry, occasionally buy or sell financial instruments, the money-market specialists are different in that they constantly stand ready either to make a market themselves, as buyers or sellers of the instruments in which they are interested, or to serve as brokers in consummating arrangements for their principals.

The specialists operate from the trading desks of banks, brokers, dealers, and the Federal Reserve Bank of New York. We have also placed in the core the organized exchanges and the mechanisms for the clearing and transferring of financial instruments and checks, because they facilitate the operations of the money market even though they do not have the same trading function as the other units. The specialist himself may be a part of a firm or organization which is devoted entirely to a single money-market operation. But more commonly, he belongs to a firm which engages in more than one money-market activity—for example, to a

Chart 1
The Money Market and Financial Functions

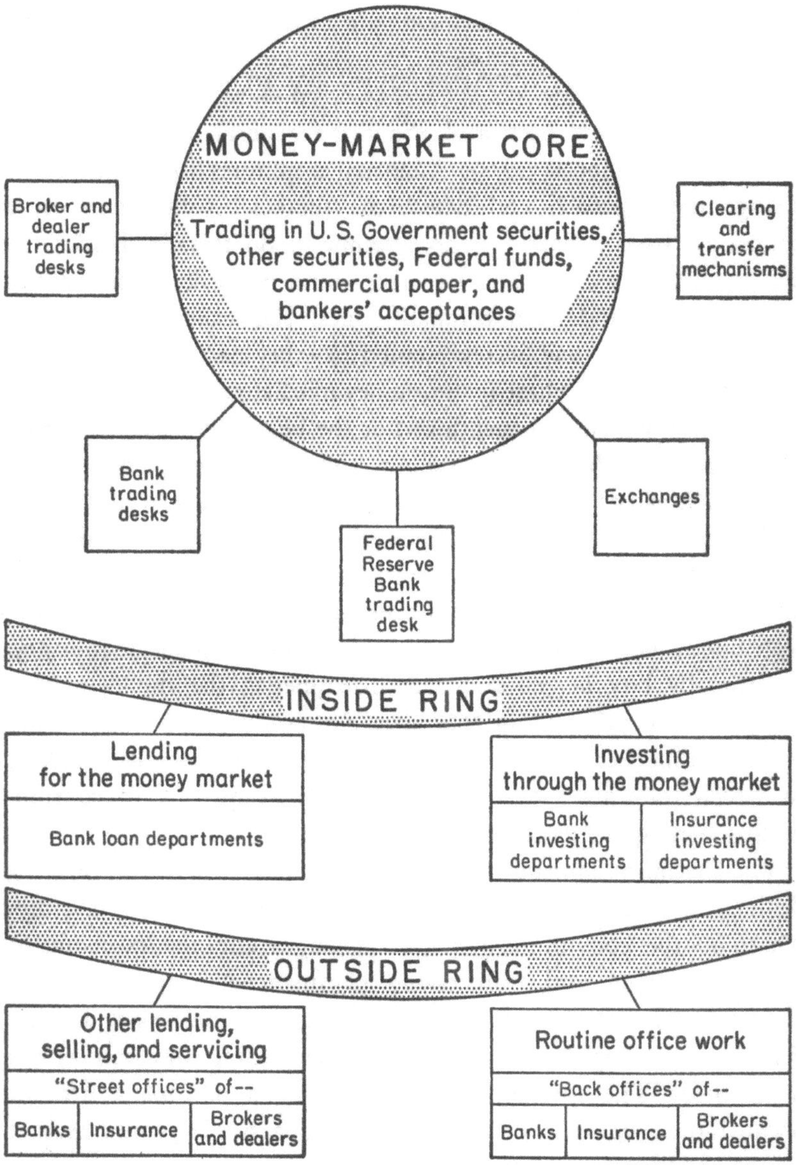

dealer firm handling bankers' acceptances, commercial paper, Treasury issues, Federal agency obligations, municipal securities, and corporate stocks and bonds. Often the specialists are members of organizations—for example, the great banks and brokerage houses—which also deal directly with the public.

The "inside ring" on the chart consists of units that deal directly and continually with the money-market core, but as secondary participants rather than direct players in the market process. These units consist of (1) those portions of the loan departments of banks which lend money to brokers and dealers for their money-market operations; and (2) those portions of the investing departments of banks and insurance companies which invest funds through the money market. The people of the inside ring are not numerous; a nose-count would be difficult but it is likely that the figure is not much different from the five to ten thousand people of the money-market core.

The "outside ring," therefore, contains nearly all the manpower of the financial community. It consists of "street offices," which deal with the public, and "back offices," which perform record-keeping and other routine functions concerned with processing the huge volume of paper handled by the financial community.[5]

There is a fourth element that must be mentioned right away, though it is not depicted on the chart. This is "top management" —the elite group of executives who establish the critical policies concerning the operations of banks, insurance companies, and other large financial organizations. Most of these men do not function exclusively in the money-market core, or the inside ring, or the outside ring, but they make decisions affecting all three, and they will figure importantly in our locational analysis.*

* In any breakdown of the financial community there is bound to be overlapping, and Chart 1 is offered as a rough indicator of major functions rather than as an array of pigeonholes by which every job can be neatly classified. For example, investment banks, though not named on the chart, may be considered as residing in the core when engaging in trading; in the inside ring when investing through the money market; and in the outside ring with respect to routine functions. "Bank trading desks" in the core and "bank loan

The persons who perform the functions of the money-market core of the financial community have a compelling need to be physically close to one another. This need, which will be elaborated within the next few pages, helps to explain not only why the money-market core is concentrated at one spot within the New York Metropolitan Region but also why so much of the nation's money-market activity takes place in one city.

As for the persons in the inside ring of the Region's financial community, their locational urges are a little more diverse. They find advantages in locating in the midst of the money-market core with which they regularly deal. At the same time, there are obvious advantages of liaison and convenience for them to be in the same building with other parts of the banks and insurance companies for which they work. When the main office is in the Wall Street area, as in the case of the big commercial banks, the inside-ring units can satisfy both needs at the same time. But if there are sufficiently strong reasons for the headquarters office to locate outside the Wall Street area, as in the case of the Region's largest life insurance firms, the inside-ring units are torn between two locations. As between the two pulls in the life insurance industry, that of the home office has proved to be the stronger, with the result that the inside ring of the financial community is split between Wall Street and the rest of the Region.

As for the multitudinous outside ring, its ties to the money-market core are weaker still. The functions performed by the approximately 300,000 people in "street offices" and "back offices"—the acceptance of deposits, the lending of money to business firms and individuals, the selling of insurance, the safekeeping of valuables, the buying and selling of stocks on behalf of the public, the administration of estates, the preparation of statements, the

---

departments" in the inside ring refer to commercial banks only, but "bank investing departments" in the inside ring and "banks" in the outside ring refer not only to commercial banks but also to savings banks and other credit institutions. As for the Federal Reserve Bank of New York, only its trading desk is shown on the chart.

paying of claims, and the incessant bookkeeping, sorting and letter-writing connected with financial operations—these have nothing inherent in themselves that require them to take place in or around Wall Street's canyon. And yet about four in every ten persons in the outside ring are found in Manhattan south of Chambers Street. Another two or three are between Chambers Street and Central Park. The rest of the outside ring is found wherever a teller stands at his window or an insurance salesman keeps his desk.

What causes so much of the financial community to cluster? And what factors are tending to pull parts of the community away from the center? To answer those questions, we begin by going back to the heart of the matter, that is, to the money-market core. In Chapter 1 we traced the development of New York as the dominant money market of the country, and in so doing we went a long way toward explaining why financial firms huddle together. We saw that money-market segments grow out of one another and overlap, and that they tend to pile up in one place that possesses great economic strength and certain other attributes. Now we move beyond the historical account in order to see what there is in the nature of finance that encourages concentration, whether in one city or one portion of a city.

THE CENTRALIZING FORCES

✔ Knowledge in a hurry

At the base of our argument is the notion that when the uncertainties of an undertaking are great, its participants have to be close together in order to operate with maximum effectiveness. Uncertainty aggravates the need for fast and frequent communication, both in negotiating for transactions and in keeping abreast of developments affecting the market. And this need creates a centripetal pull not only toward the principal money-market center—the New York Metropolitan Region—but also, within the Region, to the financial district of lower Manhattan.

Money-market specialists have an ever-present problem of adapting their resources to meet swiftly changing conditions. Sometimes the supply of funds may overflow available investment outlets; at other times unfilled investment needs may exist. Whether the specialist takes title to financial instruments or acts only on behalf of clients, his job is to see that buyer and seller are brought together through an efficient market mechanism. In the process of adjusting supply and demand, the prices of the paper in which the specialists deal are subject to rapid changes. Since the specialists, or the firms they represent, often have large amounts of funds at stake, the risk exposure is high.

The primary protection against the hazards of doing business in this taut and fickle environment is knowledge—of the play of forces affecting money-flows, of impending changes, of the attitudes of regulatory authorities, of clients' buying or selling dispositions, and of a host of other possible influences. This knowledge is, in part, the product of a counterplay of ideas among the specialists. The benefits of this exchange are derived through continuing relations rather than by the sporadic transfer of information. There is more than psychological comfort—although perhaps this too is a factor—in the intimacy that permits brokers and dealers to expose their views to the accumulated wisdom of their compatriots through frequent personal meetings and lengthy conversations.

In short, the participants in the money market are clustered together because the "costs" of buying and selling can be minimized by maintaining direct and continual contact with the market. It is desirable for them always to know "what the market is"—the terms on which business can be done. And this knowledge reduces the cost of transactions in the sense that it enables the participant to avoid being "off the market"—doing business on terms unnecessarily unfavorable. Though difficult to express quantitatively, such a cost is crucial in a market as competitive as that in which financial instruments are traded.

It is not only a matter of face-to-face confrontation, important as that is. In order to maintain continual contact on an economical basis, the participant must be where through the flick of a key he can put himself in direct telephonic communication with any of the other important members. Conceivably, such calls could be made from one part of the country to another. But the teletype—so useful in simply buying and selling securities at market prices—is not an equally satisfactory medium for discussing market conditions, and the cost of direct wires for long-distance telephoning would be prohibitive. For example, an over-the-counter house of medium size in Wall Street has, say, 120 lines running to other Street firms. At present rates, the monthly rental for these lines is $420. If the firm were conducting operations from Los Angeles and maintained the same direct lines to New York, its monthly telephone bill would be a staggering $640,000. From Dallas it would be $410,000; from Chicago $230,000.[6] Consequently, if a firm moved to California, it would probably have to eliminate all but one or two direct connections. Even if it used these wires as ties to feeder lines to cover the money market, it would lose the competitive edge provided by direct connections with each money-market listening post.

This prohibitive cost would not remain so high if a group of firms, rather than one or two isolated houses, were eventually to congregate in some city other than New York. The communication needs of the money-market specialists would then be partially met by their personal contacts in the newly established center. But the pioneer money-market firm which left the existing New York nucleus would be faced with the formidable communication problem suggested above. And the money-market firm that set up in some part of the New York Metropolitan Region other than Manhattan, even though it would not face the same telephone problem, would still be handicapped by the added difficulty of face-to-face meetings.

It is true that some money-market firms are located outside lower Manhattan, even in other parts of the country, but these usually have representatives in the Manhattan money-market core.

Our first principle, then, is that clustering tends to occur whenever the high risks of an activity can be modified through the frequent swapping of information and ideas. The principle is most applicable in the case of the specialists of the money-market core.

It is also applicable, though with somewhat less urgency, to the inside ring of units that lend funds for money-market operations or invest through the money market. And it is powerfully applicable to the echelon of "top management," the high executives who, though not engaging full-time in money-market trading, have the authority to make critical decisions for large firms. These men, too, find it desirable to keep up with the money market and, in general, to maintain close and frequent contacts with knowledgeable persons outside their own firms—a circumstance to which we shall return later in the chapter.

It would not do to suggest that two people have to be in the same skyscraper, on the same street, or even in the same part of the country for one of them to sell a piece of paper to the other. Nevertheless the delicate communication problems involved in money-market transactions do exert a centripetal force upon the participants. As an illustration, in the high competitive market for United States Treasury bills, prior to the weekly deadline for submitting bids to the Federal Reserve Bank, the dealers maintain continual communication with one another in order to keep track of the demand and supply situation up to the moment when they dispatch runners to the "Fed" with their tenders.

Furthermore, there is the added fact—an important one—that financial institutions share common customers. This fact helps to hold together not only the participants in the money-market core but also the inside and outside rings. For example, business firms that need funds can obtain them in the money-market core by tapping the resources of the securities markets or by borrowing in the bankers' acceptance market and the commercial paper market. On the other hand they can seek short-term or long-term financing directly from commercial banks or insurance companies, that is, from units of what we have called the outside ring of the financial community—"outside" in a functional sense but not necessarily in a physical sense. Some business enterprises prefer to use all these sources over a long period in order to reduce their reliance on a single source of financing. And corporations often wish to negotiate with more than one source during a short period of time. The grouping of the sources in physical proximity to one another broadens the range of negotiations that can be undertaken. Thus, out-of-town corporation officials who wish to use the facilities of more than one financial firm—or more than one department of a single firm—find the narrow boundaries of the financial district a convenience in "shopping around." And a financial firm that wishes to be taken into consideration by the "shopper" finds it helpful to have offices within those boundaries.

Corporations, in their transactions with financial organizations, are not only borrowers but also investors and lenders. As investors they participate in various segments of the money market, shifting their preferences from time to time as they uncover advantages not previously recognized; for example, in recent years they have been buying large amounts of Treasury bills and commercial paper. The brokers and dealers in the money-market core rely heavily on borrowing from the commercial banks—a fact which helps to tie the core and the inside ring together—but here again the nonfinancial corporations enter the picture, for the money-market specialists have found that corporate treasuries are helpful supplementary sources of funds. So are state and municipal treasuries. Through continued close associations, dealers in financial instruments become familiar with the financial characteristics of the nonbank lenders. Thus the dealers are better able to provide these lenders with maturities that suit their needs and also to take advantage of the lenders' seasonal periods of cash excesses.

External economies

Financial institutions, when crowded close together, not only share common customers but also share common specialized services, which reduce the costs and difficulties of doing business. The resulting economies are external to the firm that benefits from them, since they grow not from the firm's inside arrangements but from the circumstance that many other firms are concentrated in the same area. These external economies did not precede the coming of the financial district, except in the limited sense that a busy city always offers certain facilities that cannot be found in an open field or a small town. But as the financial markets grew in volume, the degree of specialization increased, and the specialized services and facilities, once there, contributed toward bringing and holding financial activities together. Accordingly, our second major centralizing influence, a companion-piece to "knowledge in a hurry," is the existence of external economies.

For convenience, the external economies that make for clustering in New York can be divided into three kinds: (1) those that spring from the high degree of financial specialization among individuals and firms; (2) those that come from joint facilities set up by groups of financial firms; (3) those resulting from services provided by other industries, such as printing.

As for the first kind, we have already had much to say about the specialists of the money-market core, operating within one or another of the money-market segments. And we have stressed the basic importance of the exchange of knowledge among the participants in the markets. What we have not pointed out is that there are specialties within specialties. There is someone who knows all about municipal bonds, even of the bonds of a particular state; a man with an extraordinary grasp of the intricacies of arbitrage; others who can speak with authority on revenue obligations, income bonds, or the investment opportunities in Japan; or, if you please, the implications of the latest changes in the ratios of ton-miles per train-hour of the western railroads. The initiated can make use of the specialized knowledge of these people whether or not he is actually associated with them in transactions.

As for the joint facilities, the sheer size and numbers of the banks and other financial institutions in New York permit them to support a variety of services which a smaller financial cluster could not maintain. A few outstanding examples will indicate the range of these activities.

The New York Clearing House, founded in 1853 as the first in the country, depends for its efficiency upon the size of the banking community it serves. It provides an exchange mechanism for checks, coupons, postal money orders, stock certificates, and items drawn on foreign banking houses, on investment brokers, and on insurance companies. It also provides its members with helpful statistical information. On various occasions in its history, the New York Clearing House members have pooled their resources to provide credit, through clearing house certificates, during periods of monetary stringency.

The large number and substantial aggregate resources of the New York savings banks have enabled them to develop a number of servicing agencies that have served as a unifying force. Important among them is the Savings Banks Trust Company, which serves as the savings banks' central bank; the Institutional Securities Corporation, originally formed to provide savings banks with extra mortgage liquidity but now active in a variety of ways in connection with their investment activities;[7] and the Institutional Investors Mutual Fund, Inc., which was organized to help its member banks invest in common stock.[8]

Because of the large number of security analysts congregated in the financial district, the New York Society of Security Analysts is the nation's leading organization in the field. It has gone a long way to help professionalize this activity; it provides daily luncheons at which outstanding corporate executives are glad to have the chance of addressing the assembled analysts; and it publishes *The Analysts Journal,* which has acquired considerable stature as a professional publication. And finally, the presence of the giant organized exchanges, the New York Stock Exchange and the American Stock Exchange, requires the close affiliation of a substantial and active body of members. These exchanges not only provide the physical facilities and mechanisms for trading and clearing securities but also perform a number of very important regulatory and guiding functions.

The third kind of external economy is derived not only externally to the benefiting firm but externally to the financial community itself. Financial activities create the need for numerous auxiliary services that must be located nearby. Financial institutions are heavy users of the prominent, multinamed law firms that are skilled in drawing the elaborate agreements underlying financial transactions; they rely on the capacities of custom printers who specialize in producing a variety of technical reports and documents; and they engage an increasing number of public relations firms which specialize in financial affairs. The clustering of financial institutions both generates the need for and provides the resources that make possible the existence of all these—lawyers, printers, and various other specialists—within a small area, and this congregation of supporting agencies, in turn, facilitates the making of financial arrangements.

External economies are a centralizing force not only for the money-market core but also for the inside and outside rings of the financial community. They help to explain both New York's continuing leadership in the nation and the continuing dominance of the Wall Street area in the financial activities of the New York Metropolitan Region. Without the special importance of information, growing out of the uncertainties inherent in financial dealings, external economies would not be the potent force they are. Conversely, without the high degree of specialization that has developed in the financial district, the communication factor would not be as important as it it. The fact is that *both* fast communication and external economies are necessary conditions of clustering.

The dual role of the elite

Even so, we have not fully explained the remarkable concentration of so much of the Region's financial employment in Manhattan, especially in lower Manhattan. The need for fast and frequent communication applies most forcefully to the elite of the financial community, including the specialists of the money-market core and the top management of large banks, insurance companies, and other financial firms. The need for external economies, too, seems to affect the elite more than it does the large forces of clerical workers in banks and insurance firms, performing for the most part functions that are routine in comparison with the hazardous, variable operations in the money market.

But if communication needs and external economies explain the locational motivations of the elite, they also go far toward explaining the location of the lower echelons, for the elite form a link between the money-market core and the bulk of the financial community. The reason for this is that the elite play a dual role. First, as a major preoccupation, they are engaged either directly or indirectly in money-market operations. Second, many of them are responsible for overseeing the other operations of their firms—the lending, the administration, and all the rest. As the makers of critical decisions, they either must be, or want to be, in the money-market core; but at the same time, as supervisors of large forces of employees, they often consider it desirable to keep these forces close at hand, for either practical or prestige purposes.

It is a rare top-ranking official, indeed, who does not like to have his immediate associates at his beck and call to resolve issues in the meetings characteristic of modern management methods. And it is the unusual associate who does not want *his* subordinates nearby to answer sudden questions that arise or to participate directly in consultations on specific assignments. The subordinates, in turn, rely upon the ready availability of their own staffs, and so it goes throughout the organization. Thus it is that the duality of the elite encourages the maintenance of skilled and routine personnel under the same roof, or at least near each other.

The locational impact of these relations varies for different types of institutions. When the money-market pull has been relatively mild, financial firms have been willing to concentrate their staffs at locations outside the heart of the financial district. Property insurance companies, for example, have clustered on the fringe of the Wall Street area, and life insurance companies have found it expedient—for reasons to be traced later in the book—to settle even farther away. On the other hand, when the money-market tug has been sufficiently strong, the dual role of the elite increases as a locational factor. The big commercial banks participate actively in the core functions of the money market, yet at the same time engage in the functions falling within the inside and outside rings of our conceptual divisions of the financial community. The very fact that these institutions find it desirable to keep their trading desks and related operations in the Wall Street area attracts other top-ranking executives to the same location, along with masses of unskilled personnel. The total effect is for the commercial banks to keep large headquarters organizations in Manhattan's financial district, even though the bulk of the employees are engaged in functions only remotely related to the money market.

The concentration of the financial community goes back to the era when New York City was still confined to lower Manhattan. Over the decades, despite the expansion of the City into new territory, financial activities—even when not related directly to the money market—continued to pile up at the point of origin. It was a natural outgrowth of conditions in this early period for executives and their employees to be congregated at one spot. Lower Manhattan was the only place where one could collect the large number of people needed for the rapidly expanding volume of work. And slow facilities for communication and travel constituted a barrier against the separation of the elite from the rest of the organization.

Nowadays, the telephone and teletype, the subway and automobile, the continued spread of the city, and the increasing compartmentalization of routine financial functions—all have made it much less urgent for executives to keep their people at their elbows.

In these circumstances, the fact that the dual role of the elite has remained such a strong integrating force is partly due to inertia and tradition, which have held many employees in lower Manhattan even though the economic reasons for their presence have faded. Top executives without question feel the spell of Wall Street, so rich in financial history and folklore. They value the prestige of being identified with such surroundings. Besides, the men of finance, renowned for their hard-headed realism, have yet a sentimental streak that makes them hesitate to break away.

But when all this has been said, the fact remains that inertia and tradition hold firms in the financial district *only so long as there are no strong reasons for them to go elsewhere*. It is our thesis that when those reasons clearly show themselves, a shift eventually occurs, regardless of sentiment. It may take the form of building up major branches outside the main financial district, or even creating a second "headquarters" office. So sentiment compromises with economics.

THE MOVEMENT OF PAPER

One more clustering influence needs to be mentioned. It is no longer one of the more important influences, and we think it will become even less important in the future, but for the present, at least, it helps to offset the forces of decentralization when they begin to nudge a given activity.

The influence we have in mind grows out of the simple physical fact that financial operations require the movement of phenomenal amounts of paper from one office to another. Money-market transactions often entail the rapid delivery of pieces of paper by hand. In the Federal funds market, for instance, the exchange of a clearing-house check for a draft on the Federal Reserve Bank of New York is accomplished by messenger. Stock certificates also typically pass by hand from brokerage houses to the stock clearing corporations of the two New York exchanges. Indeed, one of the requirements of membership in the Stock Clearing Corporation of the New York Stock Exchange—a requirement which is waived in some cases—is that an office should be maintained in downtown Manhattan in order to facilitate the physical transfer of securities. Concerning the clearing of checks, one banking official, when interviewed, expressed the case for the location of check-processing downtown near the Clearing House as follows: "Just as we want to save the commuting time of our personnel, we want to save the commuting time of our checks."

For the present, the swift and easy movement of paper must be considered as a locational factor in the crowding together of financial institutions. But more effective methods of transmittal are being developed. Treasury securities, for example, are already being sent long distances by wire. Some day the physical movement of pieces of paper may become quite obsolete.

THE DECENTRALIZING FORCES

One must not suppose that all the influences are pushing the different parts of the financial community into the New York area and into lower Manhattan. There are also centrifugal forces which, within the country, are tending to pull finance out of the New York Metropolitan Region and, within the Region, are pulling it out of the Wall Street area.

THE PRESSURES TO LEAVE THE REGION

Perhaps the most serious long-term threat to the dominance of the Region as the country's national center of finance is the more rapid economic growth of other geographic areas. The increasing absolute size of cities elsewhere begins to suggest the possibility that some of the specialized facilities and skills now uniquely belonging to New York may come into existence in other places. Out-of-town banks, for instance, now finance an increasing portion of the securities transactions of the nation.[9] In the New York money market, the dealers in search of financing have learned to tap the resources of out-of-town banks, nonfinancial corporations, and state and local governments throughout the country, often selling and buying back Government securities through technical arrangements known as "repurchase agreements."

On top of the more rapid growth of other geographic areas, state legislation relating to insurance is relatively strict in New York. Moreover, state laws dealing with branch banking have handicapped the expansion of the money-market banks of New York, thus far, to a greater degree than in some other areas.

The possibility also exists that some of the great focalizing institutional agencies located in the money market may elect to move. As we shall discuss later, the New York Stock Exchange has already twice threatened to leave the City, and should it ever decide to do so, the shift could even take it outside the Region. The Federal Reserve Bank of New York also occupies an important role in the money market and a transfer of some of its responsibilities could weaken the money-market core. Indicative at least of what could happen is a recent Congressional report which recommended that the Open Market Committee of the Federal Reserve System consider assuming direct control of open market operations, rather than delegating authority to the Federal Reserve Bank of New York.[10] Reducing the significance of such a change, however, is the likelihood that even if the manager of the open market account were officially located in Washington, most of the actual work would have to be conducted in New York.*

The pressures to leave the Wall Street area

Inside the New York Metropolitan Region, other kinds of locational forces come into play, affecting the heavy concentration of financial activities in lower Manhattan. Over time, such factors as nearness to customers, the cost of office space, the cost of labor, and the supply of manpower can be expected to bear increasingly upon locational decisions. These factors will be discussed in later chapters dealing with major industries of the financial community; we mention them now because of their possible importance in eroding the Wall Street base of finance.

The "street offices" in the outside ring of the financial community are subject to a strong drawing force toward the customers with whom much of the work of finance is done—the receiving of deposits, granting of loans, selling of insurance, providing of investment advice, and so forth. For competitive purposes, financial firms have been compelled to locate offices to suit the convenience of these customers; and the existence of such offices provides an enter-

* Even at the present time, the New York Federal Reserve Bank deals directly with the securities department of the Continental National Bank and Trust Company of Chicago. The First National Bank of Chicago, on the other hand, maintains a New York office, although pricing decisions are made in Chicago.

ing wedge for attracting administrative personnel and establishing servicing centers in the same areas.

Similarly, the "back offices" in the outside ring are exposed to the magnetism of neighborhoods where their work can be performed more economically. Most of this work is routine, increasingly requiring large unobstructed areas of space for modern equipment as well as personnel, but deriving no special advantages from remaining in the intensely dynamic, prestige-conscious atmosphere of Wall Street with its astronomical rentals. As the financial firms become more cost conscious, they may seek increasingly to perform routine functions in less expensive spots.

Officials of financial institutions now rarely mention labor costs as a significant locational influence, but these constitute a potential force which may become more important in the future as firms expand and compare alternative sites. At present, office salaries in the built-up areas of the Region outside New York City, on the whole, tend to be a little lower than those within the City.[11] What is mentioned more often than salaries as a locational factor is the availability of manpower. The financial industries are heavy users of large masses of moderately educated clerical help, mainly female. At one time, the great bulk of the employees came from locations readily accessible to the financial district. Over time, this convenience factor has been whittled away by the spread of the population and by radical alterations in transportation routes and methods. The changes have already worked in favor of midtown locations and eventually may become an even stronger force toward relocating financial activities.

Underlying all these disintegrating factors—present and potential—is the relative looseness of the ties between the money-market core and the outside ring of the financial community, mentioned earlier in the chapter. In this peripheral area, in our functional concept of the financial community, there is little real economic need for the clustering of the participants. The dual role of the elite has not been sufficient to hold activities in lower Manhattan when the attracting power of other locations became strong. And if more and more of the routine and market-oriented functions take up new stations in the City or the Region, their movement could conceivably have the effect of weaning top management away from its cherished Wall Street stronghold, and finally could even exert a splintering influence upon the money-market core itself. The money-market tail that has always wagged the dog might then find itself in the unaccustomed position of following along behind.

It might, but that does not mean it will. The money-market core is the tail in a numerical sense only; in other respects it is the heart. The self-generative circle which was set in motion when the money-market segments were arising in lower Manhattan remains impressively strong. External economies and the need for effective communication in an atmosphere of uncertainty and hazard continue to bolster the clustering tendency, which in turn creates further external economies and more opportunities for face-to-face confrontation, which further cements the cluster. The integrating forces are by no means ready for interment. We will be in a better position to forecast the net effect of all the conflicting forces on the financial community after examining in detail the behavior of specific industries, beginning with the commercial banks.

3

Commercial Banking in the United States—Output and Manpower

As we move from a consideration of the Region's role as the nation's money-market center to its position in commercial banking, our jumping-off point once again must be the national setting. Of course, not all of the Region's banking business is national in scope; banks ordinarily obtain the bulk of their business from customers located within a quite limited radius. But the banks of the New York Metropolitan Region—more particularly, the banks in New York City—supplement their local business with that obtained from clients of nationwide scope. In 1956, for instance, the Region's member banks * accounted for 32 per cent of the value of all commercial loans and 46 per cent of the value of all securities loans on the books of the nation's commercial banks. Second, because of the wealth and size of the Region, the volume of *local* business done by its banks is large compared with that of institutions in other sections of the country. In 1956, the amount of consumer and mortgage loans held by member banks in the New York Metropolitan Region, representing for the most part "neighborhood activities," was 14 per cent and 9 per cent, respectively, of the national totals. In the same year, the Region had between 9 and 10 per cent of the nation's population. The only activity in which the Region's banks are notably deficient is agricultural financing.

* In the New York Metropolitan Region, banks which are not members of the Federal Reserve System are relatively unimportant.

But various forces have been changing the Region's share of total banking activities. To a large extent, these forces are national in scope. There have been alterations in the services that the nation's banks offer; adjustments in the amount of manpower that is needed to perform particular services; and a relatively rapid economic growth of sections outside the New York area. The shifting picture throughout the country, therefore, offers the first clue to an understanding of New York's evolving position.

Banking in the United States is a big industry. In 1956, some 13,600 commercial banks employed 536,000 persons and had assets of $214 billion. Their trust departments held another $100 billion in a fiduciary capacity. Together, these sums made up about one-tenth of the nation's estimated wealth.

In a later chapter we shall want to know how large the labor force of the nation's banks is likely to be in the future, as the country expands and the banks' functions change and grow. In order to make this prediction, we must be able to define the output of the banks in a concrete way and to establish a definite relation between it and the resulting manpower requirements.

We start out with the fact that the great bulk of banking employees are engaged in clerical functions related to the sheer physical sorting, counting, clearing, and recording of an immense volume of checks and other paper. It would be gratifying, therefore, if our measure of output could be expressed in terms of pieces of paper, and if relations could be established between the number of these items and the number of people required to handle them.

We experimented at length, but discovered that such simple measures as a count of checks did not work out satisfactorily as a basis for forecasting manpower; and neither did various related dollar measures, such as debits to accounts. They all had drawbacks: sometimes they could not be adequately related to the number of employees; sometimes sufficient historical data were not available; and even when data were at hand for past years, projecting them into the future turned out to be excessively difficult.

Eventually we fell back on various bank asset series to provide us with indicators of output. A strong correlation emerged between the behavior of certain types of assets—notably loans and investments—and the total manpower of the banks. In the first place, there are of course solid links between assets and deposits; and changes in loans and investments are promptly reflected in deposit accounts, with consequent influence on the size of the clerical work force. Moreover, the "mix" of bank assets—in effect, the "mix" of bank functions—casts light on manpower needs; institutions that favor consumer lending, for example, are likely to require proportionately more clerical personnel to service their numerous small accounts than institutions specializing in large corporate clientele. In addition, data on assets are available for long periods of time and lend themselves readily to projection.* So we turn first of all to a consideration of the way in which some of the principal assets of the nation's banks have been changing in recent decades.

THE GROWTH IN BANKING ASSETS

Except for several minor setbacks and a big dip immediately after World War II, total commercial bank assets—even when expressed in constant dollars—have been expanding since the depth of the Great Depression in 1933.** Chart 2 shows the relation between this growth and that of the nation's economy as measured by the gross national product. Though banking assets have tended to rise at a slightly slower rate, the two trends have been roughly similar. Behind this general picture are mixed movements in the major components of bank assets, including consumer credit, com-

* In Appendix A, we discuss at greater length the whole problem of choosing a measure of banking output.

** We are aware that not everyone agrees about the advisability of putting bank assets in constant dollars. Some contend that bank assets are themselves a reflection of money supply, and that changes in money supply are a major determinant of the price level, so that deflating bank assets by a measure of the price level is, in effect, using a measure to adjust that same measure. We feel, however, that bank assets—especially short-term loans—are clearly affected by price changes and that allowance should be made for those changes in order to get a realistic idea of the trends in assets as a measure of banking output. For further discussion see Appendix A.

Chart 2
Gross National Product and Assets of All Commercial Banks, United States, 1929–1956

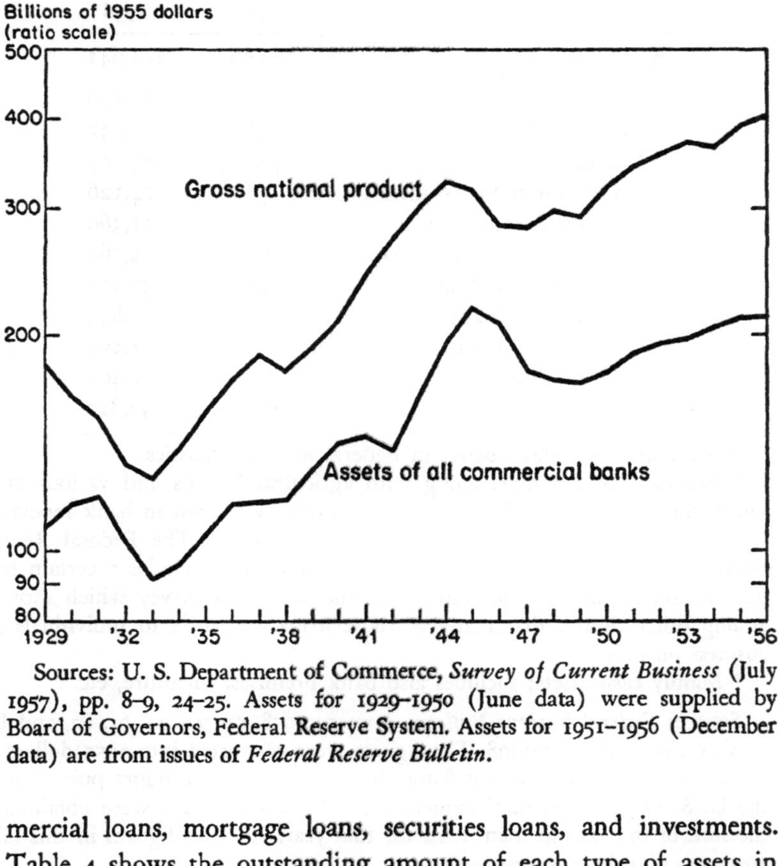

Sources: U. S. Department of Commerce, *Survey of Current Business* (July 1957), pp. 8–9, 24–25. Assets for 1929–1950 (June data) were supplied by Board of Governors, Federal Reserve System. Assets for 1951–1956 (December data) are from issues of *Federal Reserve Bulletin.*

mercial loans, mortgage loans, securities loans, and investments. Table 4 shows the outstanding amount of each type of assets in 1947 and 1956. These diverse trends, having clear importance to the future of banking, are now examined in turn.

Consumer credit

One of the major changes in the nature of economic activity in the United States since World War II has been the dramatic ex-

Table 4 Assets of Commercial Banks, United States, 1947 and 1956

(in millions of 1955 dollars)

	December 1947	December 1956
Assets, total	188,564	212,641
Earning assets, total	141,118	161,829
Investments	94,934	72,642
Loans, total	46,184	89,187
Consumer loans, total	4,646	14,126
Instalment loans	3,186	11,366
Non-instalment loans	1,460	2,760
Commercial loans	22,047	37,592
Mortgage loans [a]	11,399	21,853
Securities loans	2,488	4,155
Other loans [b]	5,604	11,461
All other assets [c]	47,446	50,812

[a] Same as "real estate loans" in Federal Reserve statistics.

[b] We have placed here, along with agricultural loans and various other kinds, the "nonconsumer" portion of the category known in bank reports to Government agencies as "other loans to individuals." The Federal Reserve Board, in publishing the figures on consumer credit, excludes a certain fraction of "other loans to individuals" on the basis of a survey which showed, among other things, that many of those loans are made to individuals for business purposes.

[c] Mainly cash assets; includes also bank premises, furniture, etc.

Source: *Federal Reserve Bulletin,* January 1958, pp. 41, 44, 61, 62, and December 1954, pp. 1294–1298. The figures were converted into 1955 dollars by means of the implicit price deflators for gross national product published by the U. S. Department of Commerce. Total loans for 1956 were obtained as the sum of the various loan items for that year. All loan figures in this table are gross of valuation reserves.

pansion of consumer credit held by banks, finance companies, credit unions, and retail stores. Consumer credit has expanded not only in absolute terms but also as a proportion of disposable personal income, upon which it depends; and it is the rise in this proportion that is especially important for our purposes. As shown in Chart 3, the rise has been almost entirely due to the spectacular growth of

Chart 3

Consumer Credit Outstanding and Its Major Components as Percentage of Disposable Personal Income, United States, 1929–1956

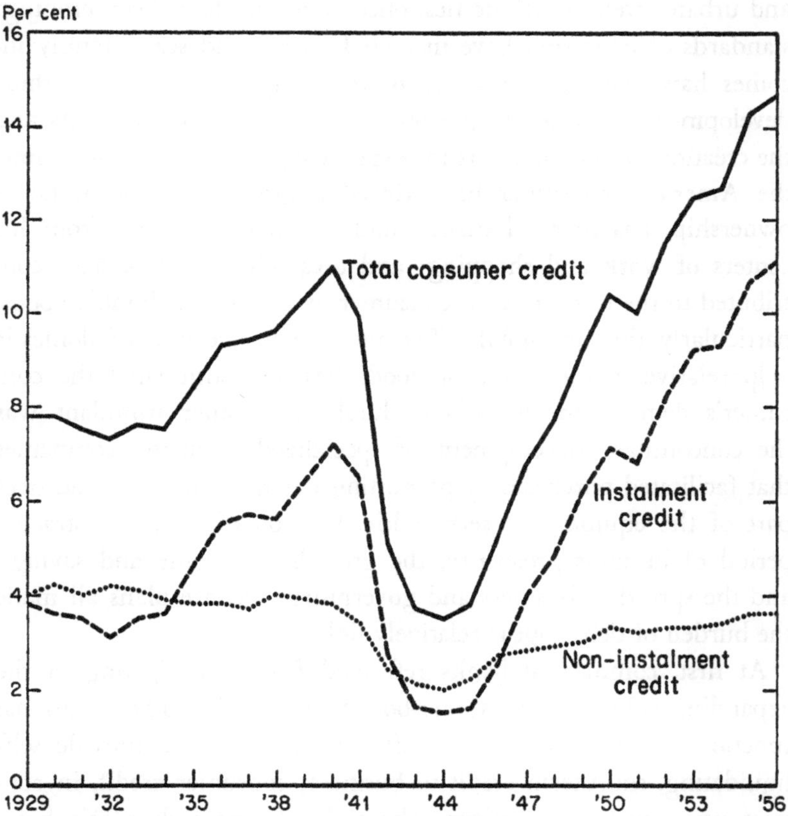

Source: *Economic Report of the President,* January 1958, pp. 131, 167.

instalment loans. Non-instalment credit (charge accounts and single-payment loans) has expanded greatly, too, in absolute terms; but its growth relative to income, although steady, has been very mild.

The popularity of instalment credit reflects deep-rooted changes in the characteristics of the consumer. Over the years he has become a buyer of "hard" goods and has been willing to assume greater debt burdens relative to his income. To create these new attitudes, strong forces were required. The nation's population has become more urbanized; improved transportation and communication have reduced the differences in living habits between farm and urban dwellers; ethnic ties, once powerful, have been eroding; standards of education have increased on a broad scale; family incomes have tended to become more nearly equal; and all these developments have led to greater uniformity in buying habits and the creation of mass markets for expensive goods. At the same time, the American consumer has evinced a greater interest in home ownership, has married earlier, and has settled farther from his centers of work and shopping; and these changes, too, have contributed to the trend toward consumer ownership of durable goods, particularly the automobile. The increase in the cost of domestic help relative to the prices of goods has also stimulated the consumer's demand for household durables. Another stimulant was the concomitant development of specialized financing companies that facilitated purchases by permitting payments to be spread over part of the equipment's service life. On top of this, a protracted period of business prosperity, the growth of income and savings, and the spread of business and government welfare plans all made the burden of debt appear relatively lighter.

At first, commercial banks refrained from participating in the expanding volume of consumer-borrowing activity. The traditional function of commercial banks, after all, had been to provide self-liquidating, short-term credit to business; consumer credit, in contrast, was a very different type of activity. In the early 1920's, however, several small institutions began to enter the field and in 1928 the National City Bank of New York opened a personal loan department. By the end of the next year, banks had established about 200 personal loan departments, though many of them fell by the wayside during the years of economic reversal that followed.[1]

Despite the depression, events in the 1930's brightened the spark lit by these early efforts. A large influx of foreign funds provided banks with substantial excess reserves at a time when their traditional investing outlets were meager. Also, the successful experience of finance companies outside the banking system furnished positive indication of the profit potential in the consumer field. Finally, an introduction to this type of activity for banks was afforded by the repayment and modernization loans established under the Federal housing program. Because of these developments, the banking community found it necessary to break unmistakably with the past, broaden its horizons, and increasingly to direct its facilities to the differing needs of individuals.

To protect their position against the competition of the other lending institutions, banks went out of their way to tear down the façade of austerity which once separated them from the public. Instead of expecting clients to make pilgrimages to their headquarters when in need of funds, they sought out new customers and helped create financing opportunities. This tendency continued with mounting force in the two decades following the depression. By 1956, Ogden Nash was proclaiming:

> Yes, bankers used to be like Scrooge before he encountered the ghost of Marley,
> But along came TV and now they are Good Time Charlie. . . .[2]

Despite this vigorous entry into a new area, consumer credit, both instalment and otherwise, is predominantly the business of institutions other than commercial banks. Chart 4 shows that the banks' share of total consumer credit rose sharply after World War II, but was still only 35 per cent in 1956. This percentage, however, probably understates the actual role of the banks because, in addition to their direct participation, they grant loans to other holders of consumer credit.

The banks consistently have granted a larger amount of instalment than of non-instalment loans. In 1956 they had about 37 per cent of the dollar value of all instalment loans outstanding and even larger proportions of some of the subdivisions of these loans, not shown in the chart. For example, they had over three quarters

Chart 4

Consumer Credit Held by Nation's Commercial Banks as Percentage of That of All Types of Holders, 1939–1956

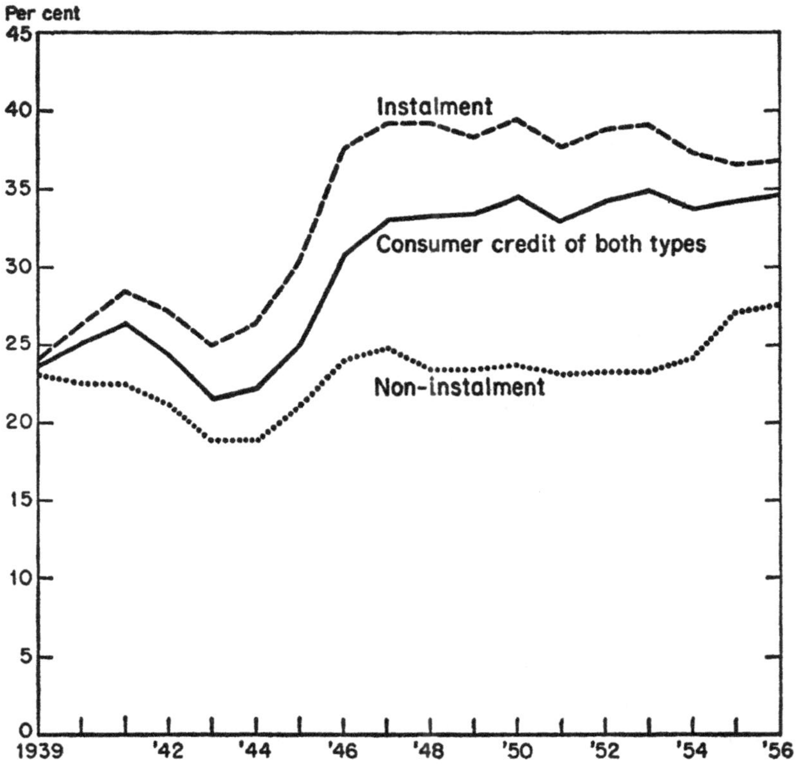

Source: *Federal Reserve Bulletin.*

of repair and modernization loans, and about 40 per cent of the outstanding automobile paper. Although the banks' shares of other types of instalment credit were much smaller, they recently have showed more interest in personal instalment loans by introducing special credit plans.[8] With respect to non-instalment loans, the share of the banks has been consistently smaller than in the instalment field, although it increased rather sharply over the past several years.

COMMERCIAL LOANS

Meanwhile, commercial lending by banks has taken a somewhat different course. Making commercial loans, of course, is the traditional function of banks and ordinarily such credit represents an important segment of total banking assets. The amount of commercial loans granted by the banks depends primarily upon the demand of business, and this demand, in turn, reflects general economic conditions.

Accordingly, as Chart 5 shows, a close affinity marks the changes in the amount of commercial loans held by the banks and the movements of the gross national product. Over the last two decades, except for the years of World War II, the ratio of outstanding bank commercial loans to gross national product has varied between 6.5 and 9.5 per cent. Within this range, there has been a tendency

Chart 5
Gross National Product and Outstanding Commercial Loans of Commercial Banks, United States, 1938–1956

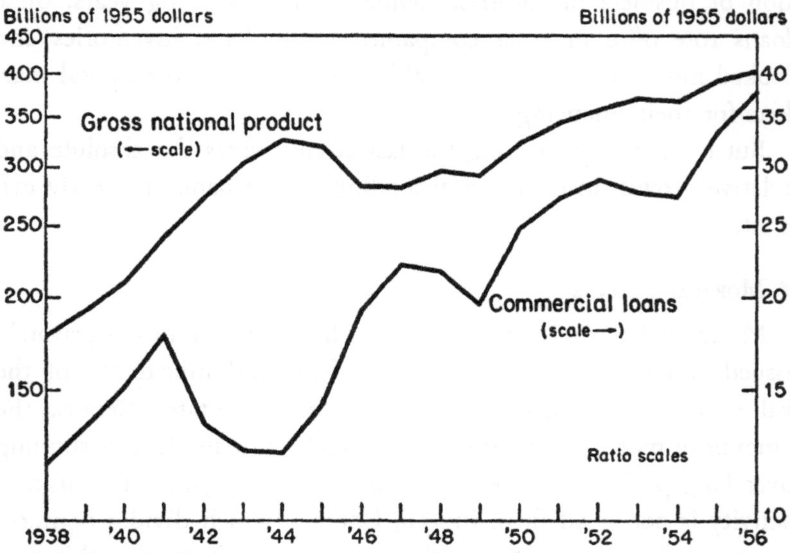

Source: *Economic Report of the President,* January 1958, pp. 117, 163.

for the ratio in recent years to be higher than that prevailing in the earlier part of the period. The general upward tilt in the ratio of commercial loans to business activity possibly reflects the more aggressive attitude of the banks in competing with other lending institutions and in broadening the kinds of loans they are willing to grant.

Aside from the direct influence of general business conditions, the volume of commercial loans is affected by the amount of capital expenditures made by business firms, the relative use of internal and external sources to finance their money needs, and the extent to which commercial banks are used to raise external funds. For example, during the middle 1930's, business firms reduced their reliance on commercial banks for financing. According to the Board of Governors of the Federal Reserve System, this reduction was due to the "increasing use of the corporate form of business enterprise, together with the growth in the importance of large concerns and in the custom of meeting financial need through security issues or out of retained earnings. . . ."[4] The decline in bank commercial loans terminating in 1954 was due in part to a substantial liquidation of business inventories,[5] while in the following years, these loans rose once more as companies accumulated inventories and looked more to their commercial banks and less to the capital markets for their financing.[6]

But by and large, during the last twenty years the absolute and relative growth in commercial lending by the banks is clearly evident.

Mortgage loans

Mortgage loans represent more than half of the country's privately issued and privately held long-term debt; and nine-tenths of the value of these mortgages is on nonfarm real estate.[7] Because the amount of mortgages outstanding depends on many factors running over long periods of time, the tie between mortgages and business activity is not at all firm. Indeed, Chart 6, which divides nonfarm mortgage debt into its two major components, shows that this debt

Chart 6

Gross National Product and Major Components of Outstanding Nonfarm Mortgage Debt, 1929–1956

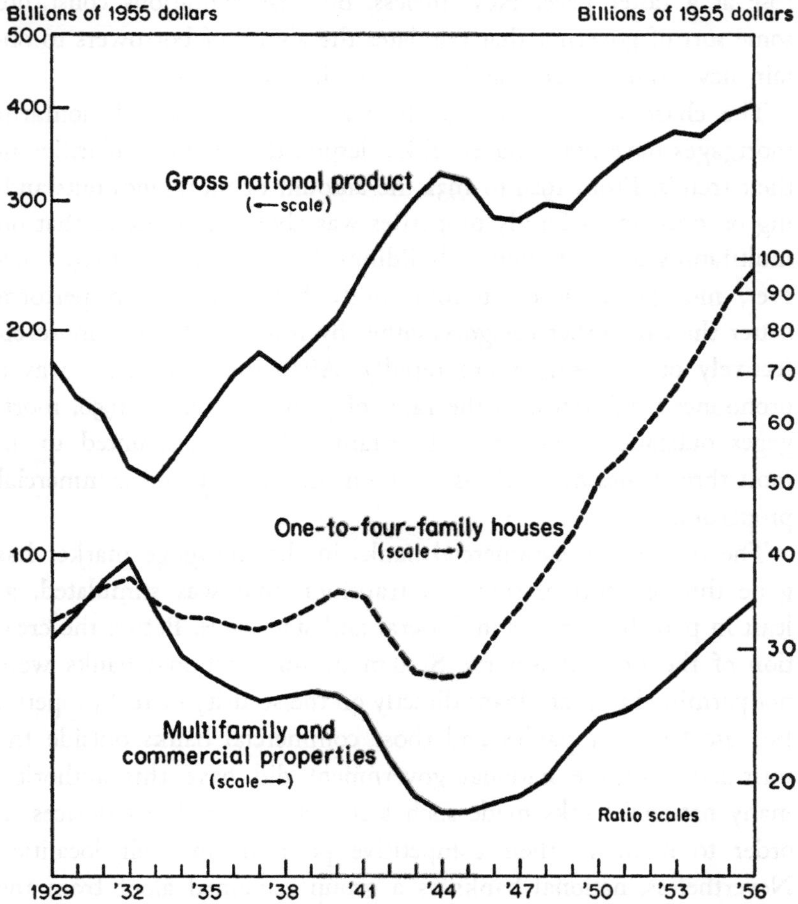

Note: Amounts were converted into 1955 dollars by means of the implicit deflators for gross national product.

Sources: J. E. Morton, *Urban Mortgage Lending: Comparative Markets and Experience,* National Bureau of Economic Research (Princeton University Press, 1956), p. 18; Saul B. Klaman, *The Volume of Mortgage Debt in the Postwar Decade,* Technical Paper 13, National Bureau of Economic Research (New York, 1958), pp. 38–39.

and the gross national product (both expressed in constant dollars) have differed markedly in their trends. During the war years, for example, such mortgage loans moved indifferently while production boomed. After the war, both moved upward, but mortgages rose at a faster pace. Nevertheless, business conditions constitute some sort of governor that regulates the ability of borrowers to obtain new commitments and meet existing obligations.

The chart also shows that the two major classes of nonfarm mortgages have not behaved alike despite the broad similarities in their trends. From 1929 to 1932 the amount of mortgages outstanding on one-to-four-family properties was about the same as that on multifamily and commercial buildings. Starting around 1933, however, mortgages on one-to-four-family houses began to perform better than the other category, either by resisting declines more effectively or by rising more rapidly. After the war, there was a pronounced difference in the rates of growth; and by 1956, mortgages outstanding on one-to-four-family houses amounted to almost three times as much as those on multifamily and commercial properties.

The role of the commercial banks in the mortgage market has gone through several stages, a transition that was stimulated, at least in part, by changes in Federal and state laws. Before the creation of the Federal Reserve System in 1913, national banks were not permitted to grant loans directly on the security of real property. Because trust companies and those commercial banks outside the jurisdiction of the national government did have this authority, many national banks made such loans through indirect devices in order to maintain their competitive positions in their localities. Nevertheless, national banks as a group remained aloof from the real estate field, and in 1913 their mortgage loans constituted only 0.7 per cent of their total resources, compared with 15.6 per cent for loan and trust companies, stock savings banks, and state banks as a group.[8]

During the ensuing years, liberalization of the legislative provisions concerning mortgage lending by national banks enabled them to make vigorous strides in this field. In 1916, for example, the Federal Government gave national banks some authority to make nonfarm real estate loans, though with limitations on the contract period, the ratio of loan to property value, and the ratio of a bank's aggregate loans to its resources. These restrictions were gradually relaxed, opening the doors for a considerable expansion in the volume of their nonfarm mortgage loans. State laws also became more lenient, but the state banks did not show the considerable improvement of the national institutions, since their legislation had been relatively broad anyhow. In 1934, a particularly sharp fillip to bank activity in this field was given by the National Housing Act, which set up the machinery for government insurance of mortgage loans. Ten years later, the guaranty program of the Veterans Administration expanded the market further.

Accordingly, all commercial banks have been participating actively in the granting of urban mortgage loans for a number of years. Chart 7 shows what percentages the commercial banks have held of the two main categories of mortgage debt since 1929. The strong and prolonged rise of the ratio covering one-to-four-family houses between 1934 and 1947 is not only attributable to the easing of legislation but also to the greater willingness of the commercial banks to move into this field. Since that time, this ratio has receded as the commercial banks found other uses for their funds and faced more aggressive competition from savings and loan associations and mutual savings banks. Meanwhile, the ratio covering multifamily and commercial properties, after a severe drop during World War II and a sharp recovery in 1945 and 1946, remained relatively unchanged thereafter. By the close of 1956, the percentage in each category was only moderately higher than it was in 1939.

The amounts of mortgage debt held by the commercial banks do not reflect all of their activity in this field. Heavy use is made of short-term bank credit in the financing of government-underwritten mortgages between the time of original closing and their assumption by permanent investors. The banks also occupy a vital role in granting short-term construction loans to builders or mortgage companies that have already obtained a "forward commitment" for permanent financing from an investor such as a life in-

Chart 7

Nonfarm Mortgage Debt Held by Nation's Commercial Banks as Percentage of That of All Types of Holders, 1929–1956

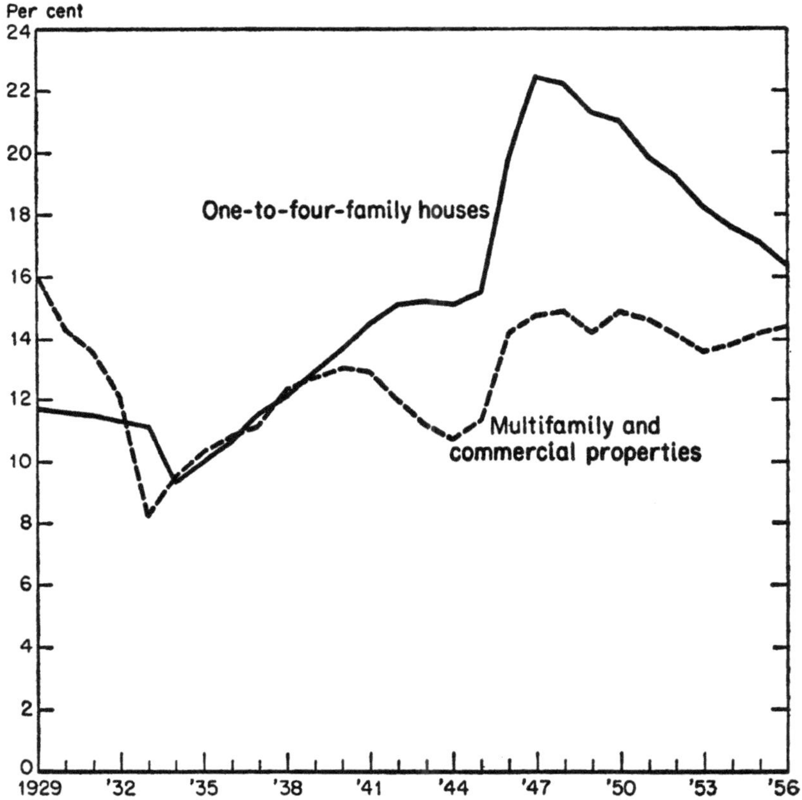

Sources: J. E. Morton, *Urban Mortgage Lending: Comparative Markets and Experience,* National Bureau of Economic Research (Princeton University Press, 1956), pp. 170–171; Saul B. Klaman, *The Volume of Mortgage Debt in the Postwar Decade,* Technical Paper 13, National Bureau of Economic Research (New York, 1958), pp. 48–49, 80–81.

surance company or a mutual savings bank. Besides, the banks sometimes grant "standby commitments" to mortgage companies that are undertaking to purchase mortgages at a future date and to carry them for limited periods until permanent investors can be found. The relative importance of this type of activity does not show up fully in the reported year-end mortgage holdings of banks.

In appraising the future of commercial banks in mortgage lending, one must bear in mind the basic fact that most banks are essentially short-term lenders. In the mortgage field they show a preference for financing mortgages over temporary periods until permanent investors can be uncovered, and a desire to act as the servicing agents of permanent investors. In these capacities, the banks have found a lucrative and comparatively safe source of income. Indicative of the reluctance of the commercial banks to share more vigorously in the direct underwriting of mortgages is the wide gap that exists between the amount held and that permissible under legal limitations. At the close of 1956, for example, the national banks had only slightly more than 60 per cent of the mortgage loans which they could have granted within existing legal requirements.[9]

Securities loans

Loans on securities are much less important than the other lending categories. In reporting securities loans, the commercial banks distinguish between those extended to brokers and dealers and to others. Brokers and dealers borrow from the banks either to lend to their customers or to finance their own securities dealings. "Others" include all other customers who borrow for the purpose of buying or carrying securities. As indicated in Chart 8, the banks have sometimes lent more to one group and sometimes more to the other. In general, these fluctuations may be explained by changes in the volume of new corporate and government financing, the prices of securities, the trading of stocks, and the margin requirements.

Loans versus investments

Banks prefer lending to investing, for various reasons: loans ordinarily bring higher returns; there is a traditional bias toward a personal relation between the banker and his clients which en-

Chart 8

Outstanding Commercial Bank Loans for Purchasing or Carrying Securities, United States, 1938–1956

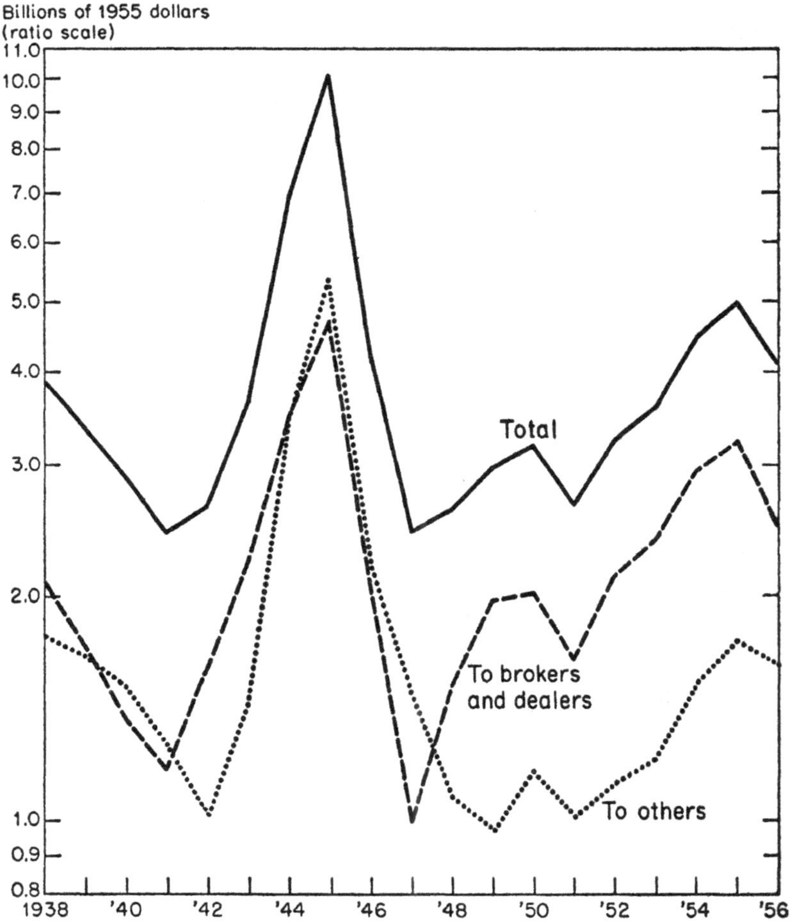

Sources: For 1938–1941, Board of Governors of the Federal Reserve System, *Banking and Monetary Statistics* (Washington, 1943), p. 109. For 1942–1956, Federal Deposit Insurance Corporation, *Assets, Liabilities, and Capital Accounts, Commercial and Mutual Savings Banks,* published periodically.

courages negotiated transactions with borrowers; and lending activity gives rise to continuing customer relations. Accordingly, when banks buy securities in the capital markets, they tend to do it with surplus funds for which they cannot find more profitable uses elsewhere.*

Banking history highlights these characteristics. Commercial banks expand their commercial loans vigorously whenever the advancing tides of business offer the opportunity; in contrast, they tend to purchase securities as business recedes or heavy Government borrowing encourages investment buying. Chart 9 shows that, in 1930, loans represented over 70 per cent of bank earning assets. Although loans continued predominant during the next several years, their absolute volume contracted severely during the depression as defaults grew and banks became increasingly cautious in assuming new commitments. On the other hand, the great expansion of the Federal debt that occurred during this period led to a growth in the volume of investments carried. By 1935, the loan portion of bank earning assets had shrunk to about 42 per cent, and it remained at this level until 1942, when the influences of World War II began to be felt. The commercial banks financed approximately 40 per cent of the $228 billion borrowed by the Treasury during the war, whereas they increased loans only modestly because corporate liquidity continued high. Accordingly, by 1945, their loan account actually was less than it had been in 1930, while investments were more than seven times as great. Thereafter, trends were generally reversed as the volume of investments fluctuated in a narrow range but was generally downward, while loans rose rapidly. By 1956, loans represented 55 per cent of earning assets.

✓ The trust function

Commercial banks have been aggressive in extending their trust activity, and today perform in more than a dozen fiduciary capacities. To illustrate: for individuals they hold securities, provide

* Exceptions to this operating principle are the portions of banks' investment accounts carried as secondary reserves.

Chart 9

Distribution of the Investments and Loans of Commercial Banks, United States, 1929–1956

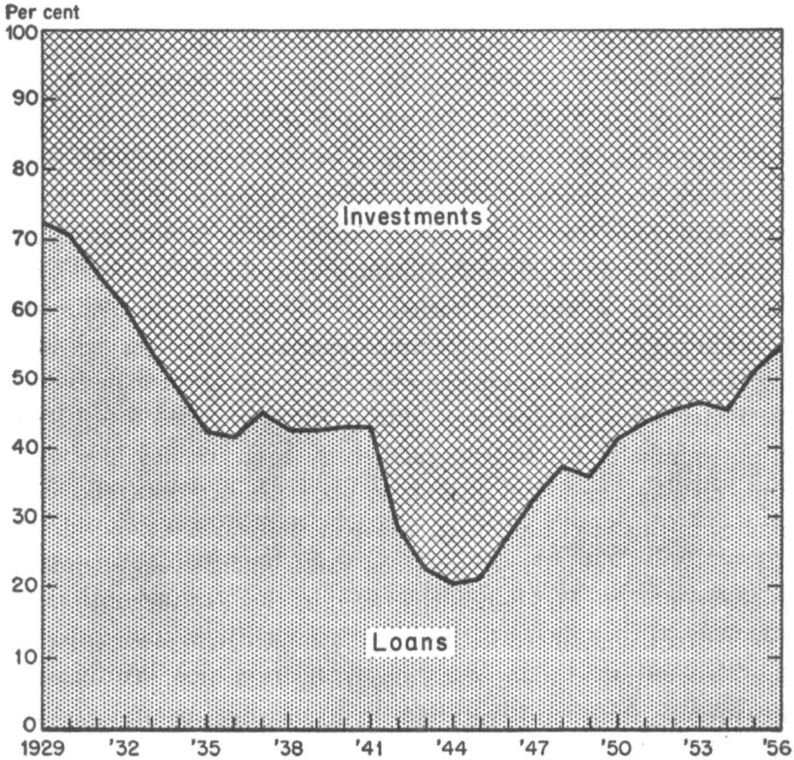

Source: *Economic Report of the President,* January 1958, p. 163. (1929–1934 data are for mid-year; 1935–1956 for year-end.)

investment advice, and manage estates and property; for corporations, they act as registrars and transfer agents, serve as trustees under bond indentures, and administer pension and welfare plans. Because of the wide range of their trust functions, the volume of such business depends upon many factors, from the number of wealthy residents and large corporations in an area to the nature of the tax laws.

Before 1913, the entry of commercial banks into the trust field was limited by the fact that national banks could not accept trust business and could only provide this service through affiliated state banks or trust companies. The Federal Reserve Act of 1913 authorized the Federal Reserve Board to permit national banks to act in a fiduciary capacity. This program laid the groundwork for a subsequent rapid growth of bank participation in trust business. As a result, the proportion of the banks' trust income to total operating earnings rose rapidly until 1937. After this spurt, despite the proliferation of trust services, a gradual reversal took place, and the ratio has been generally declining since that time. Table 5 shows this ratio at five-year intervals since 1925. Inasmuch as trust income gained substantially during this period in absolute amounts, its relative shrinkage is due to a more rapid advance in other phases

Table 5 Trust Department Income and Total Operating Earnings of Commercial Banks, United States, 1925–1955 [a]

(in current dollars)

	Trust department earnings (millions)	Total operating earnings [b] (millions)	Trust department earnings as percentage of total operating earnings
1925	$ 41	$1,919	2.1
1930	80	2,158	3.7
1935	78	1,207	6.5
1940	92	1,323	7.0
1945	120	2,482	4.8
1950	181	3,931	4.6
1955	282	6,378	4.4

[a] For the years 1925–1940 the data refer to member banks, and for the years 1945–1955 to insured banks. Comparability of the two series may be gauged by the figures for 1934, which are available in both forms; in that year the ratio of trust income to operating earnings was 5.7 per cent for member banks and 5.1 per cent for insured banks.

[b] Total operating earnings are gross figures prior to deducting operating expenses. Total earnings include interest on securities; interest on loans; service charges, commissions, fees, and collection charges; trust department and other current earnings.

Sources: Board of Governors of the Federal Reserve System, *Banking and Monetary Statistics* (Washington, 1943), pp. 262–263; also *Annual Report of the Federal Deposit Insurance Corporation*—for the year ended Dec. 31, 1945, p. 128, and for the year ended Dec. 31, 1956, p. 116.

of banking activity. The relative decline might have been even steeper had it not been for the general tendency of trust fees to rise during this period.*

The amounts in the table lump all kinds of trust income and therefore obscure the quite different rates of growth between one kind and another. Fragmentary figures suggest that personal trust funds have not risen much.[10] Instead, the absolute gain in banks' trust activities has been chiefly due to the rapid growth of trust services for corporations, including the administering of private pension funds, which have mushroomed. Since the Great Depression of the 1930's, pension plans have become increasingly attractive to corporations as a means of adding to the compensation of officers and other employees without immediately increasing the burden of income taxes. The high tax rates and the wage controls of World War II provided a great push to the development of this field, and so did a 1948 ruling by the National Labor Relations Board that pension benefits were appropriate issues for collective bargaining. Between 1951 and 1955, the book value of the assets of all non-insured corporate pension funds more than doubled.[11] In 1955, the Comptroller of the Currency noted that the management of these funds had become "a substantial part of the fiduciary business of national banks," and estimated that employee welfare or benefit accounts amounted to 15 per cent of all fiduciary business of national banks.[12]

RELATING ASSETS TO MANPOWER

Most of our discussion so far about loans, investments, and trust income bears directly on any forecast of the manpower trends of

* On the other hand, trust department earnings tend to be understated in banking statistics because they do not take into account the revenues derived from other sources as a result of trust activities. For example, prior to the time that the trust department of a bank distributes a corporation's dividend checks, the corporation will often make deposits equal to the amount of the distribution. Also, income from personal trusts may be placed in the checking accounts of the beneficiaries. The proceeds flowing to the banks from these additional deposits properly are traceable to the trust department.

the nation's commercial banks. But before we can go to the future—a subject reserved for our final chapter—we must ascertain what the changes in these banking functions have meant to manpower in past years.

What we have seen so far is a general but uneven growth in the operations of the banks, a growth in which some functions outstripped others. With respect to manpower and space needs, these differences were of critical significance. Some banking functions, as they expand, demand a much more rapid increase in payrolls and space than do others. Accordingly, the manpower required by banking is related not only to the changing *volume* of bank activities but also to their changing *mix*. And it is also related to the changing quantities of manpower required per unit of service performed. Since we have assumed that asset figures bear some consistent relation to the units of service performed—that the volume of consumer loans outstanding, for instance, is related to the size of the flow of consumer loans—our next step is to see how manpower has varied in relation to these assets.

Our analysis indicates that moderate gains were taking place in banking "productivity" by 1938 *—that is, that less and less manpower was employed for each million dollars of assets, when assets are measured in constant dollars. Although quantitative evidence is lacking for the years prior to 1938, we assume that the same tendency was present in these earlier years as well. The introduction and improvement of machines in banking offices had been going on for decades. As early as 1900, a major "break-through" had begun to take place in the technology of bank operations as the old hand-kept ledgers were replaced by tabulating machines, at first manually operated and then run by electricity. The capabilities of such devices in striking new balances and in providing records for banks and their customers were enhanced during the first three decades of the century. In 1928, the procedures for handling checks were drastically altered by the introduction of microfilming. In the 1930's, important strides were made in the mechanization of both

* See Appendix A.

bookkeeping and check-sorting. During World War II, the efficiency of the machines was temporarily offset when the banks had to hire many untrained employees to replace those entering the armed forces. But after the war, productivity rose again. A second major "break-through" is now taking place with the introduction of high-speed computers and electronic memory systems; these changes, which belong more to the future than to the past, will be evaluated in Chapter 8.

To lay a reasonable basis for speculating on the future of bank employment, we must do more than merely assert that changing manpower requirements in the past have been the outcome of changing output, changing mix, and changing productivity. The impact of each of these forces must be measured in quantitative terms.

This kind of evaluation is difficult in any field of activity. In banking, where the output of a worker cannot be expressed in such terms as bolts of cloth or bottles of beer, the problem is especially complex. We finally determined that four measures could be made to serve as indicators of both the growth and the changing mix of banking output: (1) investments; (2) consumer loans; (3) "all other loans," primarily those for commercial purposes, real estate, and securities; and (4) the income of trust departments. These assets and activities generate almost 90 per cent of the total operating earnings—the "sales"—of the banking industry.[13]

To learn how manpower needs have been changing for trust departments, we resorted to various studies conducted by the Federal Reserve Banks and to a special study of our own conducted for commercial banks in the New York Metropolitan Region. From these sources, we concluded that, in terms of current dollars, one trust department employee produced $7,000 of income in 1947, $8,000 in 1950, and $10,000 in 1956.

At this point, we began our efforts to estimate the relative weights of each of the three asset factors—investments, consumer loans, and "all other loans"—in explaining the growth of commercial bank employment as a whole. For each year, from 1947 to 1956, inclusive, we obtained the necessary asset figures and the total employment figures in each of the then 48 states and the District of Columbia. From each total employment figure, we subtracted our rough and ready estimates of the number employed in the generation of trust department income. We then sought to measure the average relation between the remaining employment and our three asset measures.

Our efforts produced ten equations, one for each year during the period. In effect, each equation stated that, on the average, banking employment in the specified year was equal to a constant figure plus the employment associated with each of the three types of assets. In each equation, the constant term was small—about 10 per cent of total bank jobs—indicating that the bulk of employment could be predicted on the basis of the three types of credit activity.

This does not mean, of course, that all bank employees are engaged in handling investments and loans. Obviously, considerable manpower is used in other activities, from janitorial services to the handling of deposits.* What appears to be the case is that most of the manpower engaged in these other activities varies in sufficiently close conformity with our loan and investment indices to permit a fairly close prediction of total manpower changes to be made through these indices.

The net result of this train of analysis is given in Table 6, which shows, for each year of the period, the average relationship by states between the number of employees in the commercial banks and the dollar amount of investments, of consumer loans, and of "all other loans." **

It is evident from the figures in Table 6 that different assets are associated with very different manpower needs. Consumer loans

* As a matter of fact, we considered using the amount of deposits as one of our indices of output, but found that it was inferior for this purpose to those we employed. See Appendix A.

** It is important to recognize that the manpower coefficients are not intended to measure the literal input-output relations of individual institutions but rather to reflect the average influence on manpower needs of variations in the kinds of service performed. It should be noted, too, that the dollar figures upon which the equations are based are expressed in constant dollars.

are linked with a heavy use of bank manpower per million dollars outstanding; other loans are very much less so; and investments are the most sparing of all in this regard.

It is clear, too, that the *changes* in the manpower requirements linked with the three types of activity have not been moving in the same direction. In the field of investments, the manpower needs of the banks per million dollars of investment have been rising. In sharp contrast, manpower needs per million dollars of loans, whether consumer or other types, have been falling.

Table 6 Average Number of Commercial Bank Employees Associated with Each Million Dollars of Investments, Consumer Loans, and All Other Loans, 1947–1956[a]

	Investments	Consumer loans	All other loans
1947	.7742	20.8686	2.1814
1948	.8480	18.8616	2.2585
1949	.8509	18.5451	1.8887
1950	.8900	17.3258	1.2851
1951	.8657	18.4671	1.6703
1952	[b]	18.7850	1.3773
1953	[b]	18.9941	1.8669
1954	1.0014	16.5302	1.2140
1955	1.2398	14.9655	1.0466
1956	[b]	15.9959	1.3670

[a] Amounts used are in constant 1955 dollars.

[b] The manpower coefficients for investments for 1952, 1953, and 1956 were not statistically significant at the 1 per cent level and therefore were omitted from the table.

Note: Some of the unevenness of the year-to-year fluctuations may be attributed to statistical sampling variations.

Source: See Appendix A.

During the period from 1947 to 1956, total manpower in the banks actually rose by 49 per cent—the net result of increases in the level of banking activity, changes in the mix of these activities, and improvements in productivity. The figures in Table 6 tell us a number of significant things about the relation between these factors and the growth of bank employment. If the mix had not changed from 1947 to 1956, and if manpower requirements per million dollars of assets had also continued the same, one might have expected the increased activity to bring an employment increase of only 16 per cent. On the other hand, if both the volume of activity and the productivity had remained the same during this period, employment in banking would have increased by 70 per cent, this time because of the changes in mix—notably the great advance of consumer loans relative to other kinds of loans, and of loans in general relative to investments. Here we have some measure of the impact which the change in bank services has been having upon bank employment.

By themselves, the combined influences of the growth in the volume of business and the changes in the mix of activities would have caused almost a doubling in the manpower requirements of the banks. The fact that employment gained by only about 50 per cent is due, of course, to the rising productivity shown in Table 6. In fact, if volume and mix had not changed from 1947 to 1956, but the manpower coefficients had declined as they did, employment in the country's commercial banks would have dropped by 23 per cent. This shrinkage corresponds to an increase in productivity, as we have defined it here, of about 30 per cent in nine years or approximately 3 per cent a year, compounded annually.

Thus, despite the picture of granitelike stability traditionally used to portray banking, one sees powerful and dynamic forces at work in the industry over the last several decades. The rise of consumer credit, the march of technology, the growth of trust functions and other activities—all these have substantially altered the banking profile in recent years. These trends have important implications for the future and will strongly influence our later projections. Commercial banking in the country sets the stage for commercial banking in the Region, to which we now turn.

4

The Region as a Commercial Banking Center

There have been various signs since World War II that the banks of the New York Metropolitan Region have not kept pace with those of the nation. From 1947 to 1956, employment in the nation's commercial banks increased by 49 per cent, but the rise in the Region's commercial banks was only 26 per cent. Measured in constant dollars, deposits in the nation's commercial banks were up 10 per cent, but deposits in the Region declined slightly. Loans and investments—also in constant dollars—expanded 16 per cent nationally but not at all in the Region. What lay behind these differences? What do they imply for the Region's future? We start this analysis by examining the movement of deposits into and out of the Region, because the credit potential of a commercial bank depends upon its available funds, which, in turn, are influenced by the extent to which it is receiving or distributing deposits.

THE ELUSIVE DEPOSITS

The Region's banks have grown to serve a national function. Their size, their location in the country's principal money-market center, and their specialized skills enable them to arrange loans of great magnitude for enterprises whose operations are nationwide in scope. They handle a high portion of America's corporate cash for investment, debt repayment, tax disbursements, and check clearance. They are depositories for correspondents, with which they are linked through wires and operating arrangements into nationwide banking systems, and also for foreign institutions accumulating dollar balances in this country. Money which the big New York banks disburse in loans or investments may be spent thousands of miles away, and money which they receive may originate in transactions just as distant. A critical link in this chain of activity, therefore, is the degree of probability that the loans and investments made by the New York banks to the country at large will eventually return in the form of deposits. For if deposit flows should dry up, a lid would be placed on the activities of the New York banks.

To understand the forces at work on the deposit movements of the New York banks, it is well to bear in mind the two-way relation between, on the one hand, the loans and investments that a bank makes, and, on the other hand, the deposits that it carries on its books. The expansion of assets leads to a corresponding rise of deposits, while an outflow of deposits may cause a bank to liquidate assets in order to replenish reserves depleted by the outflow. During Treasury financing operations, for example, the commercial banks often are permitted to pay for the new issues of Government securities they acquire by crediting the Treasury's deposit account, and this causes an expansion of both assets and deposits. When the Treasury desires to spend these deposits, it ordinarily transfers them to its account at the Federal Reserve because, with only minor exceptions, disbursements are made out of funds on deposit in the Federal Reserve Banks. These withdrawals reduce the reserves of the banks correspondingly. If the Treasury's expenditures in a given area then balance its withdrawals, the volume of deposits and reserves of the commercial banks in the area will be restored. To the extent that expenditures are made elsewhere, both deposits and reserves are shuttled to these other places. Should the transfers be sufficiently great, the commercial banks losing funds may be compelled to liquidate some of their investments or cut down on loans; the acquiring banks, on the other hand, may be able to step up their lending and investment activities. Similar results occur, of course, when private parties borrow from banks and spend the funds elsewhere.

If we go back beyond World War II for a decade or two, we can observe the deposit shifts between New York and the rest of the country and assess the major factors contributing to the transfers. In this review, one should not forget that a classification of this sort must be somewhat arbitrary, and at any time, the forces at work in one period may extend into another as well. Our concern is with detecting the principal changes that have occurred over time. Chart 10 compares the growth of deposits of "Central Reserve City Banks" in New York with that of the nation's Federal Reserve member banks as a whole.* Here we see that total deposits in the New York banks generally kept pace with or grew faster than those in the nation during the 1920's and 1930's, but that there has been a considerable slippage in the City's position ever since. Between 1920 and 1927, New York's growth in deposits just about matched that of the nation. This was the net result of forces pulling in different directions. The rapid growth of the South and West in this period tended to draw funds from New York. But the swift rise of securities prices attracted out-of-town funds to the City where they were used directly or indirectly in making loans on securities. Moreover, a relatively high portion of the considerable increase in time deposits that occurred at that time became

* Of the 50-odd banks in New York City in 1956, only 18—counting the First National City Bank's security affiliate separately—were considered "Central Reserve City Banks." Since that time, mergers have taken place between J. P. Morgan and Company and the Guaranty Trust Company and between the Chemical Corn Exchange Bank and the New York Trust Company, all four of which had been previously classified as separate institutions. In 1956, the Central Reserve City Banks held over 95 per cent of all commercial bank deposits of New York City and about 75 per cent of those of the Region. They are used in Chart 10 because data for all commercial banks in the Region are unavailable for so long a period. In July 1959, Congress enacted legislation which, among other things, provided that after three years, the classification of "Central Reserve City" would be eliminated, and that New York and Chicago would be classified at that time as "Reserve Cities" under the Federal Reserve Act. (Public Law 86–114, 86th Congress, S. 1120, July 28, 1959. 73 Stat. 263.)

Chart 10

Total Deposits of All Federal Reserve Member Banks and of New York Central Reserve City Banks, 1920–1956

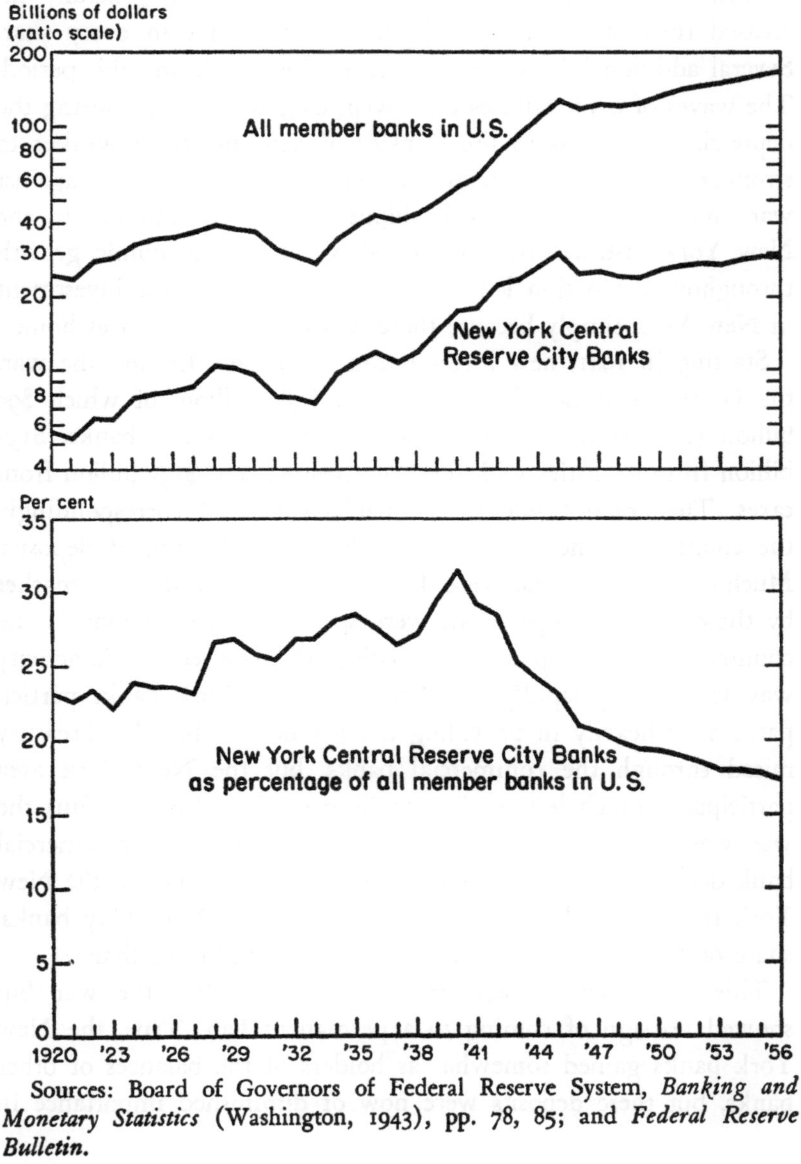

Sources: Board of Governors of Federal Reserve System, *Banking and Monetary Statistics* (Washington, 1943), pp. 78, 85; and *Federal Reserve Bulletin.*

lodged in New York; this may have been due, at least in part, to the practice of national business firms of carrying surplus funds as time deposits in the City.[1] On balance, therefore, little relative change occurred.

From 1928 through 1940, the New York banks generally increased their share of total deposits, though not in every year. Several additional forces contributed to the rise during this period. The waves of bank failures that swept over the country during the depression years led to the transfer of accounts from weaker to stronger institutions. Foreigners, trying to find a refuge against war and devaluation abroad, shipped their "hot money" to the New York institutions. And the slow rates of economic growth throughout the nation led to the deposit of funds for investment in New York simply because there was no use for them at home.[2]

Starting in 1941, new forces began to operate. During the war, the Government raised approximately $380 billion, of which $95 billion came from securities sold to the commercial banks, $132 billion from securities sold to other investors, and $153 billion from taxes. The amount sold to the banks expanded correspondingly the country's monetary supply in the form of demand deposits. Much of the funds that were drawn out of the New York market by these financing operations were spent in other sections of the country where new plants were rising and new economic activity was accelerating rapidly. In effect, the New York banks participated very heavily in providing the $95 billion that the Treasury raised through the commercial banks, but the New York area participated much less in the spending of these funds.[3] Thus the war was the catalyst that speeded the dispersion of commercial bank deposits, just as the depression had driven funds to the New York institutions. From 1940 to 1946, the New York City banks' share of total deposits shrank from 31 per cent to less than 21.

This dispersion of deposits slowed down after the war but showed no sign of coming to a permanent halt. True, the New York banks gained somewhat as holders of the balances of other banks, but these deposits were now of diminished importance in the banking system. The securities markets, which had been important in drawing funds to New York in the past, now occupied a smaller role compared with the economy's over-all growth; moreover, the improved ability to transfer funds cut down on the necessity of maintaining balances in New York to participate in these markets. Then, too, the habits of corporations in employing their cash balances were changing: large national companies which ordinarily kept substantial balances in New York were learning to operate with less funds relative to their sales volume; a number of firms also were using more of their funds to buy securities at attractive yields instead of keeping them on deposit in New York;[4] and big enterprises, for operating convenience as well as to improve their community relations, increasingly adopted the practice of maintaining balances at banks in the localities where they had plants. On top of all this, the banks outside New York have become more active competitors in meeting the servicing needs of large enterprises.

Meanwhile the rate of economic growth in the South and West continued to exceed that of the East. As a result, though most large corporations still followed their established practice in borrowing in New York, they disbursed more of the borrowed funds in other areas where their operating units were expanding. This added to the liquidity and growth potential of banks in areas of high economic activity. Since the counteracting forces that had tended to hold funds to New York in the earlier periods were now of less importance, between 1947 and 1956, as shown in Chart 11, bank assets tended to advance most rapidly in those states which experienced the fastest rise of personal income.

Besides the differences in economic growth rates and changes in the relations between banking and business, recent governmental policy has sometimes added to the deposit squeeze on the New York banks. In 1956, for example, the Federal Reserve Board, seeking to dampen the further growth of credit, restricted the lending potential of the banking system. This policy had varying effects throughout the country. One major New York City bank reported

Chart 11

Percentage Increases from 1947 to 1956 in Assets of Commercial Banks and in Personal Income, by States

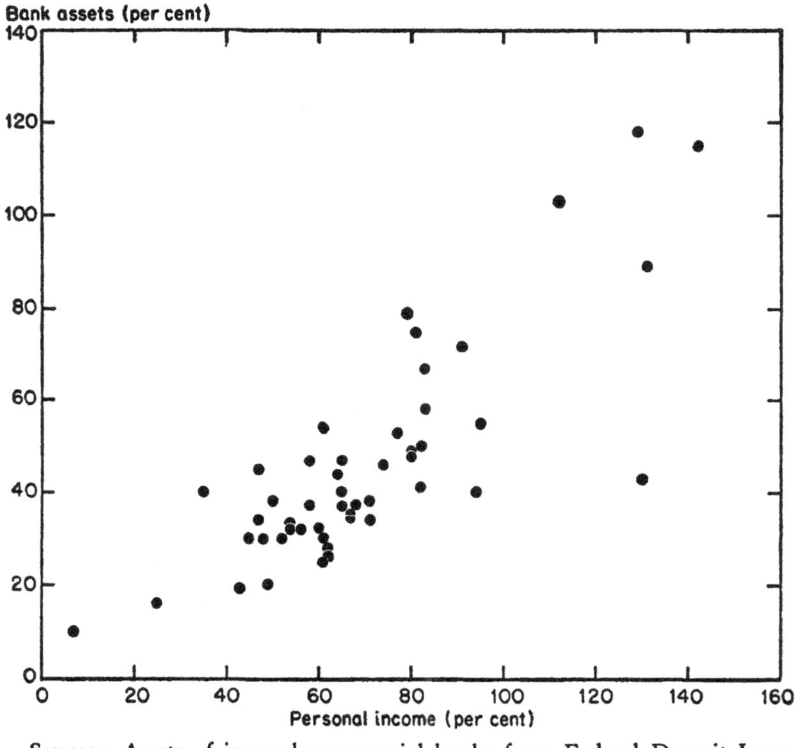

Sources: Assets of insured commercial banks from Federal Deposit Insurance Corporation, *Assets, Liabilities, and Capital Accounts, Commercial and Mutual Savings Banks,* Dec. 31, 1947, and Dec. 31, 1956. Personal income from *Survey of Current Business,* September 1955 and August 1957.

that the federal action caused many national corporations to turn from their hard-pressed local banks and to borrow from New York banks—in some cases for the first time in a number of years. As these firms shifted their balances to other parts of the country to handle their local financial needs, they contributed to the drain of funds from New York.[5]

Reflecting all these conditions, the total deposits of the Central

Reserve City Banks of New York City, calculated as a percentage of the deposits of the nation's member banks, continued gradually downward, reaching 17.4 per cent in 1956.

Pulling in the opposite direction, but not enough to halt the movement of funds from New York, has been the premier role occupied by the New York banks in the international field. Foreign central banks and governments maintain short-term balances in the United States in the form of dollar deposits, United States Treasury securities, acceptances, and other paper. So do foreign private interests. Since World War II these foreign dollars assets have built up substantially. The New York banks, which eventually receive a large part of foreign capital inflows, have benefited from the build-up, and probably will continue to benefit in the future.

The outcome of these developments is a net outflow of funds coupled with a high demand for loans. This pinch on the New York banks has exerted a pronounced effect on the assets they hold. The contrast between New York and other areas of the country is described in Table 7, which shows the change in banking activity between 1950 and 1956 in six major metropolitan areas. New York's banks, compared with banks in the "newer" areas of the nation, such as Dallas and San Francisco, had a slow growth of assets and of deposits. Yet New York's total loans rose rapidly, almost as fast as those in the newer locations, even though its major banks had to keep higher legal reserves than most banks elsewhere. To obtain funds to meet this demand, the New York institutions were obliged to hold down on their investments in United States Government obligations and to drain off their cash.

These adjustments in banking activities have major implications for the role of the New York banks in the Region's economy because if funds continue to move outward the City's banks may become shorn of their ability to carry on their national responsibilities. Moreover, as we have seen, the various forms of banking output differ widely in their manpower and space requirements. Next in order, therefore, is a closer look at the postwar changes in the Region's banking output.

Table 7 Growth of Banking Activity in Selected Metropolitan Areas, 1950–1956

(1956 as percentage of 1950)

	Total assets	Total loans	U.S. Government obligations	Cash and due from banks	Total deposits	Demand deposits of individuals, partnerships, and corporations	Time deposits of individuals, partnerships, and corporations
New York Metropolitan Region	119	169	73	112	118	110	136
Philadelphia	118	187	67	119	116	116	117
Chicago	124	189	90	112	122	119	135
Washington, D.C.	135	194	100	121	134	122	158
San Francisco–Oakland	147	179	101	151	146	147	148
Dallas	168	172	136	169	163	155	246

Note: This table covers insured commercial banks. Except for the 22-county New York Metropolitan Region, the areas are Standard Metropolitan Areas as defined by the Bureau of the Census.

Source: Special survey by Federal Deposit Insurance Corporation.

BANKING OUTPUT IN REGION AND NATION

In the preceding chapter we saw that the amount of employment growth that commercial banks experience in the nation is largely the net result of changes in four measures of banking "output," namely, consumer credit, "all other loans," investments, and trust functions. Table 8 compares the New York Metropolitan Region with the nation in each of these lines of activity during the postwar period.

CONSUMER LOANS

That consumer loans grew somewhat less rapidly in the Region than in the nation comes as no surprise if one realizes that the Region's personal income has been growing more slowly than the nation's.[6] Consumer loans are awarded primarily to local customers, and the geographical distribution of this kind of credit may be expected to follow roughly the distribution of personal income. From

Table 8 Growth of Output[a] and Employment in Commercial Banks, New York Metropolitan Region and United States

(1956 as percentage of 1950)

	New York Metropolitan Region	United States
Total loans and investments	100	116
Consumer loans	242	266
All other loans	181	182
Investments	54	77
Trust department income	176	178
Employment	126	149

[a] "Output" as defined in text. Percentages based on constant dollars.

Sources: Employment, see Appendix C, Tables C-1 and C-2. Other items, for the Region, special survey of member banks by Federal Reserve Bank of New York; for the United States, annual reports of Federal Deposit Insurance Corporation, covering insured banks.

1947 to 1956 the Region's personal income, though expanding in absolute terms, declined from 12.7 to 12.2 per cent of the national total; and in the same period the consumer loans reported by the Region's commercial banks, though they more than doubled even when measured in constant dollars, fell from 14.8 to 13.6 per cent of the national total.*

* A point about consumer loan statistics is in order. The consumer loan data for the United States, shown in Table 4, are the Federal Reserve estimates of loans made to individuals for consumption purposes. Such statistics are not available for the Region. To derive the Region's share of consumer loans mentioned above, we were forced to use the somewhat broader concept of "other loans to individuals," traditionally appearing in bank reports to Government agencies. This classification includes not only consumer loans but also such items as personal loans to finance professional practice or small businesses. Thus, the share figures for past years actually relate "other loans to individuals" in the Region to those in the nation. We assume that the Region's share of consumer loans strictly defined is about the same.

✓ All other loans

The record of the Region's banks in the category of "all other loans" tells a different story. Here one finds a marked stability in the Region's position. Throughout the postwar period, with only minor variations, the Region and the nation maintained the same growth rate, and the Region's banks managed to account for about one-fourth of the national total. Beneath this surface immobility, however, disparate movements occurred in the components.

Over 70 per cent of "all other loans" of the Region's banks are commercial loans. In 1947 these represented 31 per cent of the national total; in 1956 the figure stood at 32 per cent. This stability is accounted for by the fact that commercial loans are directed largely to a national market.

The importance of outside borrowers for New York banks is demonstrated in Table 9. About $4.4 billion, comprising about half of the commercial loans on the books of the Central Reserve City Banks on October 5, 1955, went to borrowers outside the 17-county Standard Metropolitan Area as defined by the Bureau of the Census.* In addition, though not shown in the table, $2.2 billion of the loans made within the metropolitan area by the same banks were in amounts of $1 million or more, and these accounted for another 25 per cent of their total commercial loans. In view of the size of these loans, it is reasonable to assume that most of them went to concerns which, though headquartered in the New York area, have interests throughout the country. Thus, of the $8.8 billion of commercial loans that the major money-market banks of the New York Metropolitan Region had outstanding, $6.6 billion or three-fourths may be attributable to needs generated on the outside rather than by local economic conditions. The national breadth of the coverage is highlighted in the same table, which shows that the loans to firms outside the metropolitan area were well distributed over the country.

* In contrast to this performance, less than 10 per cent of the commercial loans of the member banks in Newark, Jersey City, Paterson, and Passaic went to borrowers outside those cities.

Table 9 Outstanding Commercial Loans of New York Central Reserve City Banks by Location of Borrowers, October 5, 1955

Location of borrowers	Loans outstanding (millions of dollars)	Per cent of total
Total loans to all locations	8,758	100.0
New York Metropolitan Area [a]	4,365	49.8
New York City	3,959	45.2
Rest of area	406	4.6
Outside New York Metropolitan Area, total	4,393	50.2
Elsewhere in United States, by Federal Reserve Districts, total	4,175	47.7
New York Federal Reserve District, outside New York Metropolitan Area	148	1.7
Boston	145	1.7
Philadelphia	308	3.5
Cleveland	310	3.5
Richmond	457	5.2
Atlanta	210	2.4
Chicago	716	8.2
St. Louis	148	1.7
Minneapolis	147	1.7
Kansas City	332	3.8
Dallas	685	7.8
San Francisco	554	6.3
Territories and possessions	15	0.2
Outside United States	218	2.5

[a] Standard Metropolitan Area, which is the same as the New York Metropolitan Region except that it contains five less counties (Fairfield, Orange, Dutchess, Putnam, and Monmouth).

Source: Federal Reserve Bank of New York, *Monthly Review of Credit and Business Conditions,* May 1957, pp. 64-65.

When we turn to real estate loans—another major component of the "all other loans" category—the capacity of the Region's banks to hold their own during the postwar period is once more evident. Between 1947 and 1956, their real estate loans varied between 7.9 and 11.4 per cent of the national total, excluding farm loans, without any discernible trend. This performance may be attributed to a combination of factors. Within New York City, the big banks became increasingly aggressive in granting loans for the booming commercial and multifamily construction. Reflecting this activity, some of the banks for the first time created independent real estate loan departments. Then, too, the New York City banks' percentage of the nation's total time deposits of individuals, partnerships, and corporations rose somewhat. In this period the City banks became more competitive in developing promotional campaigns to attract savings deposits of individuals, which are less volatile than other kinds of deposits; therefore, to the extent that such savings deposits contributed to the expansion, some pressure was created for the banks to move into the long-term and comparatively lucrative mortgage field. Outside New York City, where the bulk of the Region's mortgages are held, the rapid growth of the suburbs enabled the banks in these locations to expand their residential lending.

But in the last main category of "all other loans"—namely, in loans for purchasing or carrying securities—the Region's banks, though still dominating the country, displayed a weakness during the 1950's which they had not shown in the other categories. In 1947, they accounted for 47 per cent of the national total; in 1948, the proportion rose to 62 per cent; but after that date it fell steadily back to 46 per cent in 1956.

To interpret the meaning of the recent decline, one has to distinguish between two types of securities loans—those made to brokers and dealers and those to others. In granting loans to brokers and dealers, the New York City banks tend to perform a national role, but their securities loans to others go largely to individuals and fall more nearly in the category of local "consumer" business.

Chart 12 traces the course, since 1928, of securities loans made by

Chart 12

Securities Loans of New York Central Reserve City Banks as a Percentage of Those of All Federal Reserve Member Banks in United States, 1928–1953

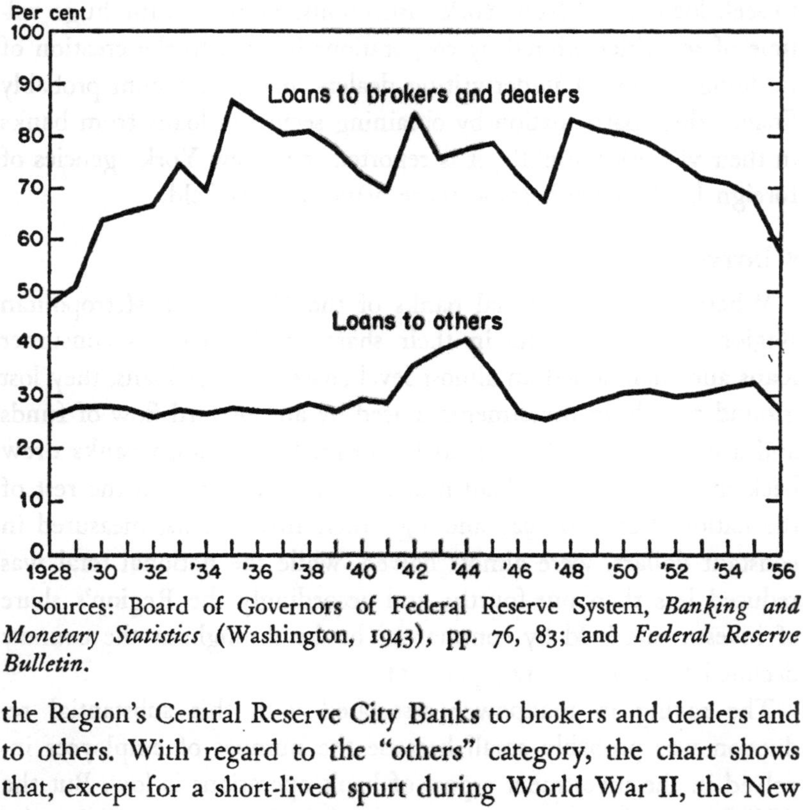

Sources: Board of Governors of Federal Reserve System, *Banking and Monetary Statistics* (Washington, 1943), pp. 76, 83; and *Federal Reserve Bulletin.*

the Region's Central Reserve City Banks to brokers and dealers and to others. With regard to the "others" category, the chart shows that, except for a short-lived spurt during World War II, the New York banks have maintained a rather constant percentage of the national total. Their share of the loans to brokers and dealers, on the other hand, has swung erratically; it rose generally from 1928 to 1935, declined to 1941, experienced fluctuations during the war years, and contracted steadily from 1948 to 1956.

Various factors may account for the recent shrinkage in these loans. During periods of monetary stringency, a scarcity of funds for lending has caused the New York banks to avoid securities loans in favor of more lucrative commercial business. As a result, some dealers have found it necessary in recent years to seek a large part of their financing outside New York City. Added to this, regional loyalties and connections have encouraged out-of-town brokers to enhance their borrowings from banks in their vicinities rather than to seek loans from New York institutions. Moreover, the huge volume of securities offered by corporations has led to the creation of far-flung groups of underwriting dealers, many of whom probably finance their participation by obtaining securities loans from banks in their vicinities. Finally, it is reported that New York agencies of foreign banks have become more active in this field.

✓ Investments

Whereas the commercial banks of the New York Metropolitan Region declined a little in their share of the nation's consumer loans and maintained an almost level share of other loans, they lost ground rapidly in investments. Faced by an outward flow of funds and a continued high demand for loans, the Region's banks drew back in the investment field much faster than banks in the rest of the nation. Between 1947 and 1956 their investments, measured in constant dollars, were almost halved, while the national total was reduced less than one-fourth; and accordingly the Region's share of investments held by commercial banks throughout the country declined from 20.6 to 14.7 per cent.

The saving in manpower associated with this substantial reduction was probably small because the number of employees involved in the investment aspect of bank operations is low. But the decline in investments has a more serious long-term meaning for the continued ability of the Region's banks to carry out their functions, because the liquidation of investments cannot go on indefinitely.

✓ Trust functions

This leaves for examination the last of our four measures of bank activity—the heterogeneous mixture of services loosely called trust functions. Here we find the Region's banks matching the nation's growth. From 1947 to 1956, trust department income in the Region, expressed in constant dollars, rose from $61.8 to $108.8 million, a gain of 76 per cent, and this activity in the nation rose at about the same rate.* Year after year, the Region's banks have earned about 35 per cent of the income generated by the nation's banks from trust activities.

The Region's ability to hold its own in trust functions is based on a number of factors. One is its early start in this field—for we have seen that the impetus gained by this advantage can be an important and continuing locational force. Another is the size of its banks. To maintain an independent trust department requires a reasonably big bank, and to provide highly specialized services, geared to particular companies and industries, calls for an even larger one. Consequently, most of the trust business is conducted by the major banks. As shown in Table 10, half of all the trust department income received by the nation's insured commercial banks in 1956 was received by banks with deposits of $500 million or more; and about 82 per cent was received by banks with deposits of $100 million or more. By contrast, these same banks were able to garner only 47 per cent of the nation's total deposits. Table 10 also shows that trust income constitutes a larger proportion of the operating earnings of the big banks than of the smaller ones.

The New York banks have a special advantage in the field of corporate trusts because of the heavy concentration of corporate headquarters in Manhattan. But this is not the only reason, for

* The estimate of the trust department income in the Region was made by adding to the trust department income of New York Central Reserve City Banks 55 per cent of the trust department income of the remaining member banks in the New York (Second) Federal Reserve District. This estimate was based on the distribution of demand deposits of individuals, partnerships, and corporations in 1956. The adjustment is of slight importance, however, for during the postwar period, the Central Reserve City Banks accounted consistently for about 88 per cent of the trust department income of all member banks in the Second District. The New York Metropolitan Region lies entirely within the Second District, which takes in all of New York State, twelve northerly counties of New Jersey, and Fairfield County in Connecticut.

much of the trust business of the New York banks comes from out-of-town corporations. Some other kinds of trust business are more prone to be performed close to the client; for example, many personal trusts entail an intimate association between trustee and trustor, and besides, certain trust functions, such as serving as administrator or executor of an estate, sometimes are required by state law to be performed within the state. But corporate trusts are another matter; these are relatively impersonal and, once established, do not require much attention from the corporate trustor.

Table 10 Distribution of Trust Department Income of Insured Commercial Banks, by Bank Size Classes, United States, 1955

Banks classed by deposits (millions of dollars)	As percentage of total trust income	As percentage of banks' operating earnings
500 or more	49.9	6.3
100 to 500	31.9	6.4
50 to 100	6.9	4.0
25 to 50	4.7	2.7
10 to 25	4.8	1.8
5 to 10	1.3	0.7
2 to 5	0.4	0.2
1 to 2	0.1	0.1
Under 1	[a]	0.1

[a] Less than 0.1 per cent.

Source: *Annual Report of the Federal Deposit Insurance Corporation for the Year Ended 1955.*

The unique position of New York City's large banks, notably their capacity to capture corporate trust business, is suggested by Chart 13, which shows the importance of corporate work to them compared with personal trusts. Indeed, the banks of New York State, among which the City banks are of course dominant, are thought to administer about 60 per cent of the nation's pension and profit-sharing funds. Furthermore, nearly half of their pension fund accounts come from employers with head offices outside the

Chart 13

Composition of Trust Department Income of Selected Groups of Banks in Three Federal Reserve Districts, 1956

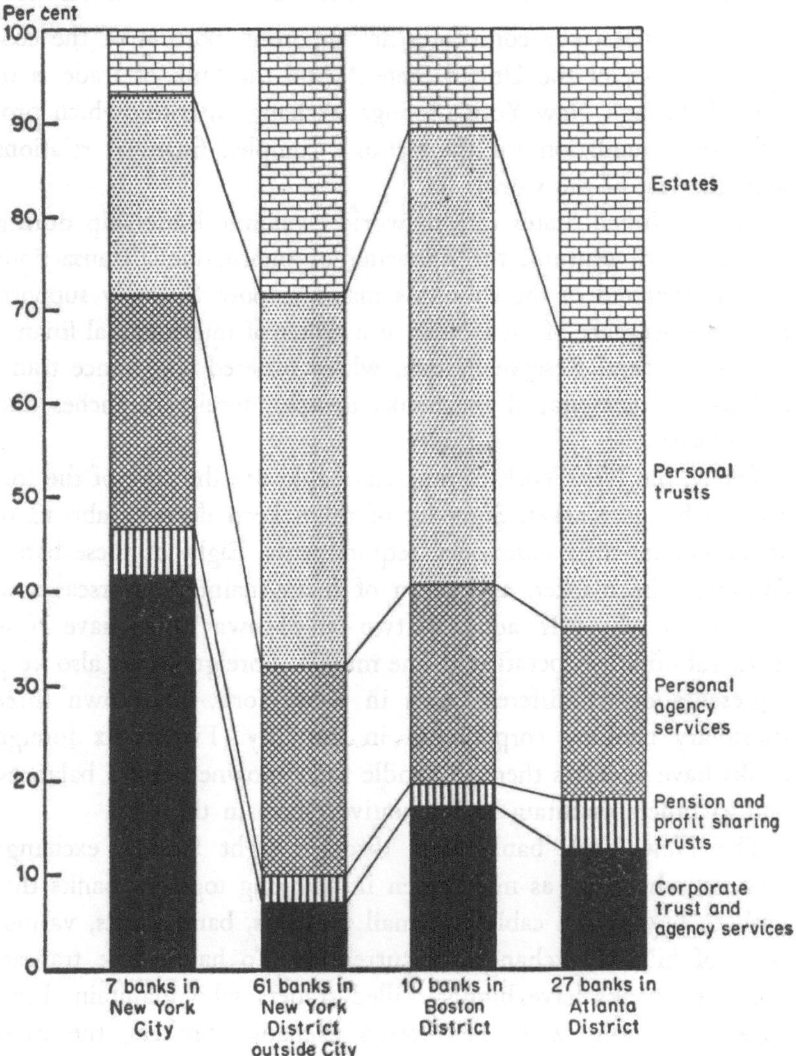

Sources: *Monthly Review of Credit and Business Conditions,* Federal Reserve Bank of New York, July 1957, p. 91; *New England Business Review,* Federal Reserve Bank of Boston, June 1957, p. 5; *Trusts and Estates,* Fiduciary Publishers, July 1957, p. 667.

state.[7] Clearly, trust functions are a field in which New York City banks hold a heavily entrenched position that is only partly dependent on the City's role as the corporate capital of the nation.

THE REGION'S ROLE IN INTERNATIONAL FINANCE

International trade constitutes an important portion of the economic activity of the United States.[8] And the bulk of trade is financed through New York's foreign exchange market, which provides the foundation for the nation's complex financial relations with the rest of the world.

As the United States rose to world economic leadership during the twentieth century, the financing of international transactions became centered in the country's major seaport. Strongly supporting the emergence of New York as a center of international finance was the Federal Reserve System, which fostered acceptance transactions and encouraged the banks to open foreign branches and subsidiaries.

Today, the New York commercial banks are the core of the foreign exchange market. Some 25 of them keep deposits abroad to accommodate their customers' requirements. Eight of these banks dominate the market, and seven of them maintain overseas subsidiaries or offices. In addition, two out-of-town banks have New York subsidiaries operating in the market. Foreign banks also keep representation of different sorts in New York. They own three subsidiary banking corporations in the City. Twenty-six foreign banks have agencies there to handle foreign-owned dollar balances, and 41 others maintain representative offices in the City.

The New York banks deal through eight foreign exchange brokers, who serve as middlemen in bringing together banks that wish to buy or sell cable and mail transfers, bank drafts, various types of bills of exchange, or currencies. To handle the transactions, the banks have highly skilled traders who maintain direct wire connections with the foreign exchange brokers, the cable companies, and one or more of the bank's leading correspondents outside New York City. In addition, the traders employ the usual telephone and teletype facilities for communicating with customers and with domestic and foreign correspondents. The New York banks, through their foreign branches and correspondents, practically cover the world.

Though there is some foreign exchange activity in big cities such as Boston, Chicago, Philadelphia, and San Francisco, the market is predominantly in the New York area. In these other cities, there are no foreign exchange brokers and the volume of transactions is small. Thus, every bank in the country that has business in foreign exchange eventually must come to New York through its City correspondents or the foreign exchange brokers. The elaborate relations underlying the foreign exchange market and the intricacy of the transactions that take place have fostered the strength of the New York City banks in this field. No serious competitor has ever appeared or now seems to be on the horizon.

New York's foreign exchange role has attracted deposits both from the interior of the United States and from abroad, and it has provided the Region with at least some partial offset to the forces serving to move funds to other sections of the country. The manpower involved in the performance of the international function is small, but its economic significance is great.

THE SHIFT IN EMPLOYMENT

Since World War II, the banks of the New York Metropolitan Region have deployed their manpower in response to a complex play of forces. Some activities, like consumer loans, have expanded throughout the nation, with New York banks lagging slightly behind in the growth. Others, like trust activities, have risen with equal rapidity in both the country and the Region. Investments actually have declined—much more in the Region than in the nation. Each of these trends has demanded or released a different increment of manpower. Moreover, overhanging all the developments have been increases in productivity which must be taken into account in evaluating any functional change.

All in all, the Region increased its commercial bank employment from 65,500 in 1947 to 82,300 in 1956, a gain of 26 per cent. (For sources, see Appendix C, Table C-4.) Using the techniques outlined in the preceding chapter, we can evaluate the relative importance of each output trend in producing this change. We find that in this nine-year period the total volume of the Region's lending and investing remained approximately unchanged, and therefore volume alone had no net effect upon manpower; that the change in the composition of these services—notably the shift to consumer loans—added 70 per cent to the manpower requirements of the Region's commercial banks; and that productivity increases intervened to cut manpower requirements by about one-quarter. The employment increase of 26 per cent was the net outcome of these elements.*

In the last chapter we analyzed the forces which lay behind changes in the nation's bank employment. In the present chapter we have explored those affecting the Region's bank employment. In both nation and Region, the changing nature of banking activity—embodied primarily in the rise of consumer "retail" loans—contributed heavily to the growth of manpower requirements. And in both instances, a mounting productivity cut back the needs that otherwise would have been created. Accordingly, the principal in-

* Of the increase of 16,800 employees, we estimate that 5,000 represent a gain in trust departments and international departments. The figures for these activities were ascertained in the questionnaire survey of the banks of the Region conducted by the authors in 1958. On the basis of this survey we estimate that employment in trust departments rose from 7,250 in 1947 to 11,250 in 1956, and in international departments from 4,000 to 5,000. When we exclude the gain of 5,000 in these two activities, the Region's banking employment rose by 22 per cent during the period. The equations by which we relate assets to manpower are based on the experience of the forty-eight states and the District of Columbia. Since international financial activity is largely concentrated in New York City, and since the influence of trust employment was eliminated in formulating the equations (see pp. 70–71), our techniques actually apply to the 22 per cent rather than the 26 per cent gain. Nevertheless the net effect of the changes in volume, mix, and productivity account for an employment rise of 27.5 per cent. Since the productivity indices were built up on a national basis, the difference between the 22 per cent and the 27.5 per cent leads us to suspect that the productivity improvement in the Region might have been slightly greater than that in the nation.

fluence which caused the differential rates of growth of banking employment between the Region and the nation was the difference in the expansion of the volume of credit. The fact that loans and investments in the nation's commercial banks (measured in constant dollars) increased by 16 per cent, while those of the Region's banks remained constant, is the largest single explanation of the difference in their employment performance.

5

Commercial Banking inside the Region

While the commercial banking activities of the New York Metropolitan Region were changing in scope and character compared with those of the rest of the nation, they were also undergoing major locational adjustments inside the Region. Such modifications made themselves felt in the Region's economic life, for the commercial banks preempt space in the most congested areas, and their locational decisions as between one part of the Region and another can have considerable effects on the value of some of the world's highest-priced real estate. More important still, the locational shifts of banking activity inside the Region have been affecting its ability to perform as the nation's financial headquarters, through a chain of causation which we shall elaborate.

Our analysis starts with the situation in New York City. After all, it is the City banks, not those in the other counties, which perform a national role. And it is the City banks, with 74 per cent of banking employment and 79 per cent of the total deposits, that dominate the Region.

CHANGES WITHIN NEW YORK CITY

Two centuries ago, most of New York City lay at the toe of Manhattan; here its residences, stores, warehouses, and counting houses were crammed close to the wharves and docks which were the City's lifeline to the outside world.

Accordingly, the first nine banks to incorporate in New York

City—all before 1816—were located on Wall Street. Eight years later, when the Chemical Bank boldly established its headquarters on Broadway opposite St. Paul's Church, some half a dozen blocks farther north, the step was regarded as an unusual act of locational derring-do.[1] In these sites the banks were not only close to the principal clusters of homes and jobs of the Region, but also adjacent to the rest of the financial community. As late as the middle of the century, most of the insurance group was located in the heart of the financial district, while the securities industry grew around the New York Stock Exchange, which has steadfastly remained within the same general area despite occasional threats of moving.

During the next fifty years the City spread with great rapidity. In 1878 the first train road, the Sixth Avenue "El," helped the City expand into semirural areas formerly accessible only by horse car. In 1883, the Brooklyn Bridge spanned the East River. The pressure of rising land values and rentals, together with the northward population trek in Manhattan, caused a number of activities to move from the financial section. Included in this migration were freight agents, freight brokers, produce brokers, merchandise brokers, commission merchants, and a major component of the financial community, the life insurance firms, which now found little attraction in the Wall Street area.[2]

All these developments affected the location of commercial banking employment, but the influence was slow in making itself felt. For a while, the banks remained aloof to the City's shifting structure. Along with many other financial participants in the money market, they clung to the narrow strip of land in the lower downtown area where they had first located. Even by 1900, the banks had done little to expand into the fast-growing section of Manhattan's midriff; in fact, there were fewer than ten bank branches operating south of 59th Street at that time.[3]

THE SPREAD OF BRANCHES

During the next 25 years, dramatic changes took place in the distribution of the City's banking. The continued march of business and population eventually broke the resistance of the banks and forced them to multiply their branches in order to get near their customers, big and little.

The greatest increase of branches took place in midtown Manhattan because of the vast growth of business that now marked that vicinity. The opening of the Pennsylvania Station near 34th Street and the Grand Central Terminal on 42nd Street; the steady expansion of the subways; the northward crawl of the retail stores, theaters, and the garment center—all these contributed to the mounting fever of activity in the area. Then, in the 1920's, came New York's boom in skyscrapers, solidifying the City's reputation as America's "front office" and heightening the economic luster of midtown.

The business firms and their throngs of employees created new demand for banking services outside the traditional financial district. Once the banks began to meet this demand, competition among them accelerated the movement. By 1926, there were 112 bank branches between Fulton Street and 59th Street.[4]

In addition, there were 12 below Fulton Street (besides the home offices there) and 68 above 59th Street, making a total of 192 branches on the whole island. By comparison, only 64 branches were to be found in all the other boroughs of New York City. But it was in those boroughs that the next big surge in branch banking took place. We find that, by 1947, the 64 had jumped to 234, surpassing by a slight margin the number in Manhattan. This growth was in keeping with the spread of population in the boroughs and the awakening interest of the banks in serving consumers.

In the years following World War II, a new boom in business facilities erupted in Manhattan. Between 1946 and 1959 some 110 office buildings of all sizes rose, and 40 more were in various stages of planning or construction; all in all this amounts to a staggering 65 million square feet of additional office area, equivalent to some 36 Empire State Buildings, or twice the footage added in the 1920's. The bulk of the new construction is in the midtown area. The changes along Park Avenue, north of the Grand Central Terminal, are particularly striking; by 1961, in this once predominantly residential strip, 18 commercial skyscrapers will have been put up, and a 50-story building will have risen above the terminal itself.[5]

More than ever, the commercial banks feel the need of keeping adequate offices in this thriving part of town to capture the banking business of corporations and their employees. In their annual reports the banks frequently comment on the importance of being at the elbows of their customers.[6] For this purpose they have established new offices, enlarged existing ones, and merged with competitors to create more strategically located branch systems. They have also tended to offer more complete services at their branches and have broadened the lending authority of their local managers.

In making these moves, the New York institutions have been aware that more might be at stake than the rivalry between two business sections of the City. They have had in mind the possibility that national companies headquartered in midtown Manhattan and capable of borrowing with equal facility in various cities might take physical convenience into account in deciding whether to do their banking in New York or some other place, say Chicago, San Francisco, or Dallas. Indicative of this notion, a major bank has stated, "We believe the further development of our national business will be enhanced by the broadened services which our enlarged system of offices in the metropolitan area makes possible, particularly in the handling of collections and credit inquiries. This system also offers the advantage of more banking locations convenient to the New York executive and branch offices of many important national corporations."[7]

In the light of the economic expansion in midtown since the war, the increase in the number of bank branches does not seem spectacular. From 1947 to 1956, as shown in Table 11, branches between Chambers Street and 60th Street increased from 152 to 174. Yet this was faster growth than occurred in the rest of New York City.

Table 11 Number of Commercial Banks and Branches in Selected Parts of New York Metropolitan Region, 1947 and 1956

	Headquarters and single-office banks		Branches	
	1947	1956	1947	1956
Region, total	480	356	626	969
New York City, total	72	66	462	497
Manhattan, total	51	50	228	244
Below Chambers Street[a]	37	37	28	28
Between Chambers and 60th	14	12	152	174
Rest of Manhattan	0	1	48	42
Rest of New York City	21	16	234	253
Region outside New York City, total	408	290	164	472
Hudson and Essex Counties	58	28	80	113
Other New Jersey counties	152	126	32	122
Nassau and Suffolk Counties	89	48	9	103
Other New York counties and Fairfield County, Connecticut	109	88	43	134

[a] Though there were some mergers in this part of town, they were apparently offset by the formation of new companies, in particular subsidiaries of foreign banks.

Source: *Polk's Banking Directory,* 1948 and 1957. The figures include all bank entries listed there for the areas given, except savings banks and the agencies and representative offices of foreign banks (as distinguished from corporate subsidiaries of foreign banks, which were counted).

✓ THE IMMOBILITY OF HEADQUARTERS OFFICES

All this time, more than half of New York City's commercial banks, including all the largest ones, have kept their headquarters offices bunched together in the Wall Street area. The northward shift of business and population has raised the question whether the banks will move their main offices in step with this trend. So far, they have shown little inclination to do so—a reaction that has been strongly supported by the decision of the Chase Manhattan Bank to put up a new 60-story building in the heart of the downtown financial district. Most of the other large banks have initiated downtown expansion programs of their own, either altering their existing buildings or acquiring added facilities nearby. To illustrate, the Chemical Corn Exchange Bank has purchased the 34-story building on Pine Street out of which the Chase Manhattan is moving. The Manufacturers Trust Company bought a 24-story building on Wall Street and occupied the first six floors as its main office. The United States Trust Company has leased most of the main floor and all of the next eight floors in a 27-story building being erected on Wall Street. On the basis of a questionnaire survey, we estimate that for the period 1953-1963, the actual and prospective expenditures of banks for downtown construction and improvements are in the neighborhood of one-quarter billion dollars.

The advantages cited for maintaining a downtown location include proximity to the New York Clearing House, to securities brokers and dealers, and to the head offices of other large New York City banks. In addition, of some importance in the short run is the bankers' interest in preserving the traditional status of the Wall Street area, an attitude compounded of an attachment to a district that has long occupied a unique niche in financial circles and a desire to protect existing real estate commitments. Though many of the downtown buildings are old and have depreciated over long periods of time, they nevertheless represent substantial values to the companies.

As a result, the financial district still houses the country's greatest concentration of banking facilities. Indeed, if one had taken a short stroll in the vicinity of Wall Street and Broadway at the beginning of 1959, he would have passed, in a very few minutes, eight of the fourteen biggest banks in the United States and all of the eleven biggest in the New York Metropolitan Region. These eleven are mapped in Chart 14. The dotted lines show the location of the impressive new plaza where the Chase Manhattan headquarters are rising.

Even so, there are signs pointing toward the midtown area as a desirable spot for a headquarters location. A dozen or so of the smaller commercial banks have seen fit to keep their main offices

Chart 14

Great Banks of the Financial District

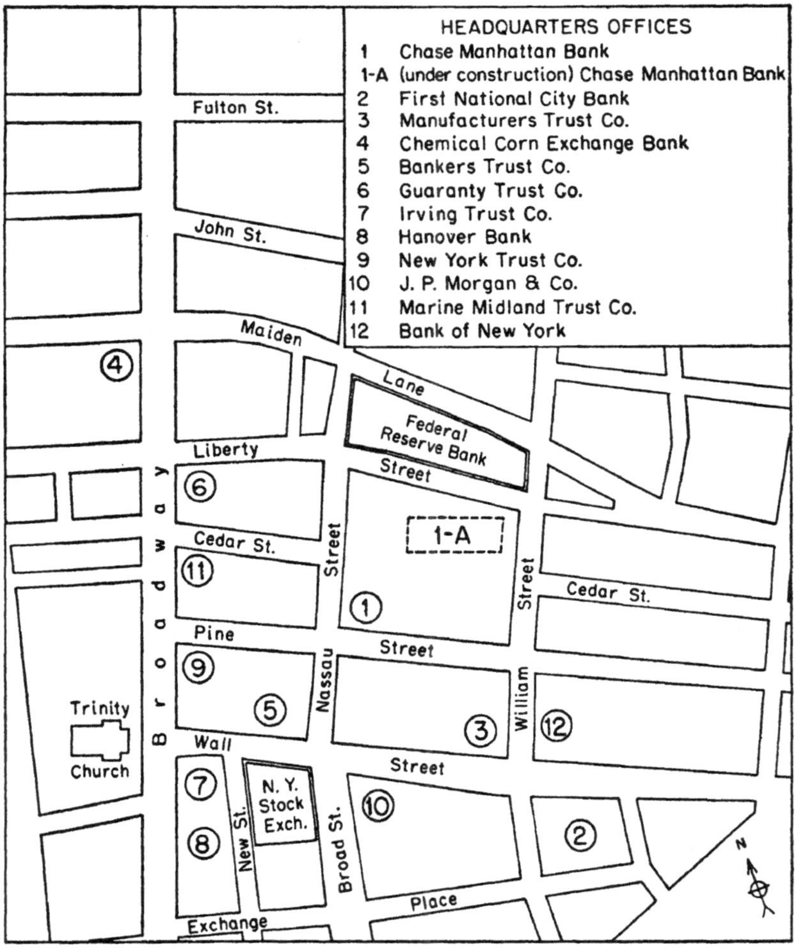

Note: Banks are listed in the order of their deposits Dec. 31, 1958, as given in *Moody's Bank & Finance Manual,* 1959. The first 11 led the New York Metropolitan Region in deposits, but No. 12 in the list was exceeded by a suburban bank, Franklin National Bank of Long Island. Since 1958, Guaranty Trust Co. and J. P. Morgan & Co. have merged into Morgan Guaranty Trust Co., but still occupy the two buildings indicated, with No. 6 as headquarters. Chemical Corn Exchange Bank has purchased the building of Chase Manhattan (No. 1, above) with a view to occupying it. In the fall of 1959 Chemical Corn Exchange merged with New York Trust Co. under the name Chemical Bank New York Trust Co.

above Chambers Street—for example, the Colonial Trust Company in Rockefeller Center. Big downtown banks maintain administrative offices in the midtown area for the convenience of senior management and directors. But most important of all is the announced policy of the First National City bank to be under a "dual head office plan." The company disclosed in March 1959 that its new 41-story executive offices rising on Park Avenue between 53rd and 54th Streets will handle out-of-town and overseas business, while the downtown building will constitute its legal head office and continue to serve brokerage, insurance, and other concerns in the area. This plan stirred the banking community. The second institution to announce dual head offices was the Hanover Bank, which leased a 30-story building under construction two blocks to the south. Hence, the beginnings of a new banking nucleus are visible on the transformed Park Avenue spur of mid-Manhattan.

THE LOCATION OF ROUTINE FUNCTIONS

The locational problems of the banks have involved more than the placement of headquarters and branches. Another task is discovering the most suitable spot for performing back-office functions, notably those concerned with the handling of paper in large volume.

To some extent these functions are tied to the basic originating activity—for example, when checks are first deposited, some preliminary processing and recording must occur at that very spot before the checks can be sent to a central point for clearance and collection. Therefore, as branches move outward they necessarily drag with them a certain amount of back-office operations. Nevertheless, there has always been back-office work that had no compulsion to be performed at the same address as a street office. This work, either by necessity or through inertia and executive decision, has generally stayed in the headquarters office. In recent years it has shown some tendency to come out, but at the same time new forces have arisen to keep it in.

With the development of more centralized methods of accounting and check-handling, the number of clerks required at a branch to support a given volume of banking activity has been reduced. And as automation in banking increases, the pull toward centralization is likely to become even stronger, resulting in a greater tendency to bring more of the bank's routine operations to a single location or at least to only a few locations.

Much of the routine function thus has become relatively footloose and may be placed in whatever location bank management believes most efficient. In some cases, completion of a headquarters building program draws these operations to the home office; in other instances, lack of room at headquarters pushes them to other areas. One factor influencing such a decision is the availability of large expanses of unobstructed floor space where the required machinery can be housed. Another is the proximity of this space to transportation facilities used by employees in getting to work.

In the face of these diverse pulls, the banks have not adopted any uniform locational policy for their repetitive activities. One procedure is to centralize them at headquarters. Another is to collect them elsewhere—in a nearby building in the Wall Street area, or at midtown Manhattan locations, or even in units set up in other boroughs to service groups of branches. The issue is dramatically portrayed in the contrasting policies of the City's two biggest banks. On the one hand, Chase Manhattan has decided to incorporate operating functions into its new downtown headquarters. On the other hand, its giant neighbor, First National City, is not only erecting a building on Park Avenue, but for some time now has been shifting personnel into the midtown area. "In recent years," observes this bank in its 1956 annual report, "as our organization has grown, we have moved several operating departments away from Head Office, making it to a greater extent an administrative rather than an operating center."[8] Eventually, it is expected that a majority of the bank's some 10,000 New York City employees will be housed in the Park Avenue structure.

❡ The balance within the city

It is difficult to keep track of these criss-crossing transfers, but some underlying facts about banking location are in evidence. When face-to-face relations with customers are desirable, such as in receiving deposits, granting consumer loans, and performing certain trust functions, there is a tendency to move the activity to the area where the customers are located. When face-to-face contacts in the hazardous conditions of the money market are essential, lower Manhattan wins in a walk. And operations that are routine and relatively footloose are torn among the conflicting advantages of downtown, midtown, and the rest of the City.

The location of all these banking functions is affected by the shifts of business activity within the City and of population in both the City and the suburbs. As we have seen, the movement of jobs has tended to enhance midtown Manhattan as a banking location. The movement of residential populations has done the same, because banking executives and clerical help alike have been moving to places where they can reach midtown more easily than downtown. In other words, the drift of the population has not been merely outward in all directions. For people who work in Manhattan office buildings, the pattern has favored Westchester County, Long Island, and northern New Jersey rather than those New Jersey communities which are linked to lower Manhattan by ferry lines.

The general shift in the residences of people who work in Manhattan is more fully discussed in another volume of this series.[9] Evidence of the transition can be seen in the contrast between the commuting patterns of 1924 and 1956. On a typical day in the earlier year, for instance, only 46 per cent of the people coming into Manhattan south of Central Park entered from north of 61st Street or from the borough of Queens, and the rest were from Brooklyn, Staten Island, and New Jersey. By 1956, 61 per cent were coming from north of 61st Street and Queens.[10]

Over the long term, the outcome as between downtown and midtown may well hinge on this question of personnel preference. The gradual residential shifts of clerical workers have not yet become a decisive factor; indeed, one of the important influences leading one major bank to centralize its check-processing and related employees in the Wall Street area was the outcome of a survey showing that almost half of these workers lived in Brooklyn. In the future, however, the changing population structure of the Region may assume increasing importance, especially if the near-chronic scarcity of office personnel should grow. And the likelihood is that this scarcity may become more acute as the middle-income people in the City's boroughs, who provide a large portion of the clerical force of the financial community, increasingly join the northward and eastward suburban parade. As the transition occurs, the banks in the financial district may experience growing difficulty in attracting and holding their clerical staffs, many of whom will then be confronted with the inconvenience of a trip on the suburban rail system plus a transfer to a subway train for a further journey downtown.

Nevertheless, as we have already implied, it would be a mistake to assume a pell-mell northward rush of banking out of the downtown financial section. True, there have been exciting changes in the center of Manhattan. The daringly modern glass and aluminum branch of the Manufacturers Trust Company, as an illustration, has no doubt made more people aware of the existence of a bank on the southwest corner of Fifth Avenue and 43rd Street than did the more conventional predecessor office located across Fifth Avenue. But in both employment and deposits, the downtown district showed impressive strength between 1947 and 1956. Indeed, statistics on thirteen large banks (those that answered a questionnaire survey conducted by the authors) show that their banking gains below Chambers Street, measured by either employment or deposits, have more than matched their growth in midtown. These figures are presented in Table 12.*

The remarkable performance of the financial district stems primarily from the fact that headquarters buildings have remained anchored there, with most of the banks actually enlarging and modernizing these structures. But the "dual head office" system could in time have a big impact on the locational pattern. A num-

* Data were not available for the First National City Bank. If those figures had been included, the showing of the downtown area might have been somewhat modified.

ber of banks have taken steps to reserve precious space in the Park Avenue-Fifth Avenue area. They have done this either by enlarging the building where the principal midtown branch was situated or by leasing quarters in another building. These measures would

Table 12 Thirteen Banks' Employment and Deposits in Selected Parts of New York City, 1947 and 1956

	Employment				Deposits			
	1947		1956		1947		1956	
	Persons	Per cent	Persons	Per cent	Billion dollars	Per cent	Billion dollars	Per cent
All parts of City, total	27,164	100.0	32,331	100.0	15.4	100.0	17.8	100.0
Below Chambers Street	19,127	70.4	23,836	73.7	10.7	69.7	12.5	70.6
Chambers Street to 60th Street	4,201	15.5	4,342	13.4	3.3	21.6	3.7	20.7
Rest of City	3,836	14.1	4,153	12.9	1.3	8.7	1.5	8.7

Notes and sources: The data by parts of the City were obtained in a special questionnaire survey. The thirteen banks which provided answers for both 1947 and 1956 have a little more than half the employment of all commercial banks in New York City, which was 50,957 in 1947 and 60,564 in 1956 (see Appendix C, Table C-4). Deposits of all insured commercial banks in the City, according to the Federal Deposit Insurance Corporation, were $26 billion in 1947 and $30.4 billion in 1956.

not necessarily entail immediate transfers of manpower from downtown; nevertheless, should the "dual head office" plan prove successful, the extra space would make future moves easy. Depending upon the turn of events, therefore, the banks at present are well situated either to dig their roots still deeper in Wall Street or to pull some of them out for replanting in midtown. Just how we expect this competition to work out over the next twenty-five years is discussed in Chapter 8.

NEW YORK CITY AND THE REST OF THE REGION

Though the movements of banking activities within New York City are important to its various sections, the hauling and pulling between the City's banks and those in the suburban counties are of greater significance for the Region's future role as the national banking headquarters.

As recently as 1947, the banking structure in the Region outside New York City consisted for the most part of a great many small, independently operated community banks, possessing in the aggregate only a modest number of branches. By that time, as we have seen, branches had been spreading in New York City for half a century, with the movement initially concentrated in mid-Manhattan and then working its way out to the rest of the boroughs. Therefore, referring to Table 11 once more, we find that in 1947 the 17 counties outside New York City, though possessing more than half of the banking offices in the Region, had only 26 per cent of the *branch* offices.

Thereafter a swift change took place as the banking structure in the suburban counties was reshaped to meet the needs of burgeoning communities. Through a series of mergers, many banks that had been independent became parts of branch systems. These systems steadily expanded, not only by means of the mergers but also by opening new offices. As a result, branch banking now predominates in most of the suburbs. In effect, therefore, a third phase has been added to the branch banking movement in the Region, this time featuring the cities and towns outside New York City. By 1956, the number of branches had leaped to almost 50 per cent of the Region's total.

In evaluating the changing complexion of banking in the suburban counties, one should not underestimate the magnitudes involved. A view of banking in the Region often tends to be distorted by the huge size of the City institutions, obscuring the fact that some of the banks outside the City are now among the largest in the country. Indeed, commercial bank assets in the New York

Metropolitan Region exclusive of New York City exceed those of most metropolitan areas—for example, Philadelphia, or Dallas, or Washington, D. C., or San Francisco. They exceed the assets of the Philadelphia and Dallas areas combined. And the rapid growth of these assets in the counties surrounding New York City has important implications for the future of bank employment in the Region's various parts.

THE DRIFT OF EMPLOYMENT

Outside New York City, as Table 13 shows, there are 89 banking employees per 10,000 of employees of all kinds and 29 banking employees per 10,000 population. In New York City both ratios are considerably greater—a reflection of the number of banking employees required to serve the City's national and international banking markets. The City banks also serve suburban clients who, even though they may have accounts in their own localities, continue to

Table 13 Commercial Bank Employment Compared with All Employment and Population in Parts of New York Metropolitan Region, 1956

	Number of bank employees	
	Per 10,000 of all employment [a]	Per 10,000 population
Entire Region	131	53
New York City	158	78
Remainder of Region	89	29
Essex and Hudson Counties	82	31
Other New Jersey counties	86	27
Nassau and Suffolk Counties	109	27
All other counties	88	30

[a] 1955 "total employment" data were used.

Sources: For bank employment, see Appendix C. Population estimates are by New York Metropolitan Region Study. Total employment is from Regional Plan Association, Bulletin 87, *People, Jobs and Land, 1955–1975* (New York, 1957), p. 43.

take advantage of the specialized facilities and staffs of experts available at the money-market banks.

Between 1947 and 1956, as may be observed in Table 14, banking employment increased at sharply varying rates in the different sections of the Region. In New York City and the older counties of

Table 14 Growth of Commercial Bank Employment Compared with Growth of All Employment and Population in Parts of New York Metropolitan Region, 1947–1956

	1956 divided by 1947			Percentage for bank employment divided by percentage for:	
	Bank employment	Total employment [a]	Population	Total employment	Population
Entire Region	126%	108%	114%	117%	111%
New York City	119	101	100	118	119
Remainder of Region	150	123	132	122	114
Essex and Hudson Counties	109	97	106	112	103
Other New Jersey counties	159	127	133	125	120
Nassau and Suffolk Counties	232	200	191	116	121
All other counties	147	120	124	122	119

[a] 1955 as percentage of 1947.

Sources: Same as Table 13.

New Jersey, the rise was relatively slow compared with the other areas, which expanded very rapidly. These differences seem to be explained by the changes in local economic activity, measured by population and working force. Table 14 sets up comparisons between these factors. When the growth rates of banking employment are related to the corresponding movements of local population and total employment, the behavior of these rates in the Region's parts is more uniform, with gains in banking employment tending to exceed gains in local population or labor supply by about 20 per cent.

This relation reflects the fact that in all the areas of the Region except New York City, the demand for banking services—and indirectly for the employees to perform these services—comes largely from local sources. As firms and individuals move, they often change banking relations, or at least add new ones, thereby causing a shift of deposits and a transfer in the locus of banking activity.

Only the experience of Essex and Hudson Counties is somewhat out of line.* Here, the growth of banking employment, when compared with that of total employment or population, has been less impressive than in other parts of the Region. The explanation of this lagging performance probably lies in the special position of the banks in the older centers like Newark and Jersey City. These banks, unlike the New York City institutions which draw upon the whole nation for much of their business, have depended heavily on the surrounding New Jersey countryside. As the counties bordering Essex and Hudson have spurted in population and jobs, their local banks have grown rapidly and taken over some of the business which formerly went to the old centers. For example, a person in nearby Morris County who formerly banked in Newark may now find adequate facilities closer by.

In New York City, a stable local population and employment were matched against a rise in banking employment of 19 per cent, a rate of change conforming with that experienced in most other counties.**

RESTRICTIONS ON THE DISPERSION OF BRANCHES

Branch banking is regulated primarily by state laws. The New York Metropolitan Region embraces portions of three states, which

* In lumping together Essex and Hudson Counties, we have brought diverse areas under one heading: the aging cities of Hudson County, the city of Newark, and the growing suburbs of Essex County. Because of the limitations of the available data, it has been impracticable to break down these areas in a way which would take account of their diversity.

** Since a large portion of the City's banking employment is not related to local economic activity, this probably means that the two components of its banking employment, the one serving the local market and the other the non-New York areas, have grown at similar rates.

have different provisions. Connecticut is the most lenient, permitting statewide branches. New Jersey is the most severe, restricting branches to a single county. New York falls between the two extremes. The effect of New York's complicated banking law is that a branch system may cover the five boroughs of New York City but may not go outside the city limits. Nassau and Suffolk Counties on Long Island constitute another integrated area within which a system may locate its branches. Westchester, Rockland, Putnam, Dutchess, Orange, and several adjacent counties represent still another unit.

The banking law has imposed a limitation on the expansion of the New York City banks. As both population and jobs have spread outward, the City banks have been prevented from following their customers to the surrounding counties of the Region. The territory to which they have been restricted, though it is tremendous in population and jobs, has reached an approximate standstill in both respects. These restraints have contributed to keeping down the growth of branches within the City from 462 to 497 between 1947 and 1956, whereas the banks of the Region outside New York City raised their branch offices from 164 to 472 in the same period. If banks headquartered in New York City were to become free in the future to place branches outside the City, their relatively sluggish growth in bank employment in the postwar period, shown in Table 14, would have less portent for their future strength.

Despite several setbacks, the City banks have continued their efforts to break out of the geographical cordon and participate in the growth of the suburban counties. Bills to amend the branch banking law have been debated in the state legislature. Also, the First National City Bank has been seeking authority to join with the dominant bank in Westchester County by forming a bank holding company.

The branch banking controversy is not limited to the New York–New Jersey area. In Chicago, for example, the banking community has been roiled by a dispute over whether to permit limited branch banking in a state that now flatly prohibits branches. On the one hand, the smaller banks oppose the change, anticipating that it would provide a wedge for statewide systems that might endanger their independent status. The major proponents are the big banks which contend that Chicago is "underbanked" compared with New York and that, in the words of the chairman of the giant Continental Illinois National Bank and Trust Company, the city "must have some form of branch banking to meet the financial competition of other cities" as well as the competition of the rapidly growing nonbanking institutions.[11] Thus, as in New York City, the Chicago banks are casting interested eyes on the city's lush suburbs and the possibilities they afford for enlarging financial "retail" outlets.

THE FLOW OF DEPOSITS

The disqualification of New York City banks from tapping the economic growth outside the City has contributed to the shrinkage in their share of the Region's deposits in recent years. Table 15 shows the strikingly different behavior of demand deposits (meas-

Table 15 Demand Deposits of Individuals, Partnerships, and Corporations in Parts of New York Metropolitan Region, 1947 and 1956

	Millions of 1955 dollars		1956 as percentage
	1947	1956	of 1947
Entire Region	24,783	22,520	90.9
New York City	21,980	18,783	85.5
Remainder of Region	2,803	3,737	133.3
Essex and Hudson Counties	1,084	1,106	102.0
Other New Jersey counties	775	1,142	147.4
Nassau and Suffolk Counties	297	586	197.3
All other counties	647	903	139.6

Note: This table covers insured commercial banks.

Source: Special compilation made by Federal Deposit Insurance Corporation for New York Metropolitan Region Study.

ured in constant dollars) between the City banks and those in the rest of the Region for the period 1947 to 1956. In contrast to the New York City group, other banks in the Region managed to expand their deposits in this period, and, except for Essex and Hudson Counties, the growth was considerable.

To be sure, when time deposits are employed as the measuring gauge, the picture changes somewhat. Table 16 indicates their

Table 16 Time Deposits of Individuals, Partnerships, and Corporations in Parts of New York Metropolitan Region, 1947 and 1956

	Millions of 1955 dollars		1956 as percentage of 1947
	1947	1956	
Entire Region	4,772	5,514	115.5
New York City	1,967	2,531	128.7
Remainder of Region	2,805	2,983	106.3
Essex and Hudson Counties	874	662	75.7
Other New Jersey counties	1,095	1,147	104.7
Nassau and Suffolk Counties	325	574	176.6
All other counties	511	600	117.4

Note: This table covers insured commercial banks.

Source: Special compilation made by Federal Deposit Insurance Corporation for New York Metropolitan Region Study.

growth by parts of the Region since 1947. This time the City shows up well. Its 29 per cent rise in time deposits is exceeded only by dynamic Nassau and Suffolk Counties. In the Region exclusive of New York City, time deposits grew by only 6 per cent; indeed, these deposits actually declined in Hudson and Essex Counties, the only group with this experience. But time deposits represent so small a percentage of total deposits in the City that they do not alter the general deposit trends very much.*

* In New York City, time deposits comprised 8.2 per cent of total deposits of individuals, partnerships, and corporations at the close of 1947 and 11.9 per cent at the close of 1956. Time deposits are far more important in the

In order to place in sharper focus New York's weakening position in demand deposits, it is important to partition the New York City deposit behavior in order to ascertain the relative weight of the national and suburban pulls. Our best guess is that the failure of New York City's banks to increase their deposits to the same degree as the banks outside the City is due rather more to national forces than to the redistribution of jobs and people inside the Region. More explicitly, we would ascribe about 85 per cent of the shortfall to national forces and 15 per cent to redistribution inside the Region.* Accordingly, it is probable that legislative enactments, enabling the New York City banks to enlarge their activities in the Region, would slow rather than halt the drain of deposits from the City.

✓ The redistribution of banking functions

The character of banking functions performed within the different segments of the Region reflects the influence of both the outflows of demand deposits from New York City as a result of national conditions and the more rapid economic development of the suburban areas. Table 17 summarizes these changing characteristics between 1947 and 1956. It is clear that the role of the New York City banks in the lending field during this period followed several distinctive patterns.

Because consumers tend to employ local institutions to finance their needs, the growth of consumer loans in the outlying areas

---

other areas and actually exceed demand deposits in the suburban counties of New Jersey.

* This estimate was made on the basis of data for insured commercial banks, as follows: the City's share of the nation's total deposits of individuals, partnerships, and corporations declined from 16.8 to 13.9 per cent, while that of the rest of the Region increased from 3.9 to 4.4 per cent, and that of the rest of the nation from 79.3 to 81.7 per cent. If these total deposits had been geographically distributed in 1956 as they were in 1947, the City's banks would have had $4,623 million more deposits than they did have, while the banks in the rest of the Region would have had $751 million less, and those in the rest of the nation $3,872 million less. The amount which represents the gain of the rest of the Region comes to 16.2 per cent of the City's loss.

of the Region, where population and income swelled, has been rapid. As a result, the New York City banks lost ground relatively in this field, with their portion of the Region's consumer loans shrinking from about 70 per cent to 64 per cent; most of this decline was in the instalment category.

On the other hand, the New York institutions came closer to keeping pace with the rest of the Region in commercial and securities loans, because of the buoying effect of lending to firms and individuals that were either outside the Region or operated on a national scope. And with respect to real estate loans and trust activity, the New York banks actually outperformed their suburban neighbors. Aided by the construction boom in office buildings in New York City and the tendency of large real estate developers to look to City banks for their borrowing needs, these institutions elevated their share of the Region's total real estate loans from 22 per cent to 31 per cent. Similarly, their specialized skills in the trust field continued to attract business and enabled them to raise their share of total trust income slightly.

Table 17 New York City's Share of Selected Banking Activities in New York Metropolitan Region, 1947 and 1956

(NYMR = 100 per cent)

	1947	1956
Investments	83%	73%
Consumer loans	70	64
Instalment	63	58
Non-instalment	76	73
All other loans	89	86
Commercial	95	94
Securities	97	94
Real estate	22	31
Trust department income	92	94

Note: This table covers Federal Reserve member banks.

Source: Special compilation made by Federal Reserve Bank of New York for New York Metropolitan Region Study.

Faced with the pinch on deposits, the New York City banks were obliged to sell relatively large amounts of securities in order to meet an increased demand for loans. In contrast to this liquidation policy, the rest of the Region as a group actually added to their holdings, as deposit inflows apparently provided sufficient funds to meet their lending requirements. The net effect of these diverse trends is highlighted by the sharp contraction in the City banks' share of the Region's investments, from 83 to 73 per cent.

THE COMPETITIVE STATUS OF THE NEW YORK CITY BANKS

As we have seen, the New York City banks have almost maintained their share of the nation's and Region's loans to business firms, despite the more rapid economic growth of other areas. One reason is the sheer size of the City banks.

Big banking offices are in a position to handle larger loans, which do not require proportionately greater servicing efforts. Customers entering into such arrangements are more likely to have well-established credit ratings, and this circumstance cuts down on the costs of approval, follow-up, and bookkeeping per dollar of credit. Offices that do a substantial amount of business can employ expert talent that attracts lucrative accounts and avoids time-consuming managerial errors. Large banks have greater flexibility of employee utilization, which makes them better able to handle peak loads occurring at different times for different specialities, without adding to their rosters. Bigger offices are more likely to have efficient automatic equipment that reduces unit manpower requirements and permits the assumption of further volume-producing services.

The major New York City banks are also able to undertake specialized services that attract clients. A large City bank, for example, may have as many as 100 officers in its trust department, with supporting staffs and connections that span the country. The suburban banks, even the big ones, can hardly be expected to match their New York neighbors in this very technical area. Moreover, as manufacturers in the Region outside the City have increased their international trade, they have relied more heavily upon the New York

City banks, which are the traditional experts in this field. Then again the City banks are better equipped to effect transfers of funds throughout the country, make collections outside of local areas, and supply information on domestic credit inquiries. Their lending charges are relatively low. Their location in the heart of the nation's financial center provides them with special insights into money-market developments. For these reasons many business executives of large firms in the Midwest, West, and South recently stated, in answer to a survey question, that "New York banks are better than other banks."[12] And this kind of reputation helps the big money-market institutions near the corner of Broadway and Wall Street to continue their dominance of the New York Metropolitan Region.

CONCLUSION

The banking story within the New York Metropolitan Region, as unfolded here, is composed of two principal parts. The first is concerned with activity inside New York City and is highlighted by the tug-of-war between the downtown financial and midtown business sections. Here the issues involved are: the extent to which branches will spread in conformance with business and population trends; the clash between centralization and decentralization policies for certain operating functions; and the challenge implicit in the location of headquarters offices, where the gauntlet is down between Chase Manhattan, with its major commitment downtown, and First National City, which is pushing a major construction program in midtown.

The second part of the story deals with the distribution of banking activity between New York City and the other areas of the Region. The major theme here is the drift of deposits to the suburbs. This flow has provided the suburban institutions with more than enough funds to meet the expanded borrowing demands of their clients in every field even while augmenting their portfolios of securities. At the same time, the channeling of deposits to the suburbs, added to the southward and westward movement of deposits in the nation, has tended to drain the liquid position of the New York City banks. These institutions, as a result, have been compelled to hold down their investment activity in order to meet a continued loan demand, much of which comes from sources outside the City.

A partial easing of this squeeze eventually may come about by the relaxing of the restrictions now barring the New York City banks from entering the adjacent suburban areas in the state. The effects of growth in other parts of the nation, however, will continue. Our extension of the banking story into the years 1965, 1975, and 1985 appears in Chapter 8. Meanwhile, we shift our attention to the next major participant in the financial community of the New York Metropolitan Region—the life and health insurance industry.

6

Life and Health Insurance

In 1956, about one-half million men and women were occupied in the private life and health insurance field in the United States.* About one-sixth, or some 83,000, worked in the New York Metropolitan Region, the nation's leading life insurance center. How did the Region achieve this leadership? What changes are taking place in the Region's national position? Within the Region, where are the insurance offices and what are the trends in their location? These are the questions for consideration.

THE INDUSTRY IN THE NATION

Life insurance in this country, though its beginnings predate the Revolution, remained in an embryonic stage until around the 1830's. Thereafter, interest began to stir, and by 1850 we find 48 companies in existence.[1] Their total assets are estimated to have been about $10 million.[2] By 1900, this amount had boomed up to $1.7 billion; and by 1930, it had reached $18.9 billion. Since that time, and particularly after World War II, the companies continued their expansion, increasing their assets about five times between 1930 and 1956 and approximately doubling their employment.[3]

* This number includes officers and employees of all life insurance carriers, including fraternal orders, and the accident and health insurance carriers. It also includes insurance brokers and agents and their employees, insofar as they are occupied in life or accident and health business. It does not include persons engaged in accident and health work of casualty companies. The bulk of employment by the accident and health carriers is accounted for by Blue Cross, Blue Shield, and similar organizations; the remainder consists of personnel of the specialized accident and health companies.

This brief picture of the growth of assets highlights the giant strides taken by the life insurance companies in this country over the last century or so. The assets of a life insurance company consist for the most part of investments in mortgages, business securities, and Government obligations. These investments are made with funds obtained from premium payments, which, in turn, are dependent in a broad sense upon the amount of income that policy buyers have.

✓ Income and premiums

The relation between income and premiums has been quite stable in the postwar period, as shown in Chart 15. True, they went in different directions in the 1930's and early 1940's, but the special conditions of the depression and war no doubt were largely responsible. The fact that they increased thereafter at about the same rate points to the strong influence of income on premium payments, though it does not necessarily rule out other influences. The available evidence suggests that the likely reason why the percentage of income spent on life and annuity insurance remained approximately constant over the postwar years is that the influences other than income have largely compensated one another.

On the one hand, the amount of life and annuity insurance in force was swelled by the growing importance of insurance as a "fringe benefit" in labor-management relations; by the explosive increase of consumer credit, causing a rise in credit insurance which gives protection against the death of borrowers; and by the vigorous promotion efforts of the insurance companies.

On the other hand, shifts in the relative importance of various types of life and annuity insurance policies have brought a reduction in the average amount of premiums paid to obtain a given amount of protection. Fringe-benefit insurance and credit insurance are generally written in group policies, which are cheaper than individual policies. By 1956, group policies accounted for 32 per cent of all life insurance in force, compared with only 9 per cent in 1930.[4] Furthermore, there has been a sharp increase in term in-

Chart 15
Disposable Personal Income and Premiums Paid to Life Insurance Carriers, United States, 1929–1956

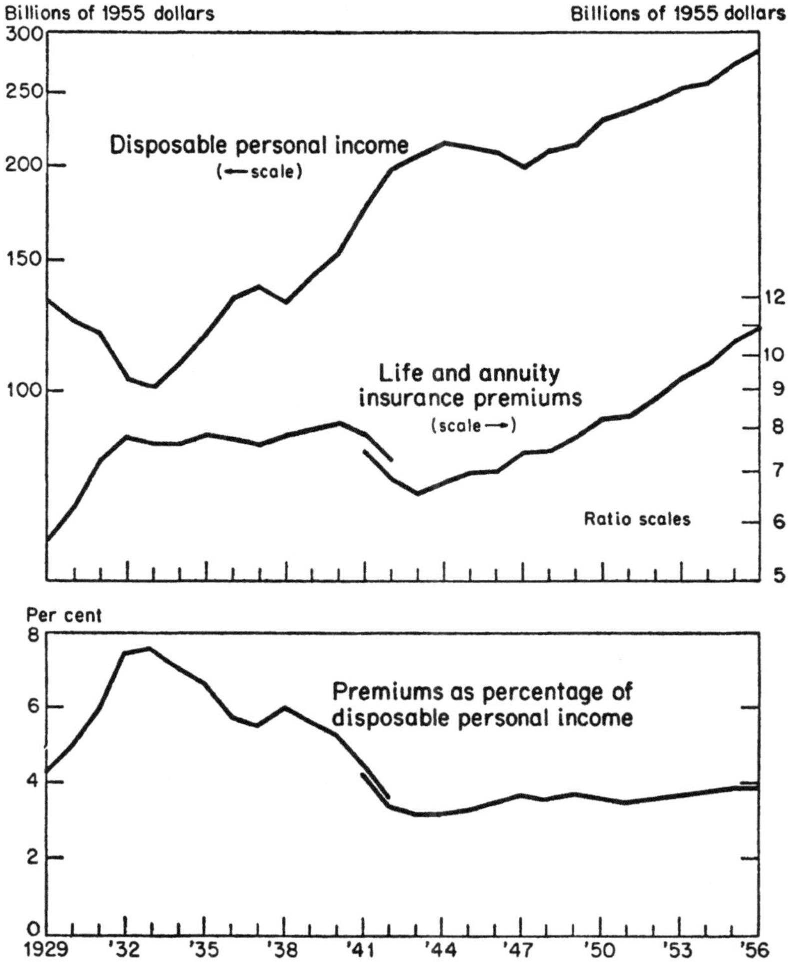

Sources: *Survey of Current Business;* also *Life Insurance Fact Book, 1957,* p. 51, and *Spectator Yearbook, 1953.* For the years 1929–1942 all premiums of life insurance companies and fraternal organizations are included; for the years 1941–1956, accident and health premiums of life insurance companies were excluded. The amounts that were excluded were determined as follows: for 1947 and later years, accident and health premiums of life insurance companies were published by the Institute of Life Insurance. For the period 1941–1946, these premiums were estimated from the data for all insurance com-

surance, which provides no savings and therefore is cheaper than other life insurance. One reason for the rise of term policies is the fact that most group insurance is term insurance; another likely reason is that inflation has influenced some individuals to forego the savings aspect of life insurance. Still another force tending toward lower premiums per unit of insurance in force is the increasing efficiency of the insurance industry, which makes it possible to provide protection at lower cost.

Though we think all these influences have roughly offset one another, we would not argue as a general proposition that, in the absence of such factors, people would always spend a constant proportion of their income on life insurance. But in the circumstances of the postwar years, this seems almost to have been the case. One straw in the wind is provided by sample surveys of the percentage of disposable income devoted to insurance by families with different income levels. These surveys suggest that, except in the very highest and the very lowest income brackets, families tend to spend about the same proportion of their income on insurance at all levels of the income ladder.[5] Though it is dangerous to project cross-sectional analyses of this sort over time, still they do carry a certain implication that increases in income will not generate much change in the proportion spent on insurance. We also find quite a direct tie between income changes and premium changes on a geographical basis. It appears that, in general, the states whose personal income increased the fastest between 1947 and 1956 had the largest gains in life insurance premiums, with roughly equal proportionate increases in both factors. This relation is shown in Chart 16.

Spectacular momentum has also been generated in the field of accident and health insurance. In 1930, the annual premiums in this field were well under one-quarter billion dollars, but by 1956 they

---

panies furnished by the Institute of Health Insurance on the basis of relations prevailing in later years. In the conversion of premiums into constant dollars, personal consumption expenditure deflators as published by the U. S. Department of Commerce were used.

Chart 16

Percentage Increases from 1947 to 1956 in Life Insurance Premiums Paid and in Personal Income, by States

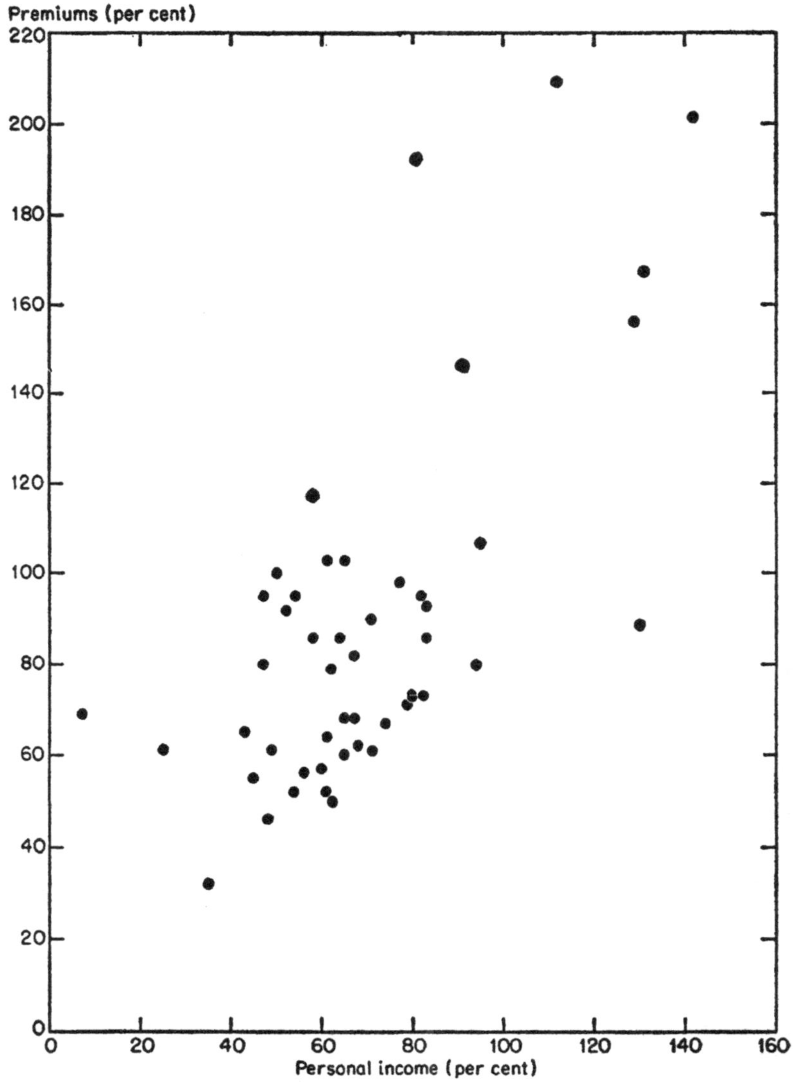

Sources of data: *Survey of Current Business,* September 1955, August 1957; Spectator Company, *Insurance Yearbook,* 1948, 1957. The dots represent the 48 states and the District of Columbia.

amounted to $4.5 billion,* compared with about $11 billion in life and annuity premiums. Between 1941 and 1956 alone, the volume of accident and health premiums, even when measured in constant dollars, rose by almost nine times. Specialized health plans such as Blue Cross and Blue Shield have partly filled the demand for this sort of insurance, but the insurance companies, too, have expanded their accident and health operations.

There is a close tie, of course, between the volume of accident and health insurance and the disposition of people to demand medical care. Expenditures on private medical care have been a fairly constant proportion of disposable personal income during recent decades. During the period 1929–1953, apart from the deep depression and the war years, this proportion varied between 3.5 and 4.1 per cent without exhibiting any upward trend. Since then, however, the ratio of medical-care expenditure to disposable personal income has shown substantial growth, reaching 4.8 per cent in 1956 and 4.9 per cent in 1957.[6] We suspect that this increase in the share of income spent on medical care has come about primarily as a result of increased insurance coverage of medical risks, although the rise of real income levels and changes in the age composition of population have probably also played a part. In any case, we may visualize private medical-care expenditure as representing a ceiling—albeit a gradually rising one—toward which the more rapidly expanding accident and health insurance premiums are moving.**

* Excluding some $400 million of accident and health premiums received by the casualty companies, which are treated in the next chapter.

** In theory, if private insurance coverage of medical risks were practically complete, the volume of accident and health premiums would about equal the actual nongovernmental payments to doctors, dentists, hospitals, and so forth. This balance would be the net result of many offsetting factors. For example, factors tending to push premium payments higher than total medical expenditures include the operating costs of providing insurance and the fact that part of the premiums go toward protecting against loss of income during illness. On the other side, factors tending to hold premiums below expenditures include the non-insurability of some risks and some persons, and the exclusion of many small medical bills under "deductible" provisions.

The gap, however, is still wide. In 1956, accident and health insurance premiums amounted to only 40 per cent of medical-care expenditures, though the proportion was up considerably from some 20 per cent prevailing in 1950. Eventually, as accident and health insurance matures out of the "new product" stage of rapid growth, the level of spending on medical care will represent an important governor on the future expansion of such insurance.

PREMIUMS AND MANPOWER

Since our final objective is to determine the economic role of insurance companies in the New York Metropolitan Region, our concern is more with manpower than with premiums. Chart 17 shows, for the life and annuity field, the relation between employment and premiums as expressed in constant dollars.[7]

The trend in the ratio of premiums per worker is the result of various factors. Changes in productivity, in the composition of the companies' business, and in the relative importance of new business versus renewals, have differing effects on employment. It requires more work, for instance, to sell and issue a new policy than to service an old one for a year; yet both generate about the same amount of premiums. Similarly, group business produces more premiums per man-day worked than does individual insurance.

Though all these factors are influential, no one of them is consistently predominant. The record since 1929, as shown in Chart 17, illustrates the varying play of the forces. Between 1929 and 1932, premiums per employee rose, probably because the collapse of new business in that period enabled the companies to cut back their staffs.*

During the next ten years, premiums per employee slipped to their 1929 level, even though insurance purchases were falling rela-

* In interpreting these developments, one may want to keep in mind that the conversion of premiums into constant dollars may distort some movements over short periods because of the cyclical patterns present in the price deflators.

Chart 17

Premiums Paid to Life Insurance Carriers, Employment, and Premiums per Person Employed, United States, 1929–1956

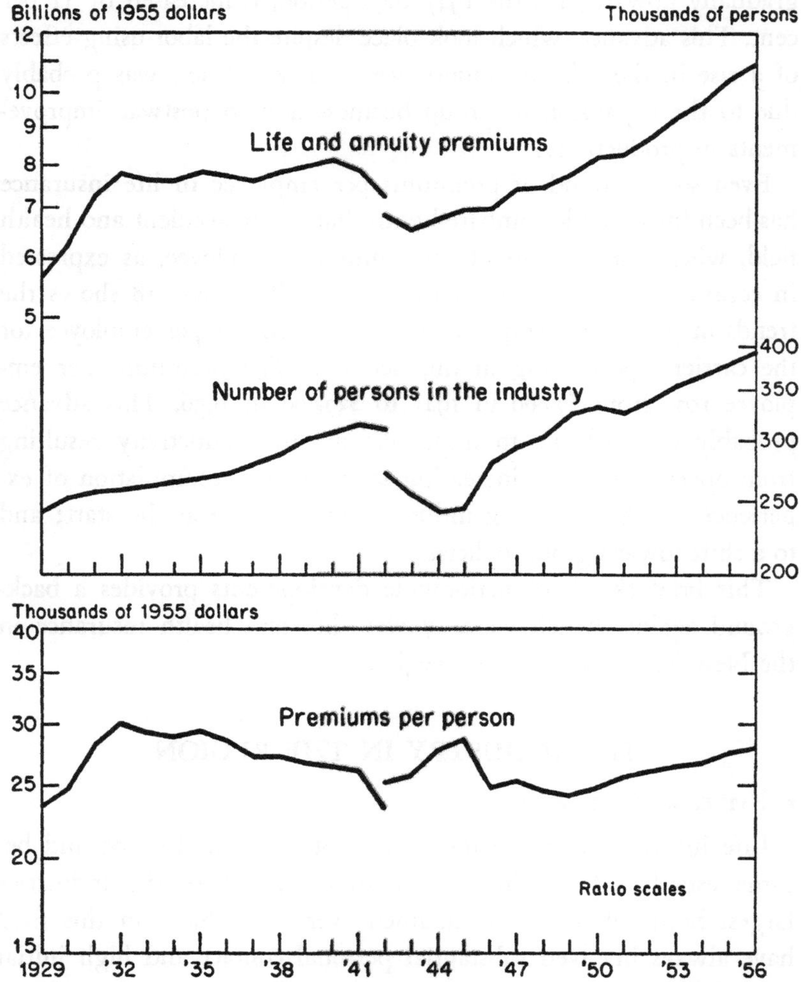

Sources: For premiums see note to Chart 15; for employment see note 7 on page 280. For the years 1929–1942, accident and health premiums and accident and health employment of life insurance companies were included; for the years 1942–1956, accident and health premiums and the estimated accident and health employment of the life insurance companies were excluded.

tive to insurance in force and group policies were growing in relative importance.

Between 1942 and 1948, the amount of premiums per employee fluctuated unevenly under the shifting influences of the war and immediate postwar developments. More recently, the ratio crept gradually upward; for the 1947–1956 period, it increased by 11 per cent. This advance, which took place despite the labor-using effects of a rise in the relative importance of new policies, was probably due to the expansion of group business and to postwar improvements in productivity.

Even so, the trend of premiums per employee in life insurance has been fairly stable compared with that in the accident and health field, where the amount of premiums per employee, as expressed in constant dollars, has been gaining rapidly. Chart 18 shows the trends in premiums, employment, and premiums per employee for the carriers specializing in this activity.[8] The premiums per employee rose from $7,800 in 1941 to $39,000 in 1956. This advance probably is ascribable to improvements in productivity resulting from operations on an increasing scale; to the accumulation of experience which the young industry did not have at the start; and to a shift toward group policies.

This brief sketch of nationwide developments provides a background against which we may view life and health insurance in the New York Metropolitan Region.

THE INDUSTRY IN THE REGION

✓ Patterns of growth

Life insurance came to the United States from Europe and became established on the eastern seaboard, where the industry's largest home offices have remained ever since. Sales in this field have always involved substantial personal contact and high initial costs. In the early period, when travel and communications facilities were poor, the need to rely on nearby markets was much greater than it is today. The high mortality of the early companies in the

Chart 18

Premiums Paid to Accident and Health Insurance Carriers, Employment, and Premiums per Person Employed, United States, 1941–1956

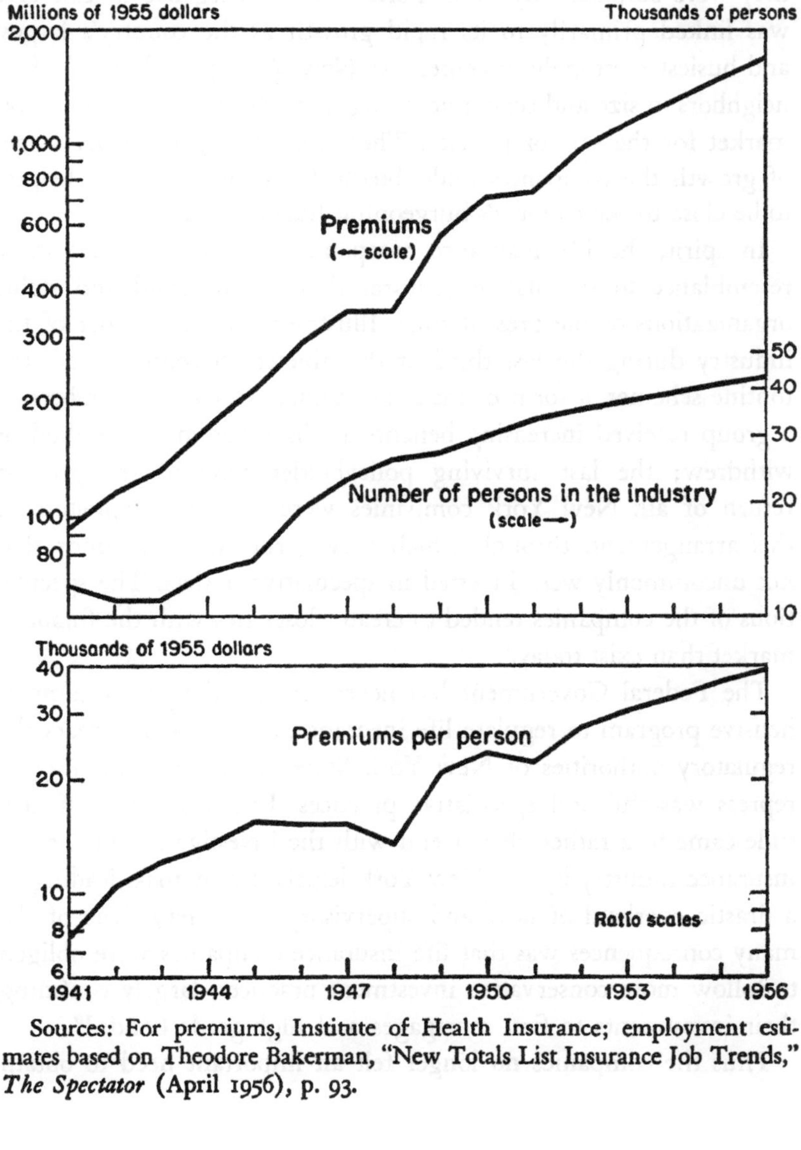

Sources: For premiums, Institute of Health Insurance; employment estimates based on Theodore Bakerman, "New Totals List Insurance Job Trends," *The Spectator* (April 1956), p. 93.

South and the West attests to the view that a certain degree of population density has been a prerequisite for the success of life insurance companies.

Originally, Philadelphia and Boston were the dominant life insurance cities, but around the middle of the nineteenth century they were surpassed by New York, whose emergence in this area was linked primarily to its rapid growth as the country's largest and busiest metropolitan center. As New York pulled ahead of its neighbors in size and economic strength, it afforded a more lucrative market for the sale of policies. Then, too, during the early stages of growth the companies undoubtedly found it somewhat helpful to be close to the country's burgeoning financial center.

In spirit, the life insurance companies of that day bore more resemblance to speculative ventures than to the staid and stable organizations of the present time. Illustrative of the temper of the industry during the last third of the nineteenth century were the tontine schemes, a form of insurance under which the members of a group received increasing benefits as the other members died or withdrew; the last surviving policyholder received the greatest return of all. New York companies were intensive exploiters of this arrangement, through which they garnered large funds that not uncommonly were invested in speculative outlets. The speculations of the companies tended to create closer ties with the financial market than exist today.[9]

The Federal Government has never embarked upon a comprehensive program to regulate life insurance, and for many years the regulatory authorities of New York State did little or nothing to repress wasteful and speculative practices. But this hands-off attitude came to a rather abrupt end with the investigation of the life insurance industry by the New York legislature in 1905, leading to a drastic overhaul of laws and supervisory machinery. One of the many consequences was that life insurance companies were obliged to follow more conservative investment practices, largely confining their investments to first mortgages and high-grade bonds.[10]

Thus the companies no longer felt an important need to obtain an hour-by-hour flow of money-market information. Meanwhile, the spread of the nation's population and the improvement of transportation and intercity communications were making it less necessary for insurance firms to be in or near the big eastern cities. But by that time the leadership of New York in life insurance had already been established, and it has persisted to the present.

It has not, however, persisted unimpaired. For some time, the industry has been spreading itself more thinly; between 1947 and 1956, while employment in the Region was increasing from 68,000 to 83,000, or by 22 per cent, employment in the nation grew by 40 per cent. Behind these differences in growth rates lies a complex pattern of forces which must be understood in order to project the future performance of the Region. These forces differ among three major components of the industry: life insurance home offices, life insurance offices in the field, and the accident and health organizations.

HOME-OFFICE EMPLOYMENT

The operations of life insurance companies fall into two distinctly different categories. One consists of work in the main office, including the top administrative and investment functions, plus a great volume of routine activities in connection with the writing of insurance, billing, and accounting. The other consists of field work and embraces the selling and servicing of insurance policies, as well as some responsibilities for collections and administration of claims. Employment in the home office, of course, depends on the total volume of the firm's business, wherever it may originate. But the field employment which the life insurance business generates in any area is primarily a function of the local population—of its number, its income, and its propensity to buy insurance. This breakdown between field and home offices is not so meaningful with respect to the accident and health carriers, dominated by such organizations as Blue Cross and Blue Shield, which for the most part conduct operations on a local basis from the home office.

The position of the New York Metropolitan Region as America's

Table 18 Employment in Home Offices of Life Insurance Companies, 1947, 1950, 1956

	United States	New York Metropolitan Region	NYMR as percentage of U. S.
1947	104,000	39,358	37.8
1950	112,000	40,127	35.8
1956	137,000	42,903	31.3

Sources: U. S. figures are estimates based on data provided by the Institute of Life Insurance; the Region's figures are estimates based on a questionnaire survey conducted by the New York Metropolitan Region Study.

outstanding center for life insurance is based on its concentration of home offices. As indicated in Table 18, employment at these offices has risen at a slower pace in recent years than the comparable employment in the rest of the country. The main reason is simply that companies headquartered in the Region have not been increasing their business as fast as those elsewhere in the nation. A glance from Table 18 to Table 19 shows the similarity between the lag

Table 19 Premiums Received by All United States Life Insurance Companies and the Eight Leading Companies of New York Metropolitan Region, 1947, 1950, 1957

	Total premiums (in millions of 1955 dollars) [a]		
	All U. S. companies	8 NYMR companies	8 NYMR companies as percentage of U. S.
1947	7,855	3,845	48.9
1950	9,109	4,319	47.4
1957	14,098	5,885	41.7

[a] Deflated by implicit price deflators for personal consumption expenditure. Includes life, annuity, and accident and health premiums.

Sources: For United States, Institute of Life Insurance, *Life Insurance Fact Book, 1958*, p. 53; for eight companies, questionnaire survey conducted by New York Metropolitan Region Study.

in the Region's home-office employment and the lag in its premium income.

The companies of the Region have been up against stiffer competition throughout the country, including their own home states of New York and New Jersey. These results are apparent in Table 20, which shows that 21 life insurance firms located in the New

Table 20 Life Insurance Premiums Paid to 21 Companies with Home Offices in New York Metropolitan Region, as Percentage of Premium Payments to All Companies, 1930, 1947, 1956

State from which paid	1930	1947	1956
New York	71.5	66.8	63.4
New Jersey	76.0	72.1	66.0
Pennsylvania	63.1	59.8	56.5
Massachusetts	56.9	49.6	45.6
Connecticut	57.7	51.4	47.3
New Hampshire	64.5	58.9	55.7
Rhode Island	56.9	48.4	46.3
Vermont	58.0	48.1	45.6
Maine	64.7	57.1	54.7
Other states	n.a.	41.9	37.1
United States	n.a.	49.4	44.1

n.a. = not available.

Source: Spectator Company, *Insurance Yearbook, Life and Miscellaneous*, 1931, 1948, and 1957.

York Metropolitan Region—accounting for practically all of the Region's home-office employment—have been giving ground in premiums in every one of the northeastern states. Indeed, the data used in preparing the table show that, between 1947 and 1956, the 21 institutions suffered relative declines in 46 states and the District of Columbia.

Why did the Region's companies trail behind the industry at large? One factor sometimes suggested is legal restriction by New

York State. The legislation makes it comparatively difficult to create new companies in the state. It also imposes relatively conservative practices with regard to investments, commissions, salaries, legal reserves, and the amount of new business written—and such provisions apply to all the major companies in the New York Metropolitan Region, whether or not domiciled in New York State, because they are licensed to do business in the state. Another important possibility is that the large national life insurance organizations have begun to experience the lack of flexibility which goes with huge size. Then again, local purchasers of life insurance might have begun to prefer a "home" concern identified with their area of the country. Such home companies may be better adapted to meet local conditions than a nationwide organization.

These are all plausible explanations and there is no certain way of testing which ones are more valid than others, because regulation, size, and markets are intermingled in a way that cannot easily be unscrambled.

We do find that the companies both inside and outside the Region which fall under the requirements of New York State have expanded less than those not subject to these restrictions.[11] These New York-regulated companies include most of the biggest in the country. Sample tests show, however, that among the insurance companies subject to regulation by New York State there has been little difference between the growth rates of the larger and smaller companies, taken as groups. This evidence suggests that regulation was more influential than size in governing growth.

We are also obliged to consider the possibility that the Region's companies may have been handicapped not only by regulation but also by having their principal markets in areas whose economic growth is sluggish compared with that of the country as a whole. If they were indeed concentrating their business in such areas, this fact could be considered one of the reasons for their relatively slow rise in premium payments; for the tie between an area's personal income and the insurance premiums it pays has been quite direct, as indicated in Chart 16, earlier in the chapter. But our investigation shows that the declining position of the New York Region's life insurance companies did not stem from an undue concentration in relatively dull markets. For we have found that when the 48 states are weighted in proportion to the premiums they paid to the Region's life insurance companies in 1947, their personal income growth between 1947 and 1956 turns out to be 70 per cent—scarcely less than the actual increase in the nation, which was 72 per cent.*

On the other hand, we find evidence that throughout the country the inhabitants of a given state were favoring "domestic" companies—that is, companies domiciled in the state—over outside companies. Though this reaction is found everywhere, it is especially pronounced in the areas of the nation which did not have major life insurance industries of their own.[12] The tendency may well reflect the fact that local companies in all parts of the country have come "of age" and now are more effective competitors of the older nationwide enterprises of the Northeast. As a rule, local men are in charge of a "foreign" company's operations in any given area; nevertheless, it may well be that a local company fits the market better, or is quicker in adapting its operations to meet changing local conditions. In addition, further competition for the older firms has been offered by the many new companies which came into being in the areas where incomes have been growing rapidly and the legal environment was favorable.

Our impression of the increased preference of the public for dealing with local companies is fortified by the experience of the Prudential Insurance Company. In 1948, Prudential began to decentralize its headquarters operations by establishing five regional "home" offices in various parts of the United States. The express purpose of this program was "to develop a closer relationship with people in their homes, farms and businesses throughout the United States and Canada. . . ."[13] It may be too early to appraise the

* The Region here is represented by the same 21 life companies used in Table 20. The only firms omitted are a few relatively tiny ones whose total premiums would be an insignificant fraction.

effects of the company's decentralization measures—three of its new "home" offices were set up as late as 1955—yet it is a provocative fact that the company has grown faster than other leading enterprises in the Region. As Table 21 shows, Prudential's increase in

Table 21 Index of Life Insurance Premiums Received by the Leading Life Insurance Companies of New York Metropolitan Region, 1947–1956

(1947 = 100)

Year	Prudential	10 leading companies (excluding Prudential)	Metropolitan	Equitable	New York Life
1947	100.0	100.0	100.0	100.0	100.0
1948	105.6	105.1	105.3	106.7	104.1
1949	105.7	107.9	108.7	108.9	106.0
1950	117.6	115.0	118.3	113.7	112.0
1951	127.8	119.7	119.5	127.6	113.3
1952	134.2	126.2	125.2	136.1	119.6
1953	145.1	134.1	132.5	146.8	127.2
1954	151.1	140.3	140.4	149.8	132.0
1955	161.2	151.5	153.3	159.9	142.1
1956	173.1	159.7	163.7	160.7	153.5
1957	184.4	168.6	174.0	166.3	162.7

Source: *Moody's Bank & Finance Manual* for the years 1948–1958.

premiums from 1947 to 1957 was faster than that of its leading competitors, including Metropolitan Life, Equitable, and New York Life. Of course, this fact is not proof that the decentralization decision was responsible, but we are inclined to believe that it was a contributing factor.

With respect to the Region's companies in general, our disposition is to conclude that remoteness from their markets has held back their growth in premiums, and that this in turn has restrained the expansion of employment of their home offices. But the decentralization of Prudential's home-office operations also helped this tendency by displacing perhaps 2,000 to 3,000 jobs which would otherwise have been in the Region.[14]

✓ FIELD EMPLOYMENT

We saw earlier that the manpower in life insurance in the Region is not confined to home offices. Almost as important in the Region's labor force is field employment, consisting mainly of jobs in life insurance field offices and partly of jobs in the establishments of independent agents and brokers selling and servicing life insurance policies. As Table 22 shows, these categories are estimated at about 35,000 jobs in the Region in 1956.

The Region has about the same share of the nation's field employment that it has of the nation's personal income and of the nation's employment of all kinds. Moreover, a mild decline has occurred in the Region's share of field employment—at least in the category of agents and brokers—a decline which parallels the Re-

Table 22 Life Insurance Employment in Field Offices of Life Insurance Companies and in Offices of Independent Agents and Brokers, 1947, 1950, 1956

	United States		New York Metropolitan Region		NYMR as per cent of U. S.	
	Field offices	Independent agents and brokers	Field offices [a]	Independent agents and brokers	Field offices	Independent agents and brokers
1947 ..	177,000	57,000	18,640	7,373	10.5	12.9
1950 ..	202,000	64,000	16,917	8,014	8.4	12.5
1956 ..	249,000	75,000	26,059	8,946	10.5	11.9

[a] Total field employment in the Region was estimated in the same way as that for the nation—as the sum of employment by the life insurance carriers, excluding the home-office labor force, but including 27 per cent of the employment reported by insurance and combination brokers and agents. See note 7 on page 280.

Sources: United States figures are estimates based on data published in *Survey of Current Business* and its *National Income, 1954* supplement, and data provided by the Institute of Life Insurance. The Region's figures are estimated on the basis of data provided by the New Jersey and New York State departments of labor, data collected by our questionnaire survey, and information published by the U. S. Department of Commerce in *County Business Patterns.*

gion's relative loss of ground in income and total jobs. This similarity is not surprising in view of the fact that the work conducted in the offices of agents and brokers consists primarily of serving the local market, and one would expect to find correspondence between the size of the local market and the amount of field activity.*

✓ Accident and health insurance carriers

The employment of the accident and health carriers in the Region, shown in Table 23, almost doubled between 1947 and 1956, rising to well over 5,000. Here again, the number of employees is intimately connected with the Region's economic life, and the Region's share of the national total again is about the same size as its shares

Table 23 Employment of Accident and Health Insurance Carriers, 1947, 1950, 1956

	United States	New York Metropolitan Region	NYMR as per cent of U. S.
1947	23,000	2,759	12.0
1950	30,000	3,707	12.4
1956	43,000	5,347	12.4

Sources: These are estimates based on Theodore Bakerman, "New Totals List Life Insurance Job Trends," *The Spectator* (April 1956), p. 93, and on data provided by New Jersey and New York State departments of labor.

of income and total jobs, though the accident and health share appears to have increased slightly instead of declining.[15] The bulk of work performed by the Region's accident and health carriers originates within the Region because Blue Cross, Blue Shield, and similar organizations, which make up most of this industry, operate in markets which are geographically limited.

Thus, we find that of the three components of the Region's em-

* The reader will note, however, the sharp rise in the Region's field-office employment from 1950 to 1956. We have been unable to find a satisfactory explanation for the change, and we suspect that it may be one of the insubstantive statistical vagaries which are constantly plaguing the analyst who deals with such data.

ployment in life and health insurance, one—the home offices of life insurance companies—has been influenced primarily by the trend of business done by the Region's companies throughout the nation and by the decision of one institution to decentralize its home-office operations. In the other two components—life insurance field work and the accident and health carriers—changes have been tied to the economic life of the Region.

WHERE IN THE REGION?

Of the 83,000 persons employed by the life and health insurance industry in the New York Metropolitan Region in 1956, about 60,000 or 72.5 per cent worked in New York City. An additional 15,000, or 18.5 per cent, worked in the New Jersey counties of Essex and Hudson, most of them in the city of Newark. The remaining 9 per cent were widely distributed among other parts of the Region.

Yet, though the number of jobs outside the big cities of the Region is relatively small, the expansion in these suburban areas has been rapid. Between 1947 and 1956, the industry's employment in the central-city areas, by which we mean New York City and Essex and Hudson Counties, increased by 20 per cent, while in the rest of the Region it rose by more than 50 per cent. This discrepancy reflects the mushrooming of agents and brokers in the suburbs and conforms with patterns found in other metropolitan areas.[16] Home offices so far have not taken to the suburbs, but neither have they remained stationary.

✓ THE RELOCATION OF HOME OFFICES

When New York was a small community huddled on the lower tip of Manhattan, it was inescapable that the life insurance companies would settle in the heart of the City. As the City pushed northward, the companies were at first aloof to the shift. As we have seen, the speculative overtones of their activities favored in some measure a location adjacent to the rapidly developing financial market. Moreover, lower Manhattan at that time afforded comparatively good travel and communication facilities. It was no wonder, therefore, that in the middle of the nineteenth century, all of the City's life insurance companies were located in what is now the financial district.[17]

Gradually conditions changed. We have already noted, in our comparison of the Region with the nation, how the ties of the insurance companies to the financial market were weakened as their investment and operating practices became increasingly conservative. Moreover, experience was beginning to permit the life insurance companies to predict their insurance risks with growing accuracy. Unlike the fire and casualty enterprises, therefore, they had little to benefit by banding together and exchanging the daily talk of the trade. Thus, there was no cohesive force which would either hold the life insurance companies to the financial district or lead them to form a separate district of their own. These factors set the stage for an exodus. By 1900, five of the twelve life insurance companies which then existed in Manhattan south of 59th Street were located north of Fulton Street.[18] Thereafter, the ties with Wall Street grew even more strained. The life companies found themselves occupying premium space in an area of rising rentals, with less and less reason to remain there. Their rapidly expanding staffs increased the importance of personnel considerations and the desirability of settling in the less expensive and increasingly accessible locations of midtown Manhattan. By 1925, as a result, the number of companies below Fulton Street had been further reduced to three out of thirteen.[19]

Today, Manhattan's life insurance companies are well distributed along the half of the island below Central Park. The most important single spot has long been the Madison Square neighborhood, where Metropolitan Life and New York Life have their impressive buildings. The biggest move now in prospect is one of about twenty blocks by the Equitable Life Assurance Society, which is about to hop northward from the vicinity of Pennsylvania Station to that of Rockefeller Center. Meanwhile, a dozen miles or so to the west, Newark is an important life insurance center in its own right. Chart 19 shows where the home offices of the New York Metropolitan Region are located.

The two major companies in downtown Newark were not migrants from the Wall Street financial district, but had their birth in the Jersey metropolis. The Prudential Insurance Company was founded there nearly a century ago by John Fairfield Dryden, a former Ohio insurance agent who had tried to establish a company in New York to sell insurance to workingmen but had been defeated when the Governor vetoed a bill which would have granted him a charter. Dryden is said to have told his wife: "Ohio was wrong for me and my ideas. Now New York has shut us out. The place to begin is where they need us most. It ought to be a thriving, growing industrial area. I think I know where that is—right across the river, in the city of Newark."[20] Even earlier, the Mutual Benefit Life Insurance Company had been founded in Newark by Robert Livingston Patterson, who had also tried to promote a company in New York but had been unable to obtain a charter from the state legislature.[21]

About 95 per cent of the Region's home-office employment is gathered in Manhattan and Newark. In Manhattan, nearly all of the personnel is stationed between 14th Street and Central Park; and the two large companies in Newark are located at the center of that city. The central-city location of life insurance home offices is mainly the result of the need to assemble a large labor force. This heavy concentration in the central cities of the Region is characteristic of the national pattern. Large institutions are restricted in their choice of home-office locations to areas with an ample supply of office workers, and hence they stay in the business sections of big cities. Only the smaller companies are found in small urban areas. Indeed, on analyzing the home-office locations of 128 firms throughout the country, we found only five instances in which relatively small urban areas contained relatively large home offices.[22]

The Region's life insurance companies are huge, and their office operations are extensive. The four biggest, Metropolitan, Prudential, Equitable, and New York Life, which also lead the nation in size,

Chart 19
Major Life Insurance Home Offices of New York Metropolitan Region

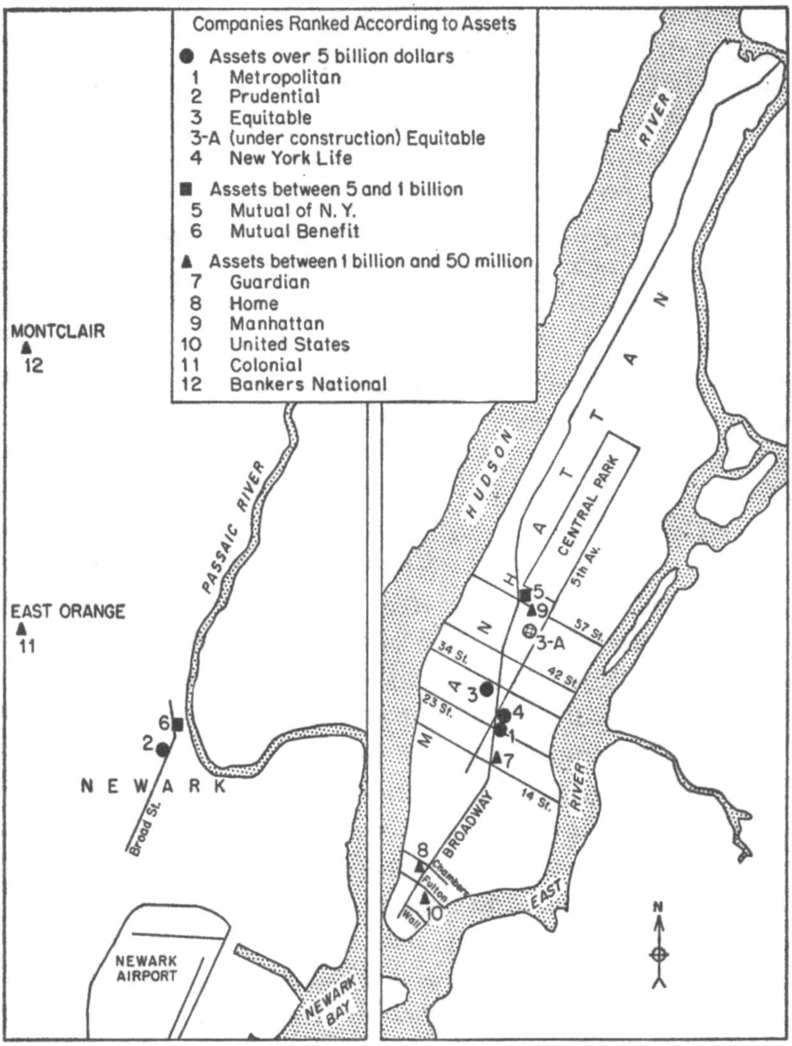

Note: Companies are listed in the order of their assets Dec. 31, 1958, as given in *Moody's Bank & Finance Manual,* 1959. The 12 companies with assets over $50 million are shown.

had about 35,000 home-office employees in 1956 out of the Region's total of 43,000. A firm with a work force of several thousand women, many of marriageable age, must count on losing and having to replace several hundred or more each year. That would not be easy in communities like White Plains, Great Neck, or Summit—indeed anywhere but in the labor markets of Manhattan or Newark with their large supplies of female workers.

Big-city locations also have an appeal because of the public relations benefits they offer. Home offices usually are prominent structures in the city landscape, intended to create a memorable and pleasing impression. From the long-established Metropolitan Life tower in Manhattan to the new buildings of Mutual Benefit Life in Newark and the regional home office of Prudential in Chicago, insurance offices have become landmarks. Several companies, when asked in a questionnaire survey about the reasons for their locations, gave some emphasis to this factor in their replies.

An insurance company, it is true, can also gain the spotlight by planting a spectacular garden office in a suburb. But the exposure to passers-by is only a fraction of that which is achieved in a city. Moreover, it has been found that even though the per-acre cost of land in the outskirts is relatively low, zoning rules and the need for parking space require a fairly extensive building site. Besides, the need to supply more amenities to employees, such as larger cafeterias and more elaborate recreational facilities, adds to the space needs of the companies.[23]

Finally, inertia also plays a part in the insurance companies' present locations. Central-city sites do have certain handicaps, which simply have not been strong enough to overcome the advantages plus the inertia. Among the handicaps in Manhattan are the higher office salaries and shorter work week prevailing there, compared with most other parts of the Region. Newark, for instance, typically reports weekly business office salaries about 4 per cent below those of Manhattan and a work week about two and a half hours longer.[24] Suburban office workers elsewhere in the Region also tend to work longer hours at slightly less pay than those in Manhattan. In the light of the labor-cost differential, Manhattan might not be nearly so attractive a location if the availability of large supplies of office workers were not a controlling consideration.

Despite the seeming advantages, on balance, of a city location, there are clear indications in the nation of a slow trek of home offices to the suburbs. So far, the movement has been confined to the smaller companies where the labor replacement problem is not prohibitive; and it has not yet affected the New York Metropolitan Region. Out of 37 life insurance companies throughout the nation which gave information on this point in response to a questionnaire survey made by the authors in 1958, there were 24 that had moved their home offices since 1940 or were in the process of doing so. Before moving, only one of these was in the suburbs, the other 23 being in the cities; but in relocating, 8 companies chose the suburbs and 16 the cities. None of the five firms in this sample having more than 1,000 home-office workers selected a suburban location.

Even so, large firms have often seriously debated whether to move to the suburbs. Before Mutual Benefit Life determined to remain in downtown Newark, for example, and before Prudential fixed on the new location of its Newark office, both considered reestablishing outside the city in the western part of Essex County. They even reserved sites for the purpose. Eventually, the existence of more satisfactory labor pools in downtown Newark contributed substantially to holding both companies there. The business district sits at the hub of an effective bus network; furthermore, the girl graduates of the city's high schools enter the labor market to a far higher degree than their suburban counterparts. Those facts made powerful arguments.

There is no question, however, that the reservoirs of labor on which America's central cities draw are more widely dispersed than they used to be. In 1910, for instance, the Metropolitan Life Insurance Company was obtaining 69 per cent of its work force from Manhattan and Brooklyn, but by 1946 the proportion had shrunk to 33 per cent.[25] This is also the likely direction of the future. As the populations of central cities alter in character and decline in absolute number, the recruitment areas of their offices—insurance and otherwise—are likely to spread more and more.

Thus there are grounds for supposing that the inducements of Manhattan and Newark to the home offices of the insurance companies may be lessening in strength. But the chinks in the armor are not wide. The still imposing advantages of city locations suggest the unlikelihood of any major resettlement program by large firms which are already established in the business districts. The smaller companies are not so tightly anchored, but even here we see no basis for expecting that the majority of them will move outward in the next decade or two.

THE DISTRIBUTION OF FIELD OFFICES

In contrast to home-office activities, employment in the industry's field activities, as illustrated in Table 24, is spread throughout the New York Metropolitan Region in somewhat the same way as total jobs. Substantial correspondence also exists between field employment and population, though the relation is not quite so close.

The location of selling and servicing offices is determined by trying to minimize the distance between salesmen and "customers." The customers, of course, may be either individuals or business enterprises. The rise of group insurance and the growing practice of businesses to insure the lives of their key men have added to the importance of businesses as life insurance buyers. On top of this, the practice of many salesmen to contact individuals at their jobs rather than at home helps explain the fact that the distribution of field personnel in the Region corresponds more closely to the distribution of total employment than to that of population.

Even so, as seen in the table, field personnel tends to concentrate more in the big-city counties of the Region than does total employment. This tendency probably is caused, at least in part, by the circumstance that insurance salesmen more often do business with persons in offices than with persons in factories or other work-places. Field offices, moreover, may house not only salesmen but also the

Table 24 Distribution of Field Employment, Total Employment, and Population, by Parts of New York Metropolitan Region

	1956 field employment [a]	1955 total nonagricultural employment	1956 population
Entire Region	100.0%	100.0%	100.0%
New York City	66.7	61.2	50.7
Essex and Hudson Counties	12.0	9.8	10.6
Other New Jersey counties	9.7	12.7	16.5
Nassau and Suffolk Counties	4.2	6.4	10.4
Other New York counties and Fairfield County, Conn.	7.4	9.9	11.8

[a] Includes, in addition to the field-office employment of the life insurance carriers, 27 per cent of the total insurance and combination (insurance, real estate, etc.) agents and brokers and their employees.

Sources: For field employment, the figures are estimates based on data provided by New Jersey and New York State departments of labor, and on data published by the U. S. Department of Commerce in *County Business Patterns*. Total nonagricultural employment is from Regional Plan Association, Bulletin 87, *People, Jobs and Land, 1955–1975* (New York, 1957). Population figures are New York Metropolitan Region Study estimates.

administrative and servicing employees of an area; and when this is true, there is additional reason to locate in a readily accessible business district in the Region.

THE ACCIDENT AND HEALTH CARRIERS

The accident and health insurance carriers maintain centralized facilities and only a small proportion of their work is performed through field offices. The carriers are located in the central cities in order to be near the subscribing organizations for their group plans; these subscribers are predominantly business enterprises. Of secondary importance, though not negligible, is the desire to have sufficient workers available and to be close to the hospitals with which the carriers deal.

Accordingly, we find that in 1956 about 83 per cent of the Region's employment by accident and health carriers was located in New York City and another 15 in Essex and Hudson Counties, leaving only 2 per cent for the rest of the Region. In 1947, the concentration was about the same.

SUMMING UP

Two major forces seem to be affecting the relative position of the Region in life insurance. One is nationwide competition: the Region's companies as a group, though growing steadily, are not matching the growth of companies—new and old—having their headquarters elsewhere, and therefore the Region's share of the nation's home-office employment is decreasing. The second force—closely related to the first—is the somewhat faster rise of personal income in the nation as a whole than in the New York Metropolitan Region; this difference has had its effect on field employment in the Region and indirectly on the Region's home-office position.

The Region's position in life insurance is affected also by the relatively loose bonds between the life companies and the money market; in locational terms they are not so closely tied, for instance, as are various activities of the big New York City commercial banks. Home-office functions can therefore spring up in other areas of the nation without much difficulty; the only major need is a center where young female office workers can readily be hired. And even this need may be weakened by the development of office mechanization.

Within the Region, the industry's structure has scarcely been touched by the tendency in some areas, as yet very mild, to move home offices to the suburbs. It is true that some of the Region's major life insurance firms have given consideration to such a shift, but eventually they relocated in the business sections of central cities. As far as the larger companies are concerned, their present home-office locations in Manhattan and Newark seem firmly fixed for some time to come. The field contingent, however, is likely to continue its suburban march as jobs and population grow in outlying areas.

7

The Rest of the Financial Community

Commercial banking and life and health insurance account for about half the manpower engaged in finance in the New York Metropolitan Region; the other half is spread over a number of different fields. In all of these fields, we find the same factors that have affected the locations of the commercial banks and life insurance office, but in different combinations and with varying shades of emphasis. Two categories stand out because they absorb about 70 per cent of the employment that is left; they are, first, the property insurance companies, and, second, the securities industry.

PROPERTY INSURANCE

We use the term "property insurance" to cover all insurance employment except the life and health and accident employment discussed in the preceding chapter. Traditionally, the field of property insurance is divided principally into two groups: (1) fire and marine; and (2) casualty. In general, fire insurance provides indemnity for losses sustained by fire and allied perils from which fire often develops. Marine insurance originally afforded protection against perils of the sea, but the scope of this coverage has been broadened considerably. Casualty insurance, as the latest of the major branches, is sometimes regarded as a residual category, picking up the risks not covered by the other branches. In general, it embraces third-party liability and certain kinds of property coverage. There are also miscellaneous lines of property insurance like title insurance and bonding.

Property insurance, all in all, generates over 70,000 jobs in the Region. Its roots in the Region go back to the eighteenth century—and its historic beginnings in America help to explain present locational patterns.

Development of the industry [1]

Ocean-going ships and their cargoes were the first forms of property insured in colonial America. As long ago as 1721, the *American Weekly Mercury* in Philadelphia ran an announcement that one John Copson had opened an office for the insurance of vessels and merchandise. Like other ventures to follow, this was an attempt to provide facilities on the famous pattern of Lloyd's of London, that is, to create a gathering place where a group of private investors might assemble to underwrite each insurance contract.

America's long coast line, poor communication facilities, and lack of political unity, however, were ill-suited to a central gathering place. Shippers would have more confidence in responsible individual companies with continuity of existence, prepared to issue contracts as required. In reponse to this need and spurred by a rapidly growing volume of exports, a group of Philadelphians organized the Insurance Company of North America in 1794. Within a few years, various other marine enterprises were formed, including the Insurance Company of New York.

The underwriting companies established themselves adjacent to the offices of the shipowners who required their protection. By 1800, marine underwriting by companies had appeared not only in Philadelphia and New York, but also in Boston, New Haven, Baltimore, Charleston, and Newburyport. The tendency was to locate in port cities and to stay close to the ports within these cities.

Fire insurance had a different set of locational compulsions. The companies developed where business was to be had, whether on the seacoast or not. Fire-fighting societies, set up by groups of property holders, already existed; and it was a logical step to the formation of companies that underwrote risks for the public, characteristically using fire brigades to help reduce those risks. The early companies were often sparked by imaginative and forceful individuals who had become interested in this field, and the accident of their presence in an area exerted a strong sway on the original locations of the companies.

The first significant colonial fire company—though there are reports of an earlier one—was founded in 1752 by Benjamin Franklin and some associates. It was called the Philadelphia Contributionship for the Insurance of Houses from Loss by Fire. This organization had no competition until 1781 when the Mutual Assurance Company was formed in Philadelphia. The first New York firm came into existence in 1787, followed within the next half a dozen years by several others. By 1794, the Baltimore Equitable Society was writing business in Maryland. In the following year, Connecticut entered the picture with the formation of the Mutual Assurance of the City of Norwich.

Up to this time, the activities of the companies remained primarily local. But the stage was now set for a change in concept which accepted the feasibility of a national fire insurance headquarters from which coverage could be written on properties located throughout the country. The transition occurred during the early 1800's in Hartford, a town of seven thousand people. It was a pleasant place in which to live and work, but there was not much to suggest that it would eventually emerge as one of the great insurance centers of the country. Indeed, the economic luster of the rising metropolises, such as Philadelphia and New York, coupled with their earlier beginning in the insurance field, suggested brighter possibilities for an insurance industry.

But Hartford at that time was fortunate in having business leaders of unusual competence, one of whom happened to be J. P. Morgan's grandfather. They became interested in fire insurance and recognized that the boundaries of the industry were national rather than local. The Hartford Fire Insurance Company, for example, was founded in 1810 and only a year later was seeking business in other sections of the country. And at the opening meeting of the stockholders of the Aetna Insurance Company in 1819, the chairman encouraged the notion that the business should not be limited to Hartford or even Connecticut but could spread into other states. This notion was in contrast with the parochial approach predominant elsewhere at that time.

The colonial companies at first sold a single line of insurance, but it was not long before they began writing different lines. The trend was foretokened by the Insurance Company of North America, which took on fire underwriting in the very next year after it had been established as a marine company. As the nineteenth century progressed, the companies extended their activities to cover additional risks on property.

The Hartford developments point up two things about the location of property insurance companies. One is that even in the pre-telephone era, their ties to the financial centers were not so close as to demand a big-city location. The other is that, wherever they developed, the bonds between the companies were strong enough to create an attraction to a common point.

This tendency to cluster, much more pronounced in property insurance than life insurance, goes back in part to the different character of the risks involved. Property risks are less readily predicted than life risks. They cover so many different situations that "experience tables" are of only limited help to the insurer in setting his rates. Indeed, many large property contracts are hand-tailored to the special requirements of the insured. On top of this, fires, floods, storms, and other disasters tend to create property insurance losses in bunches. From the very outset, therefore, the property companies have endeavored to reduce the hazards of their occupation by exchanging information regarding risk experience and by reinsuring some of their risks. To do this, they tended to concentrate in groups. The success of the Hartford pioneers encouraged the development of other companies nearby. Thus, from the coffee-house gatherings of the eighteenth century to the luncheon meetings of today, the advantage of the physical proximity of one firm to another has been an important locational influence in property insurance.

As the property insurers became national in scope, they generated employment in the field as well as at their headquarters offices. Gradually, the Hartford system of maintaining widely scattered agents with considerable discretionary authority was adopted by most of the youthful companies. The placing of such agents in New York City by out-of-town firms was difficult, at first, because of the severe rate-cutting practices carried on by the local companies and because of a special tax imposed on "foreign" companies operating there. But New York's great fire of 1835, which came near destroying the business district and wiped out 23 of the 26 local insurance companies in the process, changed the City's aversion to "foreign" firms. Shortly thereafter, the special tax on their activities was drastically reduced.

Once the property insurance industry had established itself on a national rather than a local basis, the stronger companies were able to participate in the economic advance of the country. Expansion was characterized in two ways: headquarters establishments grew, to take care of increasing operational and administrative requirements; and sales outlets spanned the country to promote sales and to service contracts.

Property insurance: recent years

"That which comes after ever conforms to that which has gone before," noted Marcus Aurelius. So it is in the property insurance field, where the record of the present is clearly traceable to the events that we have just described. The links of this chain may be noted in three major developments that the companies have been experiencing: their diversification; their tendency to converge on particular spots and lean on one another; and their rapid growth.

Diversification. Out of marine and fire insurance, many lines sprang. The most revolutionary change was the appearance of casualty forms. Accident insurance in this country is purported to have begun in 1864. Boiler insurance was brought to America by the English in 1867; plate glass insurance was introduced by the Irish in the same year; and insurance against theft appeared in 1885. In the twentieth century the rise of the automobile extended vastly the scope of insurance operations.

At first the distinction between fire and casualty lines was sharp, but it has become increasingly blurred. Starting about 1910, companies began organizing subsidiaries in a big way to invade one another's fields. Recognizing this drift, states enacted legislation authorizing fire and marine companies to write casualty lines, and the casualty insurers to enter the fire and marine fields. Companies not only broadened their offerings but also tended to consolidate various risks into single policies. Today, though some specializing still exists, the larger firms write practically every type of property insurance.

In New York State, for example, property companies may be licensed to write any or all of the following lines of insurance: accident and health, fire, miscellaneous property, water damage, burglary and theft, glass, boiler and machinery, elevator, animal, collision, personal injury liability, property damage, workmen's compensation and employer's liability, fidelity and surety, credit, motor vehicle, aircraft, and marine.[2]

Over the years, the relative importance of these activities has shifted. Marine insurance and fire insurance have receded into the background, while the casualty types have leaped ahead. In the first half of the twentieth century, the assets of the fire and marine insurance companies increased more than twentyfold, but those of the casualty and miscellaneous insurance companies gained over 100 times. At present, some 80 per cent of the volume of property business comes from casualty insurance, half of which involves some form of automobile coverage. Fire insurance accounts for about 13 per cent, and marine only 3 per cent.

The tendency to converge. As pointed out earlier, the property companies have had strong incentives to abate the risks of their business. Diversification has provided some help. Geographic dispersion, the importance of which was recognized almost at the birth of the industry, eases but does not eliminate the effects of local disasters. Even now a series of bad losses or a major catastrophe could make heavy inroads into profits and lead to bankruptcy.

To guard against these contingencies, many companies follow the practice of reinsuring portions of their liabilities with other institutions; in this way, each one acquires a portfolio of risks spread thinly over a large field. Also, the benefits of crowding together have encouraged the development of the "fleets" of associated companies which share their risks through reinsurance and gain other advantages.* A fleet, for example, typically maintains a common management and central housing, enabling the participating units to draw on a pool of services. The opportunities for savings through large-scale operations are clearly indicated in one recent study. It showed that stock companies whose annual premiums over a period of years averaged under $10 million paid out 44 per cent of their premiums in expenses, but companies with average annual premiums over $100 million paid out only 38 per cent. It also showed that for mutual companies with average annual premiums under $25 million, the average expense ratio was 32 per cent, but it was only 20 per cent for mutual companies with annual premiums over $50 million.[8]

Though the pressures to congregate are strong, they do not, of course, produce iron-tight barriers against mobility. In order to tap broader markets, individual members of a fleet may be in areas that are geographically removed from the group's base of activity. Even so, the same cities have continued to be the centers of activity in the industry. There are, at present, some 115 fleets operating in the United States, but the 20 largest handle over 40 per cent of all property insurance premiums. Of these big fleets, the dominant ones are headquartered in Hartford and New York City.

* This practice is confined to so-called stock companies, that is, those whose equity is owned by stockholders rather than by the policyholders. Stock companies constitute 75 per cent of the property and casualty field, measured by the volume of premiums, but this percentage is declining. The mutual companies, however, may be members of groups having no central administrative authority, but perhaps using common housing facilities or sharing the services of a particular staff.

Growth of the industry. During the last two decades, much of the growth of the property insurance field is directly traceable to the expansion of the over-all economy. As seen in Table 25, since 1939, except during World War II, the rising volume of premiums in non-automobile lines has tended to represent almost a constant percentage of the gross national product. The sale of automobile

Table 25 Premiums[a] in Major Property Insurance Lines as Percentage of Gross National Product, Selected Years, 1939–1956

	Automobile[b]	Fire and related lines[c]	Other property[d]
1939	0.7%	0.8%	0.8%
1943	0.3	0.5	0.6
1947	0.7	0.8	0.8
1951	0.9	0.8	0.8
1952	1.0	0.7	0.8
1953	1.1	0.7	0.8
1954	1.1	0.8	0.9
1955	1.1	0.8	0.9
1956	1.0	0.8	0.9

[a] These are "net premiums written." For each company, this means direct writing, plus premiums received for reinsurance, minus premiums paid to other companies for reinsurance. When the data reported by individual companies are aggregated for the country as a whole, they are equal to direct writings.

[b] Includes liability to others for physical damage and for bodily injury as well as coverage for physical damage to one's own car.

[c] Includes fire, extended coverage, allied lines, earthquake, glass, burglary and theft, boiler and machinery, and homeowners' policies.

[d] Includes accident (individual), accident and health (individual and group), hospital and medical, and non-cancellable workmen's compensation policies; ocean and inland marine policies; and hail (growing crop), liability other than auto, aircraft physical damage, fidelity, surety, credit, livestock, and miscellaneous policies.

Sources: *Spectator Handy Chart, Spectator Fire Index,* and *Spectator Yearbook*. Premiums are for stock, mutual, and reciprocal companies. Mutual and reciprocal totals were distributed by major groups in the same proportion as stock company totals, for which a breakdown was provided.

policies, on the other hand, has advanced even faster, and automobile premiums have risen as a percentage of the gross national product.

Increasing business has brought more manpower into the property insurance field. Here, as in life insurance, the employment consists of two parts: (1) the jobs accounted for by the insurance carriers themselves, in their home and field offices, and (2) those found in the offices of independent insurance brokers. Both segments have expanded in recent years, but at different rates. National employment by the carriers—a group which also includes a few specialty associations—rose 55 per cent between 1947 and 1956, but the property insurance employment in brokers' offices rose at a rate which can be roughly estimated at around 30 per cent. This differential in growth rates reflects, to some extent, the decline in the relative importance of stock companies, which rely almost exclusively upon independent agents and brokers. The mutuals, which are gaining in importance though they are still not so important as the stock companies, usually deal directly with their policyholders through salaried employees.

The relation since 1939 between property employment and property premiums is described in Table 26. It is clear that ties exist between the expansion in employment and the growth of output in the industry. Although short-term fluctuations in the number of employees engaged in processing claims may disturb this relation temporarily, the variations tend to iron out in the long run. Moreover, the problem of separating the time devoted to new business from that devoted to the processing of existing policies—an issue that we encountered in the life insurance industry—is of less consequence here because of the short duration of most property insurance contracts.

The volume of premiums has climbed very fast, even when adjusted for rising price levels. Part of this increase may be due to product innovation, manifest in the trend toward package arrangements of insurance contracts. The home owner's dwelling policy is a case in point. Here a single policy may encompass fire, burglary, liability, glass, and other insurance. The single contract is attractive to the consumer because of its convenience and the reduced costs which permit lower premiums. Meanwhile, employment in the industry has expanded at a slower pace than premiums. The result is a steady increase in premiums per employee.

Table 26 Property Insurance Employment and Premiums, United States, Selected Years, 1939–1956

	Employment in thousands			Premiums in 1955 dollars [c]	
	Total	By carriers [a]	By brokers [b]	Total (billions of dollars)	Per employee (thousands of dollars)
1939	283	165	118	4.3	15.3
1943	271	159	112	4.5	16.4
1947	358	221	137	6.3	17.5
1951	433	276	157	8.2	19.0
1952	451	290	161	9.0	19.9
1953	474	306	168	9.7	20.5
1954	482	312	170	10.0	20.8
1955	503	327	176	10.6	21.1
1956	523	343	181	10.8	20.7

[a] Employment by all insurance carriers except life and accident and health. Data are estimates based on *Survey of Current Business, National Income, 1954* supplement, and *Spectator Magazine* (April 1956), p. 93. For estimates of employment by life and accident and health carriers, see Chapter 6.

[b] Property insurance employment by independent brokers and agents is estimated at 65 per cent of their total employment.

[c] Current dollars were converted to 1955 dollars by using the gross national product implicit deflators published by the U. S. Department of Commerce.

In addition, there is a trend among the larger companies toward the use of electronic data-processing machines. To some extent, the inauguration of insurance policies with more comprehensive coverage has forced the use of such machines, since the combining of diverse risks has aggravated the problem of computing premiums. Another incentive toward automatic operations has been the difficulty of finding manpower to meet growth requirements. Giant computers are already being used in the industry for such purposes as classifying risks, gathering statistical information, and performing various clerical functions.

PROPERTY INSURANCE IN THE REGION

It remains now to take up the locational shifts that have occurred between the New York Metropolitan Region and the rest of the country, and those that have occurred within the Region itself.

Between the Region and the rest of the country. The Region's employment in the property insurance industry amounted to 60,800 in 1947. By 1956, as Table 27 shows, it had climbed to 72,000 persons. But this gain lagged behind that achieved by the national industry, and the Region's share declined from 17.0 to 13.9 per cent. The Region's carriers lost ground faster than its brokers, as measured in share terms: the carriers' portion shrank from 19.5 to 14.9 per cent of the nation's total, while the brokers' share slipped only a little—from 12.9 to 11.9 per cent.

Various factors account for the comparatively sluggish employment growth of the carriers in the Region. For one thing, there are

Table 27 Property Insurance Employment in New York Metropolitan Region, 1947, 1950, 1956

	Region employment			Region as percentage of United States		
	Total	Carriers	Brokers and agents	Total	Carriers	Brokers and agents
1947	60,769	43,020	17,749	17.0	19.5	12.9
1950	65,314	46,021	19,293	15.7	17.5	12.6
1956	72,646	51,108	21,538	13.9	14.9	11.9

Sources: Region estimates are based on data collected by state departments of labor under unemployment insurance programs and *County Business Patterns, First Quarter,* 1947, 1951, and 1956. The estimates for the United States are based on Theodore Bakerman, "New Totals List Insurance Job Trends," *The Spectator,* April 1956, p. 93; and *Survey of Current Business.*

probably fewer home offices in the Region than ten years ago despite an over-all growth in the country. Table 28 gives the number of home offices in leading states in 1947 and 1956. The figures show that the combined number of such establishments in New York

Table 28 Number of Property Insurance Home Offices by States, 1947 and 1956

(eight leading states ranked by number of offices in 1956)

	1947	1956	Change in number of home offices
United States, total	1,047	1,123	+76
New York	184	156	−28
Texas	55	83	+28
Pennsylvania	82	73	−9
Illinois	85	72	−13
California	46	58	+12
Massachusetts	52	49	−3
Connecticut	34	29	−5
New Jersey	32	25	−7
All other states	477	578	+101

Note: The significance of the changes in distribution of offices is affected by mergers which contribute to declines and by the inclusion in the figures of "fly-by-night" organizations with short lifespans. Nevertheless, the contrast between the shrinkage in New York State and the rise outside is sufficiently sharp to have some meaning.

Sources: *Spectator Handy Chart, Spectator Fire Index,* and *Spectator Yearbook.*

State and New Jersey fell from 216 to 181, while the number in the rest of the country rose from 831 to 942. Stimulating the growth of new companies in these other areas were rapidly expanding local economies and relatively lenient legislative provisions. In Texas, for example, where new offices mushroomed at an unusual rate, a multiple-line company need have only $200,000 in capital in order to be chartered. In California, the same company would need $1 million in capital. In New York State, a sum in the neighborhood of $3.5 million would be required.[4]

In addition to inducing the formation of new companies, the more rapid economic expansion of other geographic sections has benefited the business of the firms already in existence. As in the life field, the large property insurance companies, even though they do business nationally, tend to feel particularly the influence of local industrial activity. For example, the rise in the net premiums of the five biggest Dallas-based companies, between 1947 and 1956, was about 60 per cent greater than that of the five largest companies with New York headquarters. In order to take care of this more rapid growth in their volume of business, the companies outside New York have found it necessary to add comparatively more personnel to their home offices.

Another factor contributing to the relative shrinkage of carrier employment in the Region is the tendency to decentralize certain home-office activities—the kind that have the strongest ties to the customer. As a means of better serving their growing clientele in the West, companies are assigning some of their headquarters manpower to regional offices. Neighborhood personnel not only create more intimate underwriting ties and improve company-client relations, but also provide engineering services related to the reduction of risks and solicit business from local independent agents and brokers.[5] The shift, however, leads to a need for relatively more personnel in the local area to write contracts and to settle claims.

There are also instances in which units have been established outside New York for quite another purpose. These moves have largely involved clerical and accounting functions. The principal reasons for such transfers apparently have been to obtain more space at lower costs and to improve efficiency by concentrating these functions in a single point.

Within the Region. So much of what is important in New York's life today came from the sea. And within New York City, the property insurance industry still retains the influence of the early locational decisions which had placed it close to the port. After the great fire of 1835, the companies had an opportunity to settle in some other neighborhood, but elected to remain in lower Manhattan. Their decision was due in part to the hold of the past, and in part to a desire to be near the Wall Street financial interests which provided the necessary capital to rebuild the industry. Moreover, in those years, most of Manhattan's residents were still far downtown, while access to the growing labor markets of Brooklyn, Staten Island, and New Jersey was also an important advantage, which was not eroded until much later by the City's northward development.

In the course of time, the property insurance companies enlarged their niche in lower Manhattan. The original nucleus of the industry attracted other firms to the area; insurance associations, societies, and bureaus grew in the vicinity; and relations with major customers and important insurance brokers nearby became firmer. Individual efforts to break away from the cluster have encountered difficulties. One company which embarked upon a four-year experiment in Westchester County, during the 1950's, eventually returned to its former location in lower Manhattan. Though the exploratory move lowered rentals, the company missed the more intimate associations with clients, agents and brokers, and other insurance firms at the old stand. So the industry has remained substantially intact throughout the years, with about 90 per cent of the Region's home-office employment in the fire and marine companies and 70 per cent of that in the casualty companies concentrated below Chambers Street.[6] Of the 25 fire and casualty companies with the largest assets in the Region, 16 have their home offices in just seven office buildings in lower Manhattan—all within a few blocks of one another on Maiden Lane, William Street, and John Street. The locations of the 25 companies are shown in Chart 20.

New York City has always dominated the property insurance industry within the Region. In 1947, as shown in Table 29, the City accounted for about 83 per cent of the Region's employment. But by 1956, this portion had decreased to 75 per cent. During the same period, all the other areas shown in the table raised their shares. The

Chart 20

Major Fire and Casualty Insurance Home Offices of New York Metropolitan Region

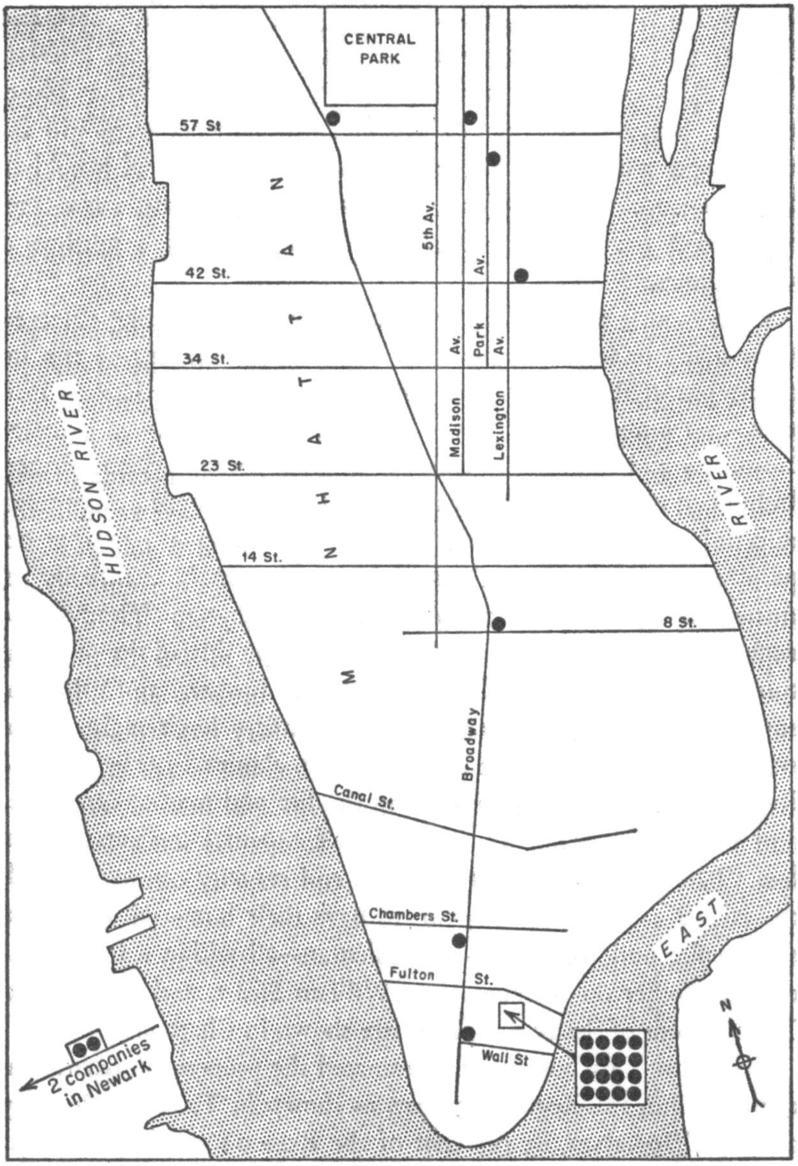

Note: The dots represent the 25 companies in the Region with the largest assets as given in *Moody's Bank & Finance Manual*, 1959. Their assets range from $517 million to $75 million.

Table 29 Distribution of Property Insurance Employment in New York Metropolitan Region, 1947, 1950, 1956

	Employment in Region	Percentage shares of Region's employment (NYMR = 100)				
		New York City	Essex and Hudson	Other New Jersey counties	Nassau and Suffolk	Remainder of Region
1947	60,769	82.5	11.8	2.1	1.1	2.5
1950	65,314	81.7	12.0	2.5	1.3	2.5
1956	72,646	74.6	12.6	5.3	2.1	5.4

Source: Region estimates are based on data collected by state departments of labor under unemployment insurance programs, and *County Business Patterns, First Quarter,* 1947, 1951, and 1956.

redistribution reflects the typical pattern—a trend from New York City to the suburbs on the part of field activities which are geared to population.

Field activities move with relative ease, but the companies are not prone to change the location of their home offices. True, a prominent insurance group recently transferred half of its 1,200 employees from downtown New York City to a New Jersey suburban area. Most of the affected employees performed accounting, clerical, and various routine functions. The administrative staff, the underwriters for the metropolitan New York area, and the top national underwriters in the group stayed behind, together with their supporting personnel. The change was prompted by various considerations: at the time of the move, space was tight in New York; avoidance of the downtown congestion was considered desirable; and the company believed that a more attractive pool of clerical labor would be available at the new location. In retrospect, the company feels that these gains were substantially achieved. More particularly, it has found that the personnel now available, as a group, are better educated and require a shorter training period. Offsetting this advantage, to some extent, has been the tendency for female employees in the suburbs to quit their jobs after marriage, compared with their counterparts in New York, who remain longer. As a result, the company has experienced a higher labor turnover in its new location.

The forces holding the Region's headquarters offices together are more powerful than those holding them to any particular location such as the Wall Street area. It is true that New York State legislation gives the property companies greater flexibility in investing than it gives the life insurance carriers, and this freedom has enabled the nonlife companies to buy relatively large amounts of common stock. Hence, a location in the Wall Street area facilitates the delivery of securities and provides the opportunity of closer dealings with securities brokers and dealers who follow carefully the course of stock prices and values. At best, however, this advantage is slim; the industry's stock transactions are hardly of the nature to require a constant interchange of ideas and information with the direct participants in the money market.

Consequently, should the Wall Street section ever become unattractive on other grounds, the communication ties of these companies to other financial institutions probably will not be strong enough to keep them there. Over the long run, the willingness of the property insurance group to remain downtown may rest heavily on the extent to which the commutation and physical facilities of this area can be maintained and improved—a question to which we shall return in our final chapter.

THE SECURITIES INDUSTRY

The locational forces bearing upon the securities industry offer a sharp contrast, in some ways, to those affecting the property and casualty insurance field. As we have seen, part of the securities industry in New York is actively engaged in facilitating transactions, and therefore occupies a key role in what we have called the money-market core of the financial community. This nucleus includes the brokers and dealers bidding for securities on the floors of organized exchanges and engaging in over-the-counter operations.

Now this nucleus is not the whole securities industry, which, as we shall define it, embraces about 38,000 persons in the New York

Metropolitan Region and about 120,000 in the nation. Money-market functions represent only a portion of the operations of the securities brokers and dealers; in addition, they carry on extensive selling, bookkeeping, advisory, and business-research activities, which presumably could be performed outside of the financial district. Nonetheless, the money-market preoccupations of the securities brokers and dealers have exerted a major centripetal pull on their other activities.

Though brokers and dealers—both those headquartered in and outside the Region—have opened offices wherever justified by population and economic growth, the industry's historical center in lower Manhattan has not been greatly dispersed over the decades. Nor has the securities industry yet gone very far toward segregating back-office activities and locating them elsewhere in the Region or the country.

THE INDUSTRY IN OPERATION

The securities industry is composed of investment bankers, serving primarily as middlemen in the purchase and sale of new issues; municipal bond houses which specialize in the underwriting and over-the-counter trading of the obligations of states, municipalities, and local "authorities" of various sorts; Government bond houses trading in United States Treasury and federal agency securities; over-the-counter houses which emphasize transactions in corporate obligations; the firms which focus their activities on the organized exchanges; commodity brokers and dealers, securities and commodities exchanges, and allied services, such as clearing, quotation, and advisory. Some companies are in many of these fields at once, running a department-store sort of operation on a huge scale. At the other extreme is the company—or individual—that pursues a narrow specialty and occupies tiny quarters with only limited communication facilities. In between, one finds every variant of size and diversity of operation.

The bulk of the industry is made up of 6,500 broker and dealer firms of all types.[7] Approximately 2,000 of these are members of organized exchanges while the rest deal exclusively in the over-the-counter market.[8] The New York Stock Exchange itself has about 650 member firms. The industry is mainly concentrated in a few metropolitan areas, with New York by far the leading center. The top ten broker-dealers account for one-quarter of the net worth of all the companies in the industry, and all but one of the ten have their principal offices in New York City.[9] Some 400 relatively large companies, most of which maintain head offices in New York City, do 91 per cent of the industry's total volume of business.[10]

On top of this is the New York orientation of the exchanges. As mentioned in Chapter 1, the two stock exchanges in New York account for about 90 per cent, by share volume, of the total trading on the country's 17 organized securities exchanges. At the close of 1956, the two exchanges employed about 1,500 persons, or about 4 per cent of the Region's manpower in the securities industry. At present, as described in Chapter 2, their power to draw firms to the downtown section of Manhattan is strong, despite the relatively small number of people they employ.

As for commodity exchanges, New York has half a dozen, Chicago has three (including the largest in the country) and no other city has more than one. The New York commodity exchanges absorb only a very minor part of the manpower employed by the Region's financial community. Their indirect role, however, may be of greater consequence. For communication and external economy reasons which have been discussed earlier, the commodity exchanges attract the commodity dealers and exporters who keep offices nearby; and the volume of trading that takes place brings a sizable demand upon credit facilities. Commodity trading also provides an important sideline to many securities firms.

The future employment of the securities industry in the New York Metropolitan Region depends upon the industry's employment trend in the nation more than on any other single factor. National employment, in turn, is affected by many things: securities offerings, transactions on the exchanges, over-the-counter trading, and so on. Of these strands, two important ones can be traced with accuracy over long periods of time—securities offerings and exchange trading. In Chart 21 we see these two measures, compared with employment in the securities industry as a whole.

As may be observed from the chart, the relation between these activities and employment is not clear-cut. Employment was over 200,000 in 1929, sank steadily to around 75,000 in 1945, and climbed to 120,000 in 1956. Since World War II, an erratic but generally rising trend of exchange transactions, combined with spectacular increases in new offerings, apparently has operated to produce the moderate rise in employment. If figures for the volume of over-the-counter trading were available, they probably would show a very substantial increase since the 1930's, providing still another reason for the growth in employment.

Any appraisal of the future level of this employment must take into account the susceptibility of much of the industry's office work to further mechanization. Many improvements have already been made in the bookkeeping operations of leading firms by the introduction of data-processing equipment. A number of companies have installed punch-card machines which are used to prepare account statements, bill customers, maintain margin-account records, and provide a variety of internal data for management purposes.

Various houses have also obtained, or laid plans to obtain, electronic computers which may be fed from magnetic tapes and are speedier and more versatile than their predecessors. The brokers and dealers with whom we have discussed the problem have generally believed that the capacity of these computers is so large that only a handful of securities houses are justified in installing them. It is therefore felt that their existence may create an incentive for firms to band together in groups for the purpose of setting up a common bookkeeping office. And, indeed, a trend in major financial centers toward the cooperative administration of certain data-handling functions is already in evidence.[11]

Indicative of other labor-saving innovations is an experiment being conducted by a group of member firms of the New York Stock Exchange aimed at reducing the physical movement of stock

Chart 21

Employment and Activity Measures in Securities Industry, United States, 1929–1956

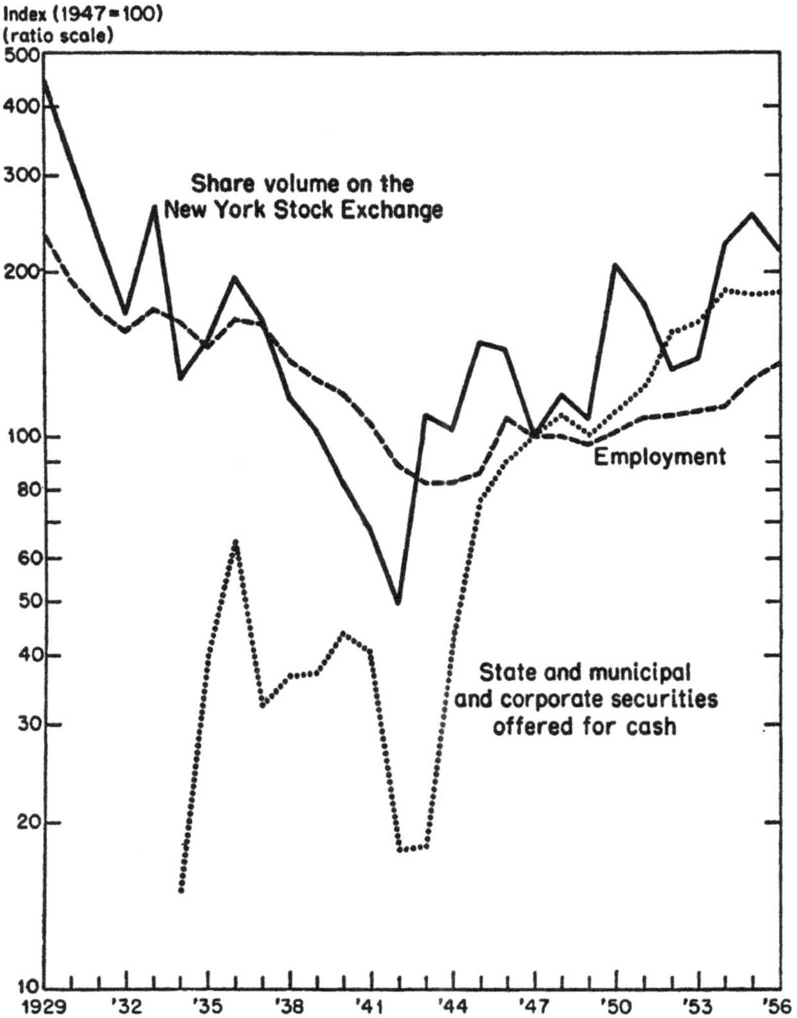

Sources: Employment index based on figures in Appendix C, Table C-1. Share volume data furnished by the Department of Research and Statistics of the New York Stock Exchange. Securities offerings taken from *Economic Report of the President, January 1958,* Table F-61, p. 185.

certificates. Under normal procedures, firms belonging to the Exchange's clearing house make physical deliveries of certificates representing the excess of a day's sales over their purchases in each issue of securities. In the method under study, transfers would be arranged through bookkeeping entries rather than by the actual movement of securities.

A variety of other experiments are in train, some to conserve labor in the offices of the member firms, others to provide savings on the floor of the stock exchanges.[12] Even the possibility of a totally automatic mechanism for the transmission and execution of orders has been proposed.[13] Along these lines, at least one major firm has experimented with a system that carries orders directly from branch offices throughout the country to the floor of the New York Stock Exchange.[14]

As yet, the adoption of automatic equipment has not led to any conservation of labor. On the contrary, a number of companies have indicated that their personnel needs initially expand when such equipment is introduced. New employees must be obtained to service these intricate machines, and various checks must be undertaken before the resulting information can be used with confidence. Even after that stage, the firms have found, at least thus far, that the result is an enlargement in their capacity to handle business rather than a shrinkage in their staffs. Besides, the typical response of firms in possession of such facilities is to find new ways of using them, even though the volume of their business is not directly increased thereby. Over the long run, however, the machines are likely to save manpower by reducing the need to add new employees as business expands.

LOCATIONAL SHIFTS IN THE NATION

As Table 30 shows, employment in the New York Metropolitan Region's securities industry grew considerably between 1947 and 1956, outpacing that of the national industry. As a consequence, the Region's share of the country's total rose moderately from 29.1 per cent to 31.8 per cent. The increase in the ratio occurred despite the fact that the relative rise in share volume on the two New York securities exchanges combined has barely managed to match the growth of trading in the country's remaining exchanges. Since 1936, the New York portion of all trading on securities exchanges has fluctuated within the general range of 85 to 90 per cent with no clearly defined, long-term trend in evidence. The New York gain occurred, too, in the face of a postwar shift in the geographical location of major securities houses. Evidence of the shift is found in

Table 30 Employment in Securities Industry, United States and New York Metropolitan Region, 1947, 1950, 1956

	U. S. employment	Region's employment	Region as percentage of U. S.
1947	88,015	25,623	29.1
1950	89,458	25,595	28.6
1956	119,758	38,138	31.8

Source: Based on *County Business Patterns* and data of the Department of Commerce.

the fact that New York State and New Jersey declined slightly in importance as the homes of the head offices of New York Stock Exchange member firms; whereas the two states had 75 per cent of these head offices at the beginning of 1947, they contained 72 per cent nine years later. Meanwhile, their share of the branch offices of member firms fell from 23 per cent to 20 per cent during the same period.

The growing importance of areas outside the New York Metropolitan Region as a source of securities trading is underlined from still another source. Table 31 shows the geographical distribution of public trading on the New York Stock Exchange for various brief periods between March 1953 and October 1957. There is, of course, considerable variability in the figures from one period to the next, but the relative decline of New York City as a source of public business is unmistakable.

Table 31 Geographical Distribution of Public Trading[a] on the New York Stock Exchange, Selected Periods

Source of trading	Distribution of trading, by number of shares, for two-day period in: March 1953	March 1954	Dec. 1954	June 1955	March 1956	Oct. 1957
New York City	30.9%	30.9%	31.2%	30.1%	29.6%	25.4%
Newark	0.8	1.0	1.0	0.9	0.6	0.8
Middle Atlantic states excluding Newark and New York City	14.9	14.9	15.1	15.9	16.4	16.9
East North Central states	13.0	12.7	13.6	13.0	13.5	14.6
Pacific states	10.2	10.1	10.0	9.6	9.8	11.4
New England states	7.2	7.0	6.4	7.7	6.1	7.0
Rest of United States	19.6	19.5	18.5	18.0	18.9	19.7
Foreign countries	3.4	3.7	4.0	4.7	5.0	4.0

[a] Includes all trading except transactions by members and member firms for their own accounts or on behalf of institutions and "intermediaries" (commercial banks, trust companies, and nonmember broker-dealers).

Note: Because of rounding, some columns do not add exactly to 100 per cent.

Source: New York Stock Exchange, *A Picture of the Stock Market,* March 1958, p. 15.

Yet the fact remains that employment growth in the securities industry of the New York Metropolitan Region has more than matched that of the nation in the postwar period. To understand this seeming anomaly, it is helpful to recognize that less manpower is used at the order-taking point than at the stages that follow.[15] After a customer delivers his buying or selling instruction to a firm's sales representative, who may be stationed in the field, numerous additional personnel are involved—including telephone clerks, traders, floor brokers, margin clerks, bookkeepers, and runners—before the transaction is complete and the securities and funds change hands. These personnel have always been heavily centered in New

York, and as the volume of transactions has grown, their numbers have tended to expand more than proportionately.

One reason for this disproportionate expansion is that there has been a tendency for firms to bring to New York some of the clerical activities once performed in the branches. This process has been aided, particularly, by the advent of mechanization; the typical consequences of the new system, as we have pointed out earlier, are to encourage the centralization of routine functions.

Moreover, the postwar growth of the securities industry has brought an expansion of certain activities which typically are found more in home offices than in field offices. Some of the bigger houses have created training departments, which require supervisory personnel and lead to the presence of pools of trainees. A number of brokers and dealers have established special departments to meet the needs of pension funds and investment companies, which have grown rapidly, and of insurance companies and savings banks, which now have authority to buy common stocks. Research departments have been enlarged to provide investment assistance to clients, usually without charge, and to furnish formal portfolio supervision, at a fee. And some firms have set up staffs to seek out "special situations" involving unusual opportunities for investing their own funds or those of their clients.

While these factors have been augmenting home-office employment, New York has continued strong in its position as the market for the negotiation of underwriting transactions. The City, because of its financial preeminence, is the place where big borrowers make their arrangements for the flotation of securities. For this reason, large out-of-town firms typically maintain sizable branch offices in New York. Despite the growth of economic activity in other parts of the country, no rival to the New York investment banking fraternity has appeared. On the contrary, the increasing ease of transportation across the country, brought on by air travel, has probably strengthened New York's position as an investment banking center.

Thus the securities industry, more than any other major financial industry, concentrates its manpower in the New York Metropolitan

Region—and increasingly so. There it has its money-market ties, its administrative superstructure, much of its operating personnel, and a considerable fraction of its customers. The sources of most of its business are elsewhere, and for that reason the industry has a network of field units, but even they, in large part, are controlled by men pushing buttons in New York.

Locational shifts within the region

Just as the New York Metropolitan Region has maintained its position in the nation, so New York City has maintained its position in the Region. From 1947 to 1956, the City's share of the Region's securities employment changed only a trifle, from 99 to 98 per cent. Less than a thousand of the Region's total of 38,000 people worked outside the city limits. From the early nineteenth century to the present time, no real challenge to the City's role has emerged.

The characteristic benefits of face-to-face communication appear unusually strong: the securities brokers and dealers find it helpful to be near the country's two dominant exchanges, banking facilities, and transfer agents; they enjoy the benefits of participating in underwriting meetings, professional lunches, and business discussions; they can participate in—or at least be continually in touch with—the money-market core that shapes the swiftly changing stream of prices. That is why some 430 of the 459 New York Stock Exchange firms that in 1956 had their main offices in the Region were located in Manhattan below Chambers Street, and another 21 elsewhere in Manhattan.

There is always a possibility that some powerful new force will dislodge the whole complex nucleus of the securities business from Wall Street and propel it in a body to another location. Two incidents help to make this imaginable. In 1933, only the Mayor's signature was lacking for the adoption by New York City of a tax of 4 cents a share on stock transfers and a tax of 5 per cent on the gross income of people in the securities business. A committee was hurriedly formed to create a New Jersey Stock Exchange in Newark, and most members of the New York Stock Exchange accepted the committee's invitation to shift their allegiance. But the bills were killed. In 1959 the ghost of this issue came out for a brief walk. The Mayor of New York, wrestling with the City's financial difficulties, proposed a tax on stock transfers. The New York Stock Exchange appointed a committee to explore ". . . the practicability of moving some or all of the Exchange's operations from New York State."[16] The idea was dropped, but even after this the Exchange continued to canvass the bids of other communities which offered sites.

The possible future effects of electronic data-processing machinery must also be considered. We have already seen that there is a trend in New York and elsewhere toward the cooperative use of computers by groups of securities firms. The movement is not yet big enough to exert an important locational impact within the Region. Should the ventures prove successful, however, and become more widely adopted, they might strip home and branch offices in the Region of much of their back-office activity and centralize it elsewhere. At first, the new centers are likely to be established adjacent to the financial district where the parents are located. At some later time, particularly if population shifts make recruitment of personnel more difficult, the centers may be established farther north, in less expensive rental areas.

Nonetheless, considering everything, the economic ties that create a dominant cluster of securities firms and facilities, and those that bind the cluster to the Wall Street area, have shown no real signs of slipping. The position of the ancient securities district in downtown Manhattan seems solid for a long time to come.

THE REMAINING INSTITUTIONS

Together, commercial banking, life insurance, other insurance, and the securities industry account for almost 90 per cent of the employment in the Region's financial community. The remaining or miscellaneous group, amounting to about 35,500 persons in 1956, is distributed among a number of activities, which, though heterogeneous, can be assembled into just two categories for locational analysis.

On the one hand are the credit institutions, including the mutual savings banks, savings and loan associations, credit unions, and finance companies; in their locational pattern these are oriented toward population, both resident and working. The mutual savings banks had 11,500 employees and the other credit agencies 16,800. On the other hand are the institutions which, for convenience, we can call "noncredit," including the bank clearing houses, safe deposit companies, foreign exchange dealers, branches of foreign banks, the investment companies, money-order companies, financial research and counseling firms, and stock-ticker services; most of these activities are geared locationally to the money market and to business enterprises. The noncredit category had 7,200 employees.

In addition to the broad locational patterns just mentioned, the institutions comprising the miscellaneous group face some of the same specific problems that we have encountered earlier in this book. Among savings banks and savings and loan associations, for example, there is disagreement over whether the legal provisions governing the establishment of branches ought to be relaxed. The big finance companies must determine the degree of centralization that is desirable for maximum efficiency. And the investment companies, like the stock exchanges, have viewed the threat of local taxation as a factor that might cause an exodus from the City.

Indeed, in 1952, after the City had raised the gross income tax on investment companies from 0.4 per cent to 0.8 per cent, six investment companies moved out of the state and did not return even though the tax was restored to its previous level in the following year. Talk of further moves has been revived because of amendments to the General City Law recently enacted by the state legislature, once more empowering the City to raise the gross income tax on investment companies. In the summer of 1959, though none of the 54 companies that would be affected had definitely stated it would move, several had leased office space outside the City and others were exploring possible sites in nearby tax-free areas.[17] In terms of employment and physical space, even a major outward migration by the investment companies would not seriously affect New York City, but it would loosen to some degree the bonds holding the financial community together; in this context the decisions of the investment companies could have serious implications for the long-term position of New York's financial community.

The Region in 1956 possessed about 14 per cent of all the persons employed by the "miscellaneous" group in the United States. Probably the outstanding feature of the miscellaneous group is its national rate of growth, which has been swifter between 1947 and 1956 than that of any other major sector of finance. National employment rose by 78 per cent, compared with 47 per cent in the Region. Part of the explanation for the slower pace of the Region's advance is its strong concentration of noncredit institutions, where employment grew rather modestly. If this group is set aside, the rate of expansion in the Region becomes 61 per cent—still behind the country at large, but a striking performance, nevertheless. For this reason, even though the miscellaneous credit institutions play a relatively minor role in the Region's financial community, the implications of their growth rate must be taken into account in forecasting their future status in the Region.

The problem of the future of the whole financial community is considered in the following chapter. There we endeavor to project our historic findings to obtain some notion of what tomorrow will hold. From now on, in the words of Mrs. Malaprop, "We will not anticipate the past! . . . Our retrospection will all be to the future."

8

The Prospects

Anyone who has attempted systematically to project the future development of an entity as complex as the Region's financial community cannot fail to come away from the experience with a sense of inadequacy and frustration. He may well come to the point of mumbling "Double, double toil and trouble" over his statistics, but unlike Macbeth's witches he will not stir up a supernatural brew. The best that he can accomplish is to frame a crude working model of the operation of the community; to translate the functions underlying his prototype into quantities; and finally to observe whether the results produced offend his more general and less articulate conceptions of how the community may develop.*

A pessimistic forecaster might cut this chapter abruptly short by citing the results of the latest conferences on controlling atomic warfare. More cheerfully, we assume that there will be a world in 1985; that there will be no major war; and that human institutions will be much as we know them at present—that is, in a condition strikingly different from that described by George Orwell for the year prior to our own furthest target date. Moreover, we make no allowance for cyclical changes in economic conditions, though we do of course take into account long-range growth.

These assumptions are only the beginning. Our forecasts of the individual financial sectors will have to be based on more specific presuppositions concerning such things as the state of technology, consumer attitudes, and prevailing legislation. Even more broadly,

* The reader who is interested in the methodology of our projection will find it helpful to read Appendix B in conjunction with this chapter. The appendix begins on page 218.

the forecasts presume some knowledge about the state of the national economy, which is where our discussion begins.

THE NATIONAL ECONOMY

The financial community of the New York Metropolitan Region does not exist in either an economic or a geographic vacuum. Its growth depends more upon national population and income trends than upon any other influences. In Table 32, we show how we expect the major economic aggregates to appear in each of our three target years, compared with the present. What we assume, in effect, is a rapidly expanding national economy, in which population will grow at a rate suggested roughly by historical trends in birth and death rates and in which output per man-year will increase at 2.5 per cent annually. The basis for these over-all assumptions is derived from the work of other groups associated with the New York Metropolitan Region Study, and we do not propose to elaborate them here.*

Table 32 Past and Projected National Economic Aggregates, Selected Years, 1947–1985

	Gross national product (billions of 1955 dollars)	Personal income (billions of 1955 dollars)	Disposable personal income (billions of 1955 dollars)	Total civilian employment (thousands of persons)
1947	281.8	224.9	199.5	58,027[a]
1956	402.6	305.9	282.4	64,979
1965	599.6	472.1	410.8	76,958
1975	878.9	692.1	602.1	88,125
1985	1,293.1	1,018.2	885.8	101,281

[a] 1948 estimate.

Sources for past years: U. S. Department of Commerce for income data and U. S. Census Bureau for employment estimates. The forecasts are by New York Metropolitan Region Study.

* The reader concerned with these basic assumptions will find them discussed in the final report in this series, Raymond Vernon, *Metropolis 1985*.

The national financial community

After we had settled upon these basic notions about the country's growth, the next step was to derive estimates of national employment for each sector of the financial community. In general, our procedure followed a consistent pattern: we first estimated the level of "output" and then converted this into employment data. In making this conversion, specific premises had to be established about the changing relation of manpower needs to output.*

Table 33 Past and Projected National Financial Employment, Selected Years, 1947–1985

	Financial employment (thousands)	Financial employment as percentage of total employment [a]
1947	1,312	2.3
1956	1,941	3.0
1965	2,368	3.1
1975	3,043	3.5
1985	3,900	3.9

[a] Total employment as given in Table 32.

Sources: See Appendix C, Table C-1.

According to our forecasts, manpower used by financial activities will increase more rapidly than the nation's total working force. This means that finance will absorb a rising percentage of the country's total. Between 1947 and 1956, the ratio of financial to total employment moved from 2.3 per cent to 3.0 per cent. Our data indicate that the gains over the next three decades will be more gradual than that, bringing the ratio to 3.9 per cent by 1985. The forecasts are shown in Table 33.

* These assumptions appear in Appendix B. In a general sense it is possible to refer to changes in the relation of manpower needs to output as changes in "productivity," and we shall do so in this chapter. Strictly speaking, these relations are only functions of changes in productivity rather than actual estimates of productivity change.

Behind this picture, the changes experienced by the various sectors of the financial community are far from uniform, as indicated in Chart 22. Employment in the property insurance field, for instance, grows quite slowly, while the miscellaneous financial institutions experience the swiftest rise of all. What lies behind these different rates of growth becomes apparent as we consider each group in turn.

THE CHANGING CHARACTER OF COMMERCIAL BANKING

The continued expansion of the nation's economy will inevitably generate a considerable growth in the activities of the commercial banks. Not all phases of the commercial banking business, of course, will move at the same rate. As Appendix B indicates, consumer credit is likely to advance faster than commercial credit, real estate loans at still a different rate, and so on. The different output changes will create their own manpower needs—needs which vary from one type of activity to the other for each added dollar of business.

Affording some offset to the enlarged manpower requirements in all these lines will be the prospective increases in the productivity of employees in the banking business. Our analysis has indicated that the manpower needs associated with each million dollars of outstanding credit in the fields we have selected as banking activity indicators declined between 1947 and 1956 at the rate of about 3 per cent a year on the average. Over the long-range future, we expect this rate of change to continue.

Our anticipation that productivity will continue to grow is based on the fact that the banking community is on the verge of another major "break-through" in demand-deposit accounting, an activity that absorbs a large portion of its manpower requirements. The new concept relies upon a standard machine "language" appearing in magnetic-ink characters on checks and deposit slips. By using a common language it becomes possible to join the banks of the country together in an effective communication system that facilitates automation. The American Bankers Association has approved the plan and spelled out the technical specifications for the

Chart 22

Past and Projected Employment in the Financial Industries, United States, 1947–1985

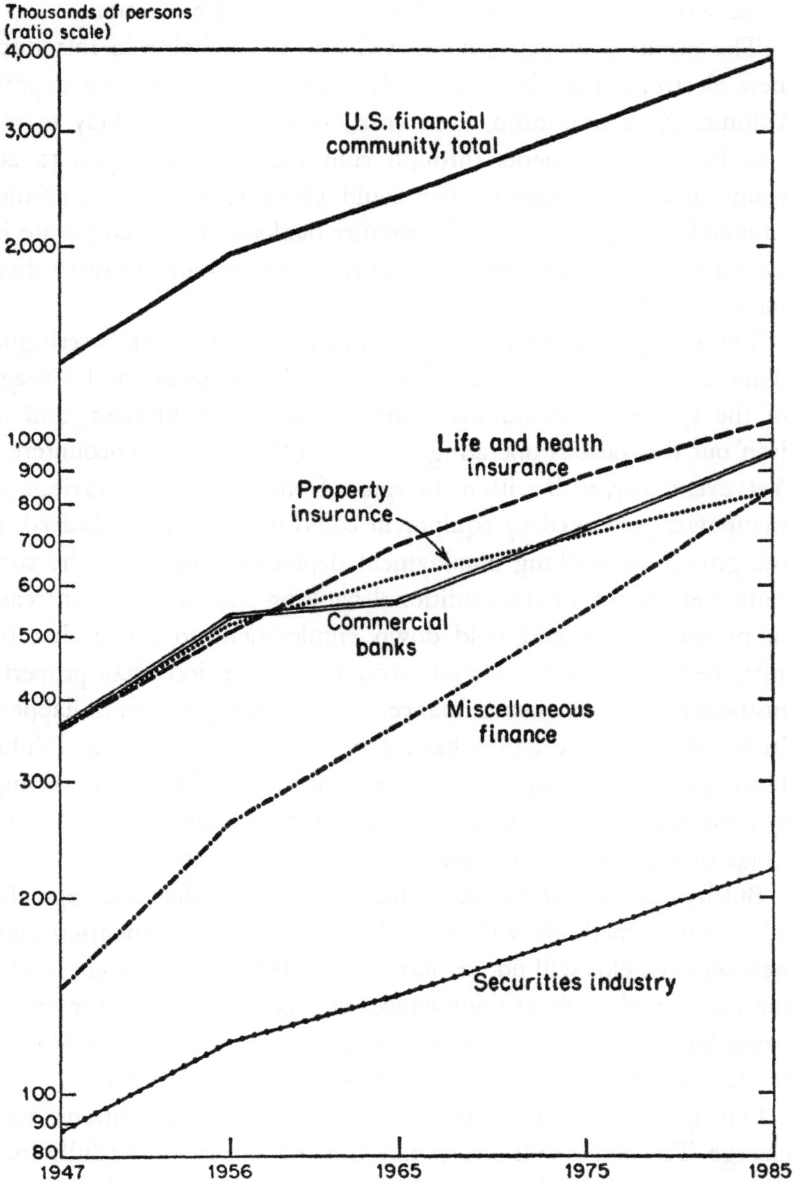

Source: See Appendix C, Table C-1.

manufacturers of the equipment. The Association has expressed the hope that almost all of the $25 billion in checks that are expected to be written in 1970 will have magnetic-ink identification.[1]

The extent to which a bank will find it profitable to introduce new electronic machinery depends largely on its size and deposit volume. At a minimum, even small institutions are likely to obtain by-product benefits through converting, for example, to account-numbering systems that could effect substantial economies in bookkeeping. Moreover, the smaller banks also may cooperate in establishing electronic computers at strategic locations to serve their joint needs.[2]

The change-over to the new methods will not come overnight. Time is required to educate bankers and customers in the usage of the system, to manufacture and install the equipment, and to iron out the various operating difficulties that will be encountered. Yet, eventually, well within the span of our forecast, the savings in manpower generated by equipment could be very great.[3] Indeed, if the growth in banking employment depended only upon the continued expansion of the traditional banking functions, the increase in productivity would hold down employment so much that by 1985 the banking sector would account for fewer jobs than property insurance or miscellaneous finance. We do not expect this to happen. In recent years, the banks have overcome their traditional inhibitions against venturing into new fields of service. As data-processing systems are introduced, the remaining reluctance to expand the range of their services is likely to be further reduced.

But by our first target date, 1965, it is probable that, although the labor-saving methods will be well underway, the expansion into new service fields will not yet have progressed very far. Accordingly, for the period 1956-1965 we expect the gain in manpower to be based largely on the expansion of existing activities and to be only modest in size, boosting the total from 536,000 to 562,000.

During the following ten years, we believe, conditions will change. The banks will incorporate the new devices more fully into their operations, and this will free large portions of their manpower for fresh activities. Thus, they will be confronted with the choice of curtailing their employment or embarking upon new functions. We assume here that they will choose new functions. By 1975, we expect that the banks will be broadening their services for businesses and individuals, particularly in developing new credit methods and assuming additional bookkeeping and bill-paying functions, and that these practices will have grown considerably by 1985. In other words, innovation in finance, which has already made itself felt in the rapid development of the miscellaneous institutions, will increasingly contribute, after 1965, to the growth of employment in commercial banking. Our manpower forecasts, incorporating these assumptions, are 729,000 in 1975 and 952,000 in 1985.

Our analysis is further based on the premise that the funds will be forthcoming to permit the commercial banks to meet their expected growth. We are assuming that the supply of money will increase somewhat more slowly than national income until 1965, but will quicken its pace thereafter and grow at about the same rate as income. For a century and a half until the end of World War II, the money supply tended to increase somewhat faster than national income.[4] Then, a reversal of the relation occurred, reflecting the rapid expansion of the economy without an equal growth of the money supply, probably because of the enormous monetary resources that had been built up during the war period. As a result, total commercial bank deposits as a percentage of the gross national product declined from 62 per cent to 48 per cent between 1947 and 1956. What our forecast implies is that the ratio will shrink still further to about 44 per cent by 1965 and will be fairly stable thereafter.

The growth of insurance

Because of the large untapped market that still exists for life and health insurance, particularly in the group and accident and health fields, we foresee a big continuing growth in the industry. Like the commercial banks, the home offices of life insurance companies have many clerical employees engaged in routine operations. These operations are susceptible to considerable advances in productivity as electronic equipment is installed. On the other hand, comparable productivity gains in the selling end seem less likely; it is true that the expansion of group business tends to reduce the number of sales personnel required relative to premiums written, but the sales process itself involves time-consuming relations between the insurance representative and his client. Our projections, therefore, are based upon only a 2 per cent rate of increase, compounded annually, in the premiums-per-man ratio for life and annuity business and upon a somewhat higher rate for accident and health insurance. The employment changes that we forecast are a 37 per cent rise by 1965, a further 28 per cent increase by 1975, and a 21 per cent gain during the final decade, resulting in a total employment in the life and health insurance industry of 1,064,000 in 1985. This projected pattern of growth is greatly influenced by the rosy prospect for the accident and health business, which is expected to mount very rapidly until a nearly complete coverage of medical risks is reached some time between 1965 and 1975, after which a more gradual growth is foreseen.

Property insurance in the aggregate has been developing more swiftly than life insurance, and premiums per man have also been advancing at a more rapid rate. Though the writing of fire protection is an old line of business, fresh opportunities are continually appearing in the property field. Most business enterprises now take property insurance much more seriously than they did a decade or two ago, and are becoming educated to provide against a variety of risks which once they ignored. For this reason the opportunities for expansion in the property field through the invention of new types of policies appear to be greater than in the life and health fields.

Employment in property insurance, however, will be held down by the larger productivity gains that are anticipated. Our guess is that the firms in this industry have lagged behind the life companies in the achievement of economies of large-scale operation, and therefore have a greater potential field to tap in this regard. Accordingly, productivity advances are projected at an annual rate of 3 per cent. The net effect of these factors is for employment to rise relatively slowly, by somewhat less than 20 per cent for each of the target periods, to 612,000 persons in 1965, 713,000 in 1975, and 832,000 in 1985.

The securities industry

The firms and exchanges involved in the business of executing securities orders have always taken a lively interest in the possibilities of using automatic devices for the handling of their business. Yet considerable room for progress along these lines remains; and should it materialize, the face of the securities industry could be drastically altered. The organized exchanges might become collections of huge electronic machines for the consummation of transactions; branch offices of securities firms would be confined, for the most part, to receiving and transmitting orders; big home offices would be largely nerve centers of accounting and administration; and smaller home offices would use central servicing agencies. Manpower requirements, in these circumstances, would be heavily reduced as the industry assumed the form of a national system of electronic intercommunications.

Our forecasts do not incorporate these extreme assumptions. Possible though they may be, we simply assume a productivity growth of 3 per cent a year, which is not much different from that prevailing in the past. On this basis, the industry would experience a modest rate of expansion: about 18 per cent by 1965 and an additional 25 per cent each by 1975 and 1985. This rate would result in employment levels of 141,000, 176,000, and 220,000 for each of these years.

Miscellaneous finance

We have seen that the miscellaneous group, including the finance companies, credit unions, savings and loan associations, mutual savings banks, and various specialized firms, has been experiencing swift growth. Many of the innovations in finance have initially appeared in this area.

But in projecting the future we have made an important modifying assumption—that the commercial banks will seek new opportunities to use their large manpower resources made excessive by automation, and will begin competing in fields heretofore exploited by the institutions in the miscellaneous group. Therefore, we do not believe that the future rate of growth of the miscellaneous companies will match their prior performance. In general, we have estimated that half of the growth in this category is attributable to the expansion of existing lines and the other half to innovation, and have further assumed that half of the future rise of the innovation portion will be shared by the commercial banks. On this basis, employment in the miscellaneous group will rise about 40 per cent by 1965, an additional 50 per cent by 1975, and another 50 per cent by 1985, to levels of 364,000, 544,000, and 832,000, respectively.

THE REGION AND THE NATION

Our forecast of the financial community of the New York Metropolitan Region, like our forecast of the nation's financial activity, takes as its point of departure the projected economic status of the Region. Our yardstick for gauging its future performance is personal income. Here, we assume a continuation of the tendency for the Region's personal income to rise a little less rapidly than that of the United States. In 1947 and 1956 the Region's personal income as a percentage of the nation's ran as follows:

1947	12.7
1956	12.2

And our projections for the three target dates are:

1965	11.8
1975	11.5
1985	11.3

By assuming this decline, we betray the essential circularity of some of the reasoning which perforce goes into the making of our forecast. Quite clearly, the economic performance of the Region depends upon the contribution of each of its parts. And one of its parts is the financial community. Accordingly, we find ourselves in the position of assuming a conclusion (aggregate personal income) in order to project a part (the financial community's activity) which will contribute toward the conclusion. Yet, circular though this reasoning may be, its implications cannot be resolved in any portion of the forecasting procedure of this book. Only in a full projection for the Region as a whole, such as will be published in the final and summary volume of the New York Metropolitan Region Study, can all the parts be examined together, and a determination made whether the initial assumptions about the conclusion and the final conclusion itself are consistent—and, if not, what must be done about it.

If we are prepared to swallow these initial assumptions about the Region's *aggregate* performance, the problem still remains to determine how the financial community will function in this setting.

Out of the welter of influences determining the performance of the financial community of the New York Metropolitan Region, two kinds engage our special attention. One is concerned with the money market, and the other with the relative economic tugs of different areas of the nation.

Will the money-market center leave New York?

Since the existence of the nation's money-market center in New York City has helped to hold together the Region's financial community, our forecast of the future of finance in the Region must take into account the possibility that the market will no longer be in New York. A major shift took place once before when the country's financial apex moved from Philadelphia. What are the prospects of another change occurring by 1965 or perhaps 1985?

It will be remembered that in our view, the heart of the money market in New York is a core of several thousand specialists who spend their full time in the criss-crossing interplay that enters into maintaining active markets in financial instruments. As has been emphasized, these specialists over the years have developed a smoothly functioning and highly efficient mechanism. In the unpredictable and venturesome atmosphere of their business, they need to be next-door to one another in order to share information and gain the external economies that stem from common services. The movement of such a complex apparatus in a piecemeal fashion is made unlikely by the fact that an individual specialist rarely will risk going off by himself. The alternative to a piecemeal movement is an organized effort vigorous enough to move the whole mass at once—and this, too, is hard to imagine.

What developments could conceivably start the money-market specialists moving, either piecemeal or as an organized entity? Politics could enter the scene to some extent if the Federal Reserve Open Market Committee should supervise its money-market activities more closely from Washington. Adverse legislation in New York State might weaken the strength of local institutions; for example, the short-lived threat of a City tax on bank checks in the early part of 1959, if enacted, might have caused some large corporations to switch their bank accounts elsewhere. The competitive vigor displayed by the New York participants in meeting the requirements of national clients may decrease, thereby encouraging the appearance of rivals. But none of these developments seems to be in the offing at present.

The units in the inside ring of the financial community, as diagrammed on page 30, deal directly and continually with the money-market core. It is possible, therefore, that if a strong enough concentration of financial institutions performing lending and investing functions develops elsewhere, it could drag portions of the money-market core from New York or foster the creation of units of its own. In insurance, as we have seen, Hartford has long been a leading center, but the investment activities of insurance companies have never been sufficiently active or great to lead to the development of an indigenous money market. In banking, the rise of a mighty center might provide the instrument of change, for the New York banks play a crucial role in the money market. Some huge banks have already developed in other sections, and indeed the biggest in the country is located in California. But no group has yet developed in any one spot with sufficient strength to create the basis of a rival money market.

The force with the best chance of setting off a chain reaction is economics—just as it was 125 years ago. Should the economic base of outside areas continue to develop faster than that of New York, the banks in these places would eventually become more formidable challengers. At some critical point in size, one of the new banking clusters might be in a position to establish its own trading desks, undertake more extensive investments, begin to assume greater responsibility in advising its correspondents, and generally spread its influence in the nation. The accumulation of substantial funds in this new center would attract representatives of New York securities houses. The importance of having the trader at the salesman's elbow, and the economies realized through reaching price decisions in proximity to major buying and selling interests, could lead to an increasing number of local dealers and could break down New York's trading dominance.

But our guess is that the New York money market is too firmly entrenched to be jarred loose within the next quarter-century. Though the economic importance of the New York area may decline relative to that of other areas in the aggregate, no believable projection that we have tested brings any other single locality within challenging distance of New York during the period of our forecast.

Moreover, in measuring the economic strength of a metropolitan area, one must take into consideration not only the number of people who live and work there, but also the concentration of population and jobs in the hinterland. It is reasonable to suppose that the commercial banks in any metropolitan area have a stronger competitive position in corralling the business of customers in nearby states than the business of customers in more remote markets. Life insurance companies, as we saw in Table 20 on page 133, also have a stronger competitive position in states near their home offices than in those which are more remote; and the same seems to be true of property insurance companies. Accordingly, gauging the size of a financial market is like estimating the mass of a mountain range: it is not only the altitude of the highest pinnacle that counts, but also the lesser peaks and foothills.

Even if another area should surpass New York's summit, it would have to contend with the resources of the densely packed Middle Atlantic hinterland. New York stands near the center of Megalopolis—the merging metropolitan areas ranged down the eastern seaboard from Boston to Washington.

But how about the possibility that some outside factor could change the course of events by weakening New York's position in the field of international trade? We have seen that the City's port activities contributed heavily to its economic rise. It would be a quirk of fate, indeed, if foreign trade enabled some other metropolis to capture financial leadership.

An explosive growth of trade with the Orient would benefit West Coast cities; but an expansion of sufficient magnitude to stimulate the emergence of a new money-market center does not appear likely within our forecast span. The St. Lawrence Seaway will bring more trade to ports on the Great Lakes. We do not visualize, however, that any one of those ports will gain enough trade to overcome New York's economic leadership. Moreover, our analysis suggests that the influence of the Seaway on the New York Port will be moderate, leading to a major diversion of no more than a few bulky commodity lines, notably ore and grain.[5] Some of the major interior banks may see fit to enlarge their staffs of specialists in international finance. The heart of the international financial market, however, will continue in New York.

Thus, it does not seem likely that economics, the major historical force leading to the development of the money-market center in New York, will be the factor to cause its shift out of the City by 1985.

CHANGES IN THE REGION'S RELATIVE POSITION

Assuming that New York remains the dominant money-market center, financial employment in the Region will reflect alterations in both the local economy and countrywide conditions. In addition, changes in productivity, assumed to be the same as for the nation, will have an influence on employment. Taking these factors into account, we summarize in Chart 23 our projections of financial employment in the Region for each of the target years and in each of our major industry groups.

The life and health insurance industry, as a result of a steady growth, will continue to employ the largest amount of financial manpower. Closely following will be the commercial banks, whose rate of expansion probably will be somewhat slower than that of life and health insurance until about 1965 and speed up thereafter as they take over an increasing amount of the services which otherwise would be attributed to the miscellaneous sector. The employment rise of the property insurance companies is likely to be somewhat behind that of the other members of the financial community, though they will hold their rank in the Region. The Region's miscellaneous companies, like those of the nation, appear to be headed for the most rapid advance of all the sectors. The securities industry will also have a relatively swift growth in the Region.

All in all, the Region's financial employment, which was 311,700 in 1956, is expected to grow as follows:

1965	368,700
1975	444,000
1985	537,100

These employment trends, in general, reveal a somewhat slower rate of rise in financial employment than was projected for the nation at large. Only in the securities field do the Region's institutions tend to match the growth of those in the rest of the country. Employment in the miscellaneous area is expected to increase at a considerably slower rate than that of the nation; in the other sectors, the differential is marked, though not as great. Therefore,

Chart 23
Past and Projected Employment in the Financial Industries, New York Metropolitan Region, 1947–1985

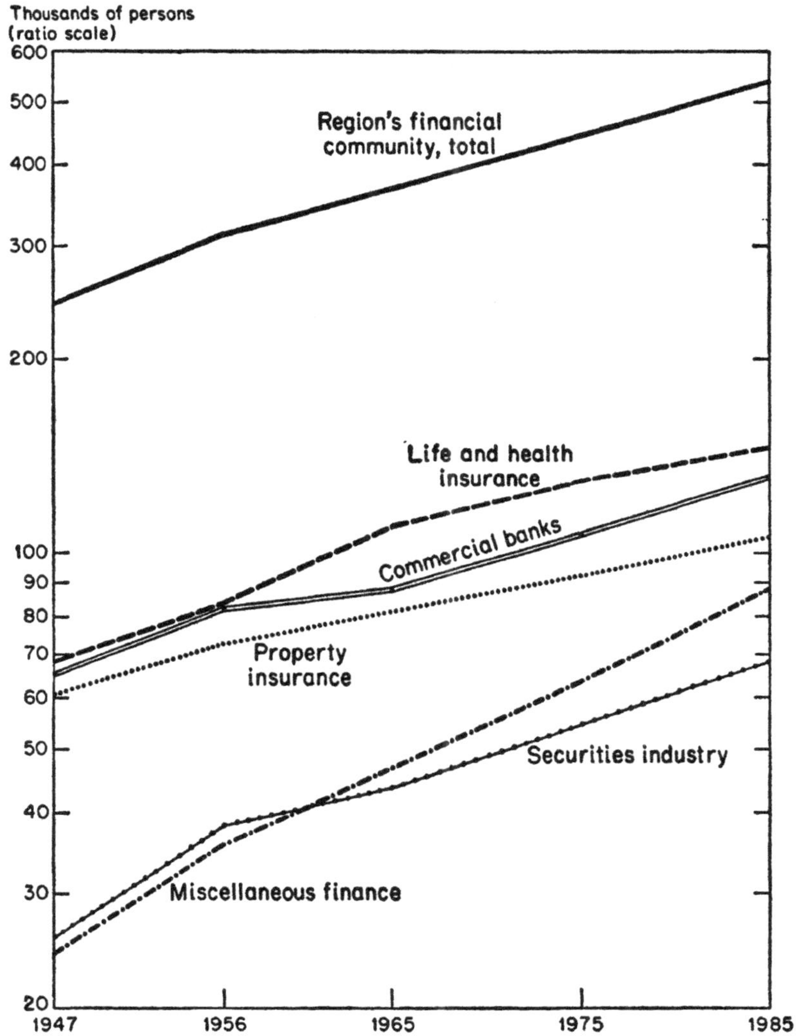

Sources: See Appendix C, Table C-2.

as shown in Table 34, the Region's share of national financial employment is expected to drop from 16.1 per cent in 1956 to 13.8 per cent in 1985. It will shrink in every sector except the securities industry. All of the declines in percentage shares, however, will be substantially slower than they were during the period from 1947 to 1956.

Table 34 Financial Employment in New York Metropolitan Region as Percentage of National Financial Employment, Selected Years, 1947–1985

	Total	Commercial banks	Life and health insurance	Property insurance	Securities industry	Miscellaneous finance
1947	18.6	18.2	18.9	17.0	29.1	16.6
1956	16.1	15.4	16.5	13.9	31.8	13.8
1965	15.6	15.6	15.9	13.3	30.9	12.8
1975	14.6	14.6	14.6	12.9	31.0	11.6
1985	13.8	13.6	13.7	12.7	31.0	10.5

WITHIN THE REGION

Inside the Region, the distribution of financial activity is determined by various forces. One is the need to perform functions in close proximity to one another in order to achieve easy communication and external economies. Another is the impulsion to be close to the customer. Still others have to do with savings in operating costs. These forces, pulling sometimes together and sometimes in different directions, have so far had the net effect of creating a highly centralized community, largely crowded into a small area of lower Manhattan, with lesser concentrations in mid-Manhattan and downtown Newark. There are possibilities, however, that this densely concentrated distribution will change in the future.

THE FORCES AT WORK

The characteristics of financial institutions do not necessarily support the notion of huge headquarters organizations grouped together. There is considerable logic in the idea of decomposing the financial community into segments that may be located in accordance with their respective economic needs. This might mean that the direct money-market participants would be left together, that the consumer-oriented activities would continue to track the consumer as they are already doing, and that the great bulk of the personnel performing routine functions would be located where space and labor costs offered the greatest economies.

After all, only a minor portion of the financial community is engaged in the kind of money-market activities that require banding together in order to reduce risks. It is entirely conceivable, therefore, that this tightly knit group will remain intact but that in time the other functions will break away to a much greater extent than they did before 1960. If customer proximity, labor supply, and the cost of space came to influence decisions more importantly than heretofore, the face of the financial community could be radically changed, with the dominant Wall Street district gradually dispersing into smaller clusters spread throughout the Region.

Such trends, uncovered in our analysis of the financial community, have repeatedly bobbed up in the chapters of this book. The banks of the Region have established branches, to the extent that legal limits have permitted, to accommodate the needs of clients. Some institutions have decentralized certain of their repetitive back-office activities. More than one major commercial bank has made known its intention of transferring most of its routine operations out of the financial district, partly because of the changing commuting pattern of the labor supply. The life insurance companies have long since been spreading northward. Companies in other sectors of the financial community, including the stock brokers, savings banks, and savings and loan associations, have followed the paths of customer and employee convenience in developing branch offices.

But there are countervailing pressures to resist these outward drives. Dispersion must overcome some major resistances: the superiority of the money-market arena over the rest of the financial community as a prestige point for the elite; the desire to protect existing real estate values; the major external economies that come from congregating together; the physical conveniences in speeding the flow of paper so vital in the financial industry; and the advantages of offering customers a concentrated group of facilities.

Furthermore, there are new forces for centralization—at least for centralization *somewhere,* whether Wall Street or not. Important among these is the trend toward office automation, discussed earlier. Though some electronic equipment can be used in branches, a complete data-processing system usually can be supported only at a major installation, and this circumstance favors big headquarters buildings or nearby special space, in or close to central-city locations.

On balance, we are inclined to believe that the notion of a major cluster of financial institutions in the Region will survive. This still does not necessarily mean, however, that physically it must remain in its present location in the Region.

Will a new financial center emerge in the Region?

Thus, before we can predict the distribution of financial employment within the New York Metropolitan Region and within New York City, we must make up our minds on the extent to which the downtown financial section will wane in importance and the extent to which a new center will rise at midtown. Our own conclusion is that, although the challenge of the midtown section will grow over the next quarter-century, the dominance of the downtown financial district will continue during that period.

We make this prediction despite the fact that there are certain weaknesses in the downtown position. For instance, doubt exists about the ability of the institutions in the Wall Street area to attract and hold additional supplies of employees, including their executive personnel. We would feel more secure in our forecast if some of the plans for developing new residential areas close by the financial district, such as that proposed by the Downtown-Lower Manhattan Association, were to materialize. The projection also would be on more solid ground if mass-transit innovations were introduced to keep the white-collar worker within tolerable commuting time from the tip of Manhattan. Along the same lines, easier access and parking for automobiles in the overcrowded area could add another cable to the anchor which holds so much of the financial community in its traditional location.

The biggest question mark in the picture is the future course of the commercial banks. Until the decision of the First National City Bank to establish dual headquarters, the question seemed to be "either-or" as between downtown and midtown. Confronted with this Hobson's choice, no bank chose to make the break. But the idea of keeping two sets of administrative offices seemed to provide the means of having the best of two locational worlds. As a result, the City's biggest banks have either laid plans for dual headquarters or taken steps to nail down office space in choice Park Avenue or Fifth Avenue buildings in order to provide flexibility. So the number of bank employees who will shift from downtown to midtown is highly uncertain. One thing seems reasonably sure: if a massive banking exodus were to develop, the repercussions on the rest of the financial district would be forceful.

Though it is plain that thousands of jobs will move uptown, we do not believe that by 1985 the midtown area will have supplanted lower Manhattan as the City's major financial section. Inertia weighs heavily against moving. It is not easy to break the tradition of a long and successful past. We have observed the strong neighborhood loyalties that have been developed for the Wall Street area, and the vigorous pride in its rich history. These are qualitative but powerful forces. More tangibly, moving is expensive, particularly when complicated equipment has been installed. Existing operating relations are the outcome of long years of development, and in most instances work well. The elite, who can make final locational decisions, and whose presence keeps large numbers of employees close by, still find it useful to be in the midst of money-market activities. Finally, the decision of most of the big banks to maintain and even expand their headquarters locations in the financial district is an important lodestone for keeping the activity downtown, one whose effects are likely to be felt throughout the 25-year period which is our present concern.

For that period, at any rate, we expect the inertial locational forces in the downtown community, buttressed by the new Chase Manhattan commitments, to prevail. If our projections were for a longer period, however, we would feel obliged to give greater weight to the growing remoteness of the homes of employee personnel and to the continued expansion of the corporate community in midtown New York.

Distribution of employment in the region

Nonetheless, even during the next 25 years, there are bound to be shifts in the location of financial employment in the Region, reflecting closely the economic growth of its different parts. The effects of these changes are shown in Table 35 for each of our target dates.

Table 35 Percentage Distribution of Financial Employment, by Parts of New York Metropolitan Region, Selected Years, 1947–1985

	1947	1956	1965	1975	1985
Entire Region	100.0	100.0	100.0	100.0	100.0
New York City	79.0	77.2	71.8	68.3	64.9
Essex and Hudson Counties	12.6	10.5	10.6	10.1	9.7
Other New Jersey counties	3.5	5.0	7.5	9.4	11.1
Nassau and Suffolk Counties	1.5	2.8	4.2	5.3	6.6
Remainder of Region	3.4	4.5	5.9	6.9	7.7

Sources: See Appendix C, Table C-3.

The changes are significant. All major areas will show an absolute increase in financial employment; but their shares will change. In 1956, New York City absorbed over three-quarters of total financial employment in the Region; by 1985, this ratio is expected to have become about two-thirds. Hudson and Essex Counties are also expected to decline relatively. On the other hand, the share of the other New Jersey counties will move up fast, bringing the total New Jersey share to about 21 per cent, compared with 16 per cent in 1956. The shares of the New York counties outside the City are also likely to rise sharply.*

As we further narrow our vista, the details of our future picture become clearer. Table 36 shows a projection of financial employment for three parts of the City: (1) the many-towered triangle below Chambers Street, about six-tenths of a square mile in area,

Table 36 Financial Employment in Three Parts of New York City, Selected Years, 1956–1985

	Employment in thousands				Employment as percentage			
	1956	1965	1975	1985	1956	1965	1975	1985
Entire City ..	240.7	264.7	303.4	348.5	100.0	100.0	100.0	100.0
Below Chambers Street	130.1	128.6	145.2	165.2	54.1	48.6	47.9	47.7
Chambers to 60th Street	78.0	100.0	115.1	131.3	32.4	37.8	37.9	37.7
Rest of City ..	32.6	36.1	43.1	52.0	13.5	13.6	14.2	14.9

Sources: 1956 figures are estimates based on questionnaire surveys, interviews, and data provided by the City Planning Commission of New York City. The projections were made by assuming a shift of employment of commercial banks from downtown to midtown Manhattan, as explained in Appendix B, and by allowing for minor changes in the distribution of other financial employment.

representing the traditional financial district; (2) that part of Manhattan from Chambers Street to 60th Street, about five miles long and two miles wide, in which is situated the midtown business district; (3) all the rest of the City, including upper Manhattan and the other four boroughs.

The City harbored about 240,000 financial jobs in 1956, with 54 per cent of them below Chambers Street and another 32 per cent

* For projections of employment by parts of the Region in commercial banking, life insurance, and the other sectors of the financial community, see Appendix C, Tables C-4 through C-8.

between Chambers and 60th. By 1965 the City is expected to add about 24,000 jobs to this total, nearly all of them between Chambers and 60th. During this initial period the old financial district seems headed for an actual loss of personnel, primarily because of the northward trek of bank personnel.

Over the whole period from 1956 to 1985, our projection is that 108,000 will be added to New York City's financial roster. We think that during this 29-year span, the area between Chambers and 60th will again make the biggest net gain, say 53,000; but the smaller area to the south, resuming its manpower growth after 1965, is expected to show a net gain of 35,000. This long-term increase will be sufficient to keep the Wall Street area, in 1985, still ahead in numbers and far ahead in density.

Squeezing 35,000 more daytime population south of Chambers Street is something to contemplate. The area already has a working force of perhaps 350,000, financial and otherwise. Customers and visitors swell the number even more; exactly how much more is uncertain, but some estimates of the section's total daytime occupants have exceeded a million. Whatever the exact number may be, it is clear that the increased volume of financial business will raise the number of customers and visitors in addition to the new financial workers. The daytime pedestrian jam in the financial district is probably one of the worst in the world. During lunchtime, ambulatory traffic moves at a plodding rate; so do vehicles. The addition of even 50,000 persons to this glutinous mass would add perilously to the difficulty of movement.

The prospect would be even more serious were it not for the expected departure of various nonfinancial enterprises which now occupy space on the fringes of the financial district—for example, light manufacturing, warehousing, and fish and fruit markets.[6]

But even if, on balance, the size of the work force in the area does not change very much, its composition will. Those who replace the warehousemen, shippers, and factory workers will be, principally, stenographers and clerks. As a result, there will be an enlarged demand for office space and for restaurants and shops.

Moreover, the enhanced activity will put heavier demands upon the services of the printers, lawyers, and other professional help that support the financial industries.

We estimate that by 1985 the downtown financial community, to take care of its growth, will require an additional 10.7 million gross square feet of floor space, more than 50 per cent in excess of the amount presently in use by the community below Chambers Street.[7] Though new construction equal to about three-fourths of this amount is already under way or planned, some of this space will be used by nonfinancial services and corporate offices. The financial community, therefore, will still have to acquire a substantial amount of space even beyond that being currently built or planned. As a result, the physical appearance of the downtown financial section will be altered gradually as new office buildings reach skyward and more shopping facilities spread through the neighborhood to replace the structures abandoned by the departing industries. The change will be stretched over a long period of time and in large part will represent the substitution of one kind of business activity for another. It is not expected to be as striking, therefore, as the transformation of midtown's Park Avenue from a residential to a business area.

THE NEW YORK CITY BANKS AND THE DEPOSIT SQUEEZE

The giant banks of New York City, despite their competitive advantages and their ability to attract national business, are confronted with another problem, the answer to which is, at least partially, beyond their control. As we have seen, these institutions receive much of the funds required for their operations from deposits which originate locally. Since we assume that deposits will continue to flow outward as a result of faster economic development elsewhere in the nation, we project that the City banks will hold about 11 per cent of national deposits in 1985, compared with 15 per cent in 1956. At the same time, the City banks presumably will continue to handle a high portion of the loans made by the nation's banks. Accordingly, the City banks will have to hold down their investments, and their share of the investments of the nation's banks is expected to fall from 11 per cent to about 7 per cent between 1956 and 1985. During the same period the investments of the City banks, expressed as a ratio of their earning assets, will shrink from 33 per cent to an estimated 22 per cent. Banks use investments as secondary reserves to provide for both forecastable and more remote cash needs. Investments also serve as a means of gaining additional income without impairing operating flexibility. It is questionable how much lower the City banks would be willing to see their investment accounts drop.

The position of the large banks of New York City will be somewhat eased—at least relatively—by legislation enacted by Congress in 1959. Within the next few years, under the 1959 legislation, the reserve requirements of these banks will be placed on a par with the requirements of banks in other large cities.

We assume that within New York State there will be some relaxation of present restrictions to enable the New York City banks to enter the nearby counties and participate in the deposit expansion which is expected to continue there. Should this occur, their future deposit movements would be likely to reflect some of the growth projected for the New York Metropolitan Region, rather than that for the City. This would mean that the decline of the City's deposits relative to those of the country would be more moderate. But since the relief which is possible by an extension of offices into the suburbs is not so great as to meet the liquidity problem, we foresee continued pressures on the banks arising from fund shortages.

Permitting New York City banks to reach into the suburbs could have conflicting effects on the location of banking jobs. In crossing the city limits, the big banks probably would try to absorb some established institutions. Their shift to the suburbs, therefore, might have little initial effect on bank employment in those areas. There are grounds for the view, however, that eventually the increased substitution of banking systems for unit banks in the suburbs and the further enlargement of these systems will generate more bank employment for the same volume of business. This would be caused in part by the ability of larger systems to undertake more services in small communities, and in part by their tendency to create more offices relative to population. The expansion of employment in the suburbs, however, would be offset by the centralization and consolidation of management; this move would be in the direction of transferring to home offices in New York City some of the administrative functions previously performed in the suburbs.

Chances are the net effect would be slightly to dampen the increase of bank employment in the suburban areas that would have been expected if the legal restrictions had remained unaltered, and correspondingly to increase the number of banking personnel in New York City. Any transfer of administrative personnel to the center would probably get a boost from the introduction of electronic data-processing installations. On balance, however, we believe that almost two-thirds of the Region's increase in commercial bank employment between 1956 and 1985 will take place outside New York City.

PAST AND FUTURE

So ends our forecast. A structure of the future has been fabricated from the bricks of the past. This is manbuilt stuff. And a thousand and one unforeseen problems and circumstances could hammer at our scheme of things and maybe demolish it.

But there are strong reasons for building our images of the next 25 years from the designs of the past. The financial community is a complex organism that has evolved over a long period of time. It changes slowly. And the forces currently at work are not likely to become suddenly obsolete.

We may not have detected all these forces; or if we have isolated them properly, our interpretations of their impact may be wrong. But these are the typical occupational hazards of a forecaster. If the analyst is to be of any help to those who must plan, there is no alternative to a little boldness. We have the satisfaction of knowing that, at the worst, we are on an equal footing with others in our ignorance of what is to come, while at the best, the insights derived from our studies may help in some degree to reduce the areas of uncertainty. It seems reasonable to hope that our projections will provide some basis, rough and preliminary though it may be, for contributing to a clearer view of the New York Metropolitan Region of 1985.

Appendix A

Output and Manpower in Commercial Banks

FINDING A MEASURE OF OUTPUT

In any business firm there is some fairly definite relation between output and manpower. Over time, this relation may change as the people employed become more expert at the jobs they are doing or as new machines are introduced that cut down the number of persons required to produce a unit. By determining this relation and anticipating its changes, one can convert estimates of output into estimates of employment. Before making this transition, however, a suitable measure of output must be ascertained.

THE QUALITIES REQUIRED OF A MEASURE OF OUTPUT

For use in forecasting employment, a measure of output should have several qualities. It must be sensitive to changes in the general level of economic activity, so that it may be geared to the estimates of major economic aggregates; it must bear a determinable relation to inputs of manpower; it must reflect variations in service "mix" as well as amount; and it must be readily available over a sufficiently long period to enable the determination of historical trends and relations.

The measure may be expressed in terms of physical units or dollars. Physical units are insensitive to price changes and are a more direct reflection of actual activity. Dollars have the great advantage of being a common unit that permits many activities to be expressed on the same denominator; their major disadvantage of fluctuating with the price level may be overcome in part by attempting to convert to a "constant dollar" base.

POSSIBLE INDICATORS OF BANKING OUTPUT

In the service industries, in general, analysis of the relation between output and manpower is complicated by the lack of a clearly defined product for the industry. In banking, the problem is aggravated by the range of activities performed. As a result, a variety of output measures are possible. In terms of "physical" units, use may be made of the number of accounts, number of checks, and the turnover of deposits.* The number of accounts provides a direct gauge of the operations entailed in servicing them and an indirect estimate of the attendant bookkeeping and clearing activities. The number of checks gives a clearer portrayal of the internal processing load because a given account may generate a varying number of checks. Deposit turnover is a common index that affords some notion of both economic and banking activity but does not reflect physical operations as do the two previous units. All three measures concentrate on deposits and evaluate only obliquely some of the other major banking functions, such as lending and investing.

Measures of banking activity expressed in dollars which may conceivably be related to output include deposits, debits, the total amount of assets, and the total amount of earning assets, that is, loans and investments. As a major source of bank funds, deposits may provide an indicator of output, but they are an inadequate gauge during periods of high liquidity when changes, conceivably, could be due to a piling up of dormant funds rather than to an acceleration of activity. Moreover, deposits do not discriminate among different kinds of banking functions. Debits do not distinguish between a large number of small transactions or a small number of large ones. Total assets provide a comprehensive reflection of over-all activities, but they are like deposits in that they make no differentiation for the dissimilar manpower requirements necessary to perform various kinds of functions. The total of loans

* For a further discussion of this subject, see Richard E. Speagle and Ernest Kohn, "Employment and Output in Banking, 1919–1955," *The Review of Economics and Statistics* (February 1958), pp. 22–35.

and investments behaves for practical purposes very much like total assets. All these dollar measures overlook the variations in the services performed by banks and the significance of turnover; they also ignore some banking activities, like the trust functions.

A dollar unit of banking output may also be derived from the income statement. The Department of Commerce employs a measure representing the dollar value added by different industries, including banking. This measure roughly represents gross current operating earnings less intermediate purchases from other sectors. An advantage of this notion is its conformity with the concepts of national-income accounting. It has been demonstrated, however, that after adjustments are made for price level and interest rates, the changes over time of the gross product originating in banking resemble closely the fluctuations of an index representing loans and investments because, with interest rates held constant, the gross income of banks is substantially a function of its earning assets.*

THE MEASURE SELECTED

It is not easy to strike a balance among these qualities and come up with the measure of output that most accurately reflects both the level and mix of banking activity. This difficulty underscores the reasons for the lag in developing suitable techniques for estimating factor requirements in banking. Our own solution has been to borrow from various of the devices in order to formulate an aggregate measure, the components of which reflect the disparate productivity characteristics of banking functions.

For this purpose, a bank is viewed as participating in four principal activities: investing, lending to consumers, lending to all others, and serving in fiduciary capacities. The investments of a bank are largely confined to Government bonds which are purchased in large blocks, enabling a small personnel force to generate a substantial volume of business. Banks may organize a separate department for their consumer credit business, and the trend seems to be in that direction. These loans are likely to require a high expenditure of

* Speagle and Kohn, pp. 28–29.

manpower relative to the amount granted because they are of modest size, are made to individuals whose credit ratings are apt to be less certain than those of business firms, are often repaid on an instalment basis, and may entail an added collection burden. "All other loans" are a conglomerate classification, including primarily those for commercial purposes and those on real estate and securities. It was found by a trial run that a much finer breakdown of these loans was not feasible. These loans range widely in size, terms of payment, and credit experience; manpower needs vary in accordance with these features but in general tend to be much lower, compared with the amount outstanding, than those for consumer loans. As for trust departments, their personnel requirements are not directly related to lending activities and are largely dependent on the total dollar amount of trust business handled.

This four-way approach relates commercial bank employment to the volume and kind of service performed by a bank and assumes that the underlying operational activities vary with them. The output indicators employed seem reasonable in the light of the qualifications originally laid down for selection of a measure of performance. These data reflect changes in business activity, are related to manpower inputs, recognize differences in service mix, and are conveniently available. Since the results of the trust activity of a commercial bank do not appear in its balance sheet, income data are employed to measure this function. To account for shifts in the price level, all the series are expressed in constant dollars. As discussed in the note on page 50, there may be some disagreement about the advisability of converting asset data to a constant dollar base. To the extent that this question is raised, there seems to be less doubt about applying this procedure to loans, where changes in amount are likely to follow rather directly changes in the price level. In the case of investments, on the other hand, the changes may be more directly related to Federal debt policy than to the price level. Nevertheless, we decided to conduct the analysis in terms of constant dollars partly to achieve comparability with our projections and partly for the sake of internal consistency.

DETERMINING THE MANPOWER RELATIONS AND MANPOWER REQUIREMENTS

After we determined the three types of credit activity, expressed in terms of assets, to be used as indicators of banking output, our next procedure was to ascertain manpower relations that could be applied to convert the credit items into estimates of employment requirements. For this purpose we prepared a compilation of the banking employment and the amount of investments, consumer credit, and all other loans—our three basic measures—that the insured commercial banks of each state and the District of Columbia had at the close of each year from 1947 to 1956. For each year, we fitted a regression equation to the 49 observations for employment and for the three measures of banking activity. The ten years produced ten equations, each of them in the form

$$Y = a_0 + a_1 X_1 + a_2 X_2 + a_3 X_3$$

where Y is the estimated number of banking employees in a given state, a_0 is the constant of regression, a_1, a_2, and a_3 are the average number of employees per one million of 1955 dollar investments, consumer loans (instalment and single-payment loans to individuals), and all other loans, respectively, and the X's are the corresponding amounts of investments, consumer loans, and all other loans in millions of 1955 dollars held by a state's banks.

Initially, we introduced the gross earnings of trust departments as a fourth variable to explain the variations in employment. We found that the use of an income concept along with three asset measures, statistically, did not provide clean-cut results. Accordingly, we excluded the gross earnings of trust departments, on the one hand, and the estimated employment in trust departments, on the other. For this purpose, employment in the trust departments was determined separately on the basis of data provided by the questionnaire conducted by the authors and by the studies made by the several Federal Reserve Banks, notably those of New York and Boston. By this means we estimated that, in terms of current dollars, gross income from fiduciary activities per trust department employee was $7,000 in 1947, $8,000 in 1950, and $10,000 in 1956. The data for the intervening years were obtained by interpolation.

The manpower requirements per million of constant 1955 dollars of investments, consumer loans, and all other loans, gauged by

Table A-1 Estimating Equations for Determining Banking Employment, 1947–1956[a]

(employment data in number of persons)

	Constant of regression	Employment per one million of 1955 dollars of: investments	consumer loans	all other loans	Proportion of total variance by states explained by the equation
1947	597	0.7742	20.8686	2.1814	0.994
1948	608	.8480	18.8616	2.2585	.996
1949	533	.8509	18.5451	1.8887	.996
1950	599	.8900	17.3258	1.2851	.995
1951	668	.8657	18.4671	1.6703	.995
1952	744	(.6752)[b]	18.7850	1.3773	.981
1953	914	(.0182)[b]	18.9941	1.8669	.991
1954	772	1.0014	16.5302	1.2140	.992
1955	817	1.2398	14.9655	1.0466	.990
1956	950	(.7235)[b]	15.9959	1.3670	.986

[a] Excludes trust activities.

[b] Not significant statistically at 1 per cent level.

Source: Multiple regressions computed from data published by the Federal Deposit Insurance Corporation, converted to constant dollar base.

means of these multiple regressions for the various years, are shown in Table A-1, which is an enlarged version of Table 6 in Chapter 3. For instance, in 1955 in any state or the District of Columbia, the estimated employment by commercial banks equals 817 plus 1.24 times investments plus 14.97 times consumer loans plus 1.05 times all other loans, where investments and loans are in millions of dollars. The table contains the constant of regression and the percentage of the variance in the employment data which is explained by the equation.

The table indicates that the average manpower requirements associated with each million dollars of credit differed substantially among the different types of credit. Moreover, the unit manpower requirements have been changing over time, reflecting largely changes in labor productivity. In our analysis of these trends, we omit the manpower relations applicable to investments for the three years 1952, 1953, and 1956 because they were not of the same statistical quality as the others. Since the probability that these relations did not differ from zero was less than 0.99, these results were not accepted as significant.

RELIABILITY OF THE MANPOWER RELATIONS

The formulas developed from the relations shown in Table A-1 are quite successful in explaining the differences in banking employment between states. In fact, as may be seen from the figures in the last column of that table, in all cases more than 98 per cent of the interstate variations that occurred during the period covered is explained. For example, we estimated the employment for 1955 in various states by means of the formula for that year and compared the results with the reported data for the year. The close correspondence between the actual and estimated employment is shown in Chart 24.

Finally, by applying the manpower relations for each year to the amounts of investments, consumer loans, and all other loans at the nation's commercial banks, we obtained estimates of the total number of personnel associated with each function. The remaining employment (exclusive of the trust department), not covered directly or indirectly by these functions, was derived by multiplying the constant of regression by 49, the number of geographical units covered. These estimates of total employment and of the breakdown of employment by function appear in Table A-2. They may be compared with the actual employment of the nation's commercial banks in Table A-3 and with the breakdown of the percentage distribution of earnings in Table A-4. The distribution of income and the distribution of personnel by function are broadly similar. Thus,

Chart 24

Correlation between Actual Banking Employment and Employment Estimated from Manpower Relations, Selected States, 1955

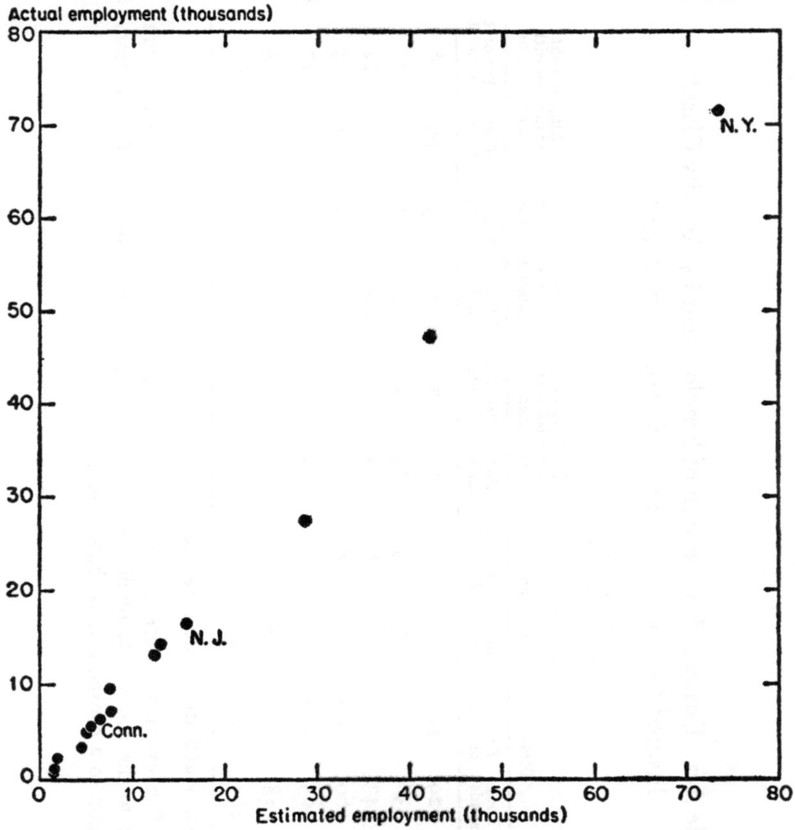

Note: States were selected by taking every fourth state in the alphabetical list of the 48 states and the District of Columbia, and adding Connecticut, New Jersey, and New York.

Sources: Estimated employment is from relations—including regression constant—in Table A-1 for 1955. Actual banking employment is from Federal Deposit Insurance Corporation, *Annual Report, 1956,* less estimated employment in trust departments.

Table A-2 Estimated Allocation of Employment by Activity Class,[a] Insured Commercial Banks, Selected Years, 1947–1955

	Total		Employment other than loans and investments (computed from regression constant)		Employment associated with investments		Employment associated with consumer loans		Employment associated with all other loans	
	Thousands	Per cent of total	Thousands	Per cent of total	Thousands	Per cent of total	Thousands	Per cent of total	Thousands	Per cent of total
1947 ..	329	100	29	9	72	22	143	43	85	26
1948 ..	338	100	30	9	69	20	147	44	92	27
1949 ..	343	100	26	8	73	21	169	49	75	22
1950 ..	360	100	29	8	73	20	196	55	61	17
1951 ..	383	100	33	9	67	17	200	52	83	22
1954 ..	438	100	38	9	85	19	246	56	69	16
1955 ..	461	100	40	9	96	21	256	55	69	15

[a] Fiduciary activities were excluded.

Note: The estimates were obtained by applying the regression coefficients from Table A-1 to the assets data published by the Federal Deposit Insurance Corporation. A conversion to a constant dollar base was made.

Table A-3 Employment by Insured Commercial Banks, Continental United States, 1947–1956

	Total employment	Estimated employment in trust activities	Total employment, excluding estimated trust component
1947 ...	349,698	20,672	329,026
1948 ...	359,506	21,311	338,195
1949 ...	365,577	21,947	343,630
1950 ...	382,589	22,586	360,003
1951 ...	407,343	24,196	383,147
1952 ...	433,455	25,794	407,661
1953 ...	454,542	27,402	427,140
1954 ...	466,941	29,003	437,938
1955 ...	491,685	30,618	461,067
1956 ...	519,871	32,209	487,662

Sources: Total employment is from annual reports of Federal Deposit Insurance Corporation. Trust employment figures are estimates based on our own survey and the surveys conducted by the various Federal Reserve Banks.

Table A-4 Sources of Income of Insured Commercial Banks, 1947–1956

(in percentage of total current operating earnings)

	Total current operating earnings	Interest on securities	Interest and discount on loans, including service charges and fees on loans	Trust department earnings	All other
1947	100.0	40.6	41.4	4.7	13.3
1948 ..	100.0	35.2	47.0	4.6	13.2
1949 ..	100.0	33.7	48.8	4.4	13.1
1950 ..	100.0	31.6	51.1	4.6	12.7
1951	100.0	28.0	55.2	4.4	12.4
1952 ..	100.0	27.9	56.5	4.1	11.5
1953 ..	100.0	27.4	57.5	4.0	11.1
1954 ..	100.0	27.7	56.5	4.3	11.5
1955 ..	100.0	26.4	58.0	4.4	11.2
1956 ..	100.0	23.7	61.0	4.5	10.8

Sources: Annual reports of the Federal Deposit Insurance Corporation, 1954 and 1956.

exclusive of trust income, during the period approximately 85 per cent of bank earnings, on the average, came from loans and investments and about 15 per cent from all other activities, while about 90 per cent of the estimated employment was associated with lending and investing activities.

Clearly, all the personnel of a bank are not directly performing the functions represented by our basic asset categories, but are engaged in many indirect bookkeeping, clearing, and other clerical activities. In effect, by allocating all banking personnel into service categories broken down into "final product" classes, we include in each service class, people engaged in the intermediate stage of production. The fact that the manpower relations based on this allocation have a very high degree of statistical significance confirms the feasibility of the procedure. Moreover, the data used in our analysis were taken by states which include large groups of banks; consequently, it is likely that the peculiarities of individual institutions with respect to assets and deposit composition, as well as divergences from the average relation, are averaged out.

FACTORS BEHIND THE EMPLOYMENT TRENDS

The changes in employment that occurred may be quantitatively attributable to the effects of changes in the volume of credit, mix of credit, and the unit manpower requirements. The volume of credit is represented by the constant dollar amount of loans and investments. Over the period from 1947 to 1956 this total grew by 15.6 per cent. The credit mix is represented by the percentage distribution of the total loans and investments among the three classes of credit. This distribution is shown for 1947 and 1956 in Table A-5. The unit manpower relations were already shown in Table A-1.

In Chapter 3, we explained how we assigned quantitative weights to the influence of these changes by holding two of them constant and permitting the third to vary. There, we went through this procedure starting with 1947 as the base and moving to 1956. As an additional check, in this appendix, we reverse our choice of the base year. For this purpose, we start with the actual employment in 1956

Table A-5 Percentage Distribution of Loans and Investments by Type of Credit, 1947 and 1956

(insured commercial banks)

	1947	1956
Total loans and investments	100.00	100.00
Investments	67.11	44.67
Consumer loans	4.95	11.36
All other loans	27.94	43.97

Source: Based on annual reports of the Federal Deposit Insurance Corporation.

and calculate the weights obtained by measuring the changes, moving back to 1947. As indicated in Table A-6, the two estimates made by choosing alternative base years bracket the actual change in employment rather closely.

Table A-6 also shows that when the 1947 volume and mix, along with the 1956 coefficients (manpower relations), are used in 1956, employment falls from 100 per cent in 1947 to 76.75 per cent in 1956. When the 1956 volume and mix, along with the 1947 coefficients, are used in 1947, employment recedes from 100 per cent in 1947 to 74.58 in 1956. Since volume and mix are held constant in both cases, the resulting shrinkage in employment is traceable to the effect of the decline in the manpower relations for the two periods. Because our coefficients cover a large part of commercial banking activity, this decline probably is a reliable function of the change in productivity that actually occurred.

There are reasons to believe that the increase in productivity represented by this function may be on the conservative side. For one thing, within each of our output categories, changes in the mix of credit services occurred in the direction of more labor-intensive activities. Investments in non-Federal Government securities grew sharply, while those in Federal issues declined; consumer instalment loans expanded more than single-payment loans to individuals; and the volume of real estate loans increased more than the volume of

Table A-6 Change from 1947 to 1956 in Employment of Commercial Banks Attributed to Loans and Investments, Calculated from Different Assumptions

	Employment in 1956 relative to 1947 (1947 = 1.0000)
A. Actual employment in 1947 and employment in 1956 estimated on the basis of:	
(1) 1956 volume; 1947 mix and coefficients	1.1564
(2) 1956 mix; 1947 volume and coefficients	1.7004
(3) 1956 coefficients; 1947 volume and mix	0.7675
(4) Compound result (1.1564 × 1.7004 × 0.7675)	1.509
B. Actual employment in 1956 and employment in 1947 estimated on the basis of:	
(1) 1947 volume; 1956 mix and coefficients	1.1563
(2) 1947 mix; 1956 volume and coefficients	1.6523
(3) 1947 coefficients; 1956 volume and mix	0.7458
(4) Compound result (1.1563 × 1.6523 × 0.7458)	1.425
C. Actual employment in 1947 and 1956	1.466

remaining loans in the "all other" category. Because we did not explicitly take these changes in credit mix into account, our changes in manpower relations probably underestimate the gains in productivity. Then, too, our measurement of employment by the number of persons instead of manhours may understate the growth of labor productivity to the extent that the number of manhours per man has been declining.

We have computed an index of our function of labor productivity implied by changes in the unit manpower requirements for the period 1938–1956. This index is shown in Chart 25. In the computation of the index, unit coefficients for constant-dollar trust department income were included in addition to coefficients for the three types of credit. (See note in Chart 25.) The movements of the index suggest that labor productivity was growing in the few years before World War II, that it declined during the war and then continued to increase over the postwar period with one major interruption in 1951,

Chart 25
Index of Function of Labor Productivity,
Insured Commercial Banks, 1938–1956

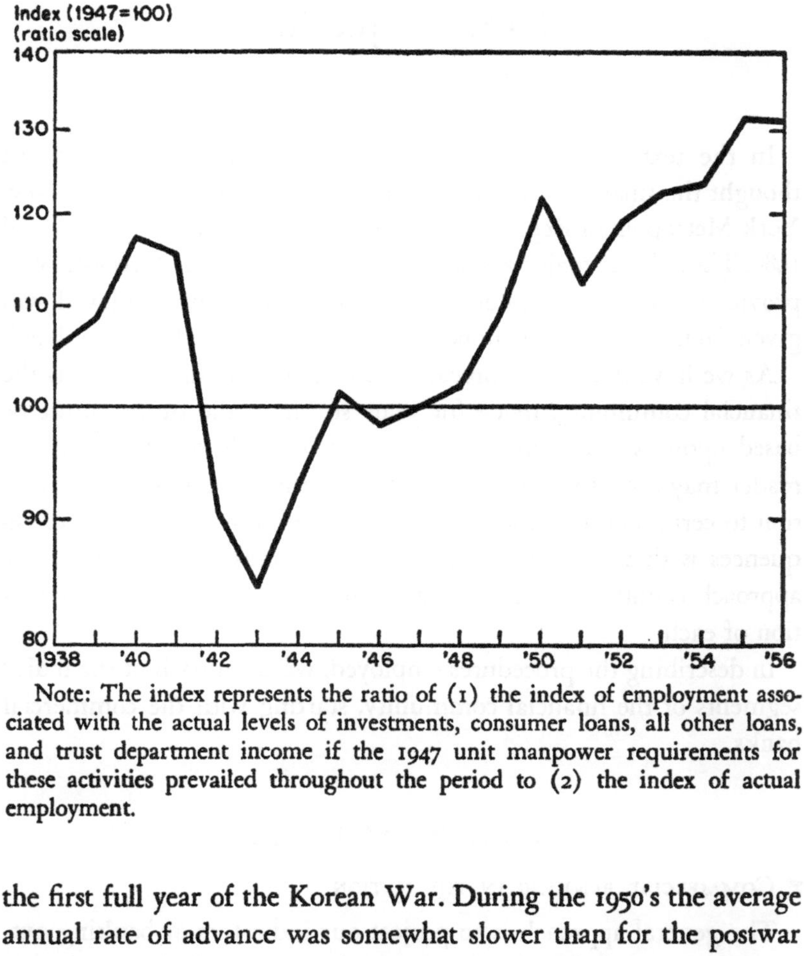

Note: The index represents the ratio of (1) the index of employment associated with the actual levels of investments, consumer loans, all other loans, and trust department income if the 1947 unit manpower requirements for these activities prevailed throughout the period to (2) the index of actual employment.

the first full year of the Korean War. During the 1950's the average annual rate of advance was somewhat slower than for the postwar period as a whole: compared with an average of about 3.0 per cent per year for the period 1947–1956, the average of annual changes was 1.6 per cent for the years 1950–1956 and 2.3 per cent for 1953–1956. It is quite likely that the relatively rapid increases which occurred in the late 1940's represent a rebound from the low levels reached during the war.

Appendix B

Methodology and Assumptions of the Projections

In the text, we presented summary charts describing how we thought the financial community of the nation and that of the New York Metropolitan Region might appear in the years 1965, 1975, and 1985. Though the major assumptions underlying these forecasts were provided, no step-by-step account of the calculations employed was given. In the present appendix, we submit the methodology in detail.

As we have stressed, a forecast of a complex organism such as the financial community, made for years so far in the future, must be based upon assumptions that could be vigorously debated. While a reader may accept many of our presuppositions, he may take exception to certain others, and may desire to fashion a new chain of sequences with some new links inserted. To make this possible, our approach is outlined in steps that permit the independent consideration of each.

In describing the procedures employed, we cover each of the major segments of the financial community, starting with the commercial banks.

I. COMMERCIAL BANKING

COMMERCIAL BANKING IN THE NATION

The general approach is to project our indicators of banking output—consumer credit, all other loans, investments, and trust income—and to convert them into employment requirements by applying to them the appropriate manpower relations shown in Chapter 3 and Appendix A. Since historical data were used to determine the ratios, we adjust the results in order to account for the expected changes in these relations between output and manpower.

Consumer Credit

First we examine the nation's total consumer credit—held by retail stores, banks, finance companies, and others. As noted previously, the long-term trend in the ratio of total consumer credit to disposable personal income has been following a steep upward incline. We have assumed that this rate of growth will not be fully matched in the future. Two major wars, a great depression, and a technological revolution have concentrated into the four previous decades economic and sociological changes that otherwise might have stretched over a much longer period.

The ratio of non-instalment credit to disposable personal income has expanded mildly from 2.8 per cent in 1947 to 3.6 per cent in 1956. A further gradual rise is projected to 3.8 per cent in 1965, 4.0 per cent in 1975, and 4.2 per cent in 1985. The ratio of instalment credit to disposable personal income rose from 4.0 per cent in 1947 to 11.1 per cent in 1956. The great backlog of pentup demand for automobiles created by the depression and World War II has now been largely met and future production is likely to depend more strongly on income growth and replacement requirements. On this basis, a moderate further growth of instalment credit relative to disposable personal income to 13.0 per cent in 1965, 15.0 per cent in 1975, and 17.0 per cent in 1985 is assumed. The projected ratios would be the highest attained, but they are set high to reflect a continued growth in the country's standard of living, further technological progress, and the consumer's cumulative desire for the ownership of durable assets. Much larger ratios appear unlikely, lest the burden of repayment created by the expanded volume of credit encroaches upon the consumer's financial ability to satisfy other needs.

These assumptions, when applied to the projections of disposable personal income already given in Table 32, produce the forecasts of non-instalment and instalment credit shown in Table B-1. The 1956

Table B-1 Forecasts of United States Consumer Credit

(in millions of 1955 dollars)

	Non-instalment credit	Instalment credit	Disposable personal income
1956	10,166	31,346	282,400
1965	15,609	53,399	410,800
1975	24,083	90,313	602,100
1985	37,204	150,587	885,800

figures are given for purposes of comparison. All the figures are in millions of 1955 dollars. (In fact, all our figures in this appendix are, unless otherwise indicated, in 1955 dollars.)

Of these totals, how much will the commercial banks finance? In view of the vigor displayed by rival financial institutions, the banks are not likely to add very much to their share of the market; through aggressive action, however, they may be able to buy more of the paper now held by retailers, and by spreading their branch outlets, improve their competitive position in granting personal loans and repair and modernization loans. Although the banks were slow to enter the consumer credit field, once they made the break, many of them were alert to improve their marketing procedures. For example, starting about 1956, various institutions broadened their lending methods in this area by adopting special devices such as creating personal lines of credit against which borrowers could draw checks and granting so-called "instant loans" whereby a depositor can borrow by simply flashing a credit card. For these reasons, it is estimated that by 1965, 1975, and 1985, the banks will expand slightly their percentage shares from 28 per cent in 1956 to 29, 30, and 31 per cent of non-instalment credit, and from 37 per cent to 38, 39, and 40 per cent of instalment credit, where they consistently have been more important. Thus, the amounts of total consumer credit, in millions of 1955 dollars, at the nation's commercial banks in 1965, 1975, and 1985 (with the actual 1956 figures given for comparison) shape up like this:

1956	$14,126
1965	24,819
1975	42,447
1985	71,768

Based upon these trends, the amount of consumer loans held by the commercial banks will be rising considerably over each period —76 per cent by 1965, 71 per cent by 1975, and 69 per cent by 1985.

Commercial Loans

Changes in the volume of commercial loans are the outcome of various interrelated factors including the level of production, the amount of expenditures made by business firms, and the source of financing of these expenditures.

Our forecast is based upon the assumption that business spending will continue to keep pace with the expansion of the national economy and that firms will maintain a policy of relying upon internal funds for the major part of these disbursements. External sources will provide the differential needed to maintain capital expansion, inventory accumulations, and accounts receivable; the ratios relating these factors as a whole to the gross national product, it is assumed, will approximate those prevailing in 1947–1956. Over this period, excluding the recession years 1949 and 1953–1954, commercial loans outstanding at the year-ends constituted on the average 8.1 per cent of the gross national product. Applying the same percentage to the forecasts of gross national product given in Chapter 8, we get

Table B-2 Forecasts of Commercial Loans by United States Banks

(in millions of 1955 dollars)

	Commercial loans	Gross national product
1956	37,592	402,600
1965	48,569	599,600
1975	71,191	878,900
1985	104,739	1,293,100

the forecasts of commercial loans for 1965, 1975, and 1985 that appear in Table B-2.

These trends indicate that by 1965, the amount of these loans held by the commercial banks would rise about 29 per cent; by 1975 another 47 per cent; and by 1985 an additional 47 per cent.

Real Estate Loans

It is expected that building activity will continue to be an important factor in the business picture, particularly because of the Government's long-run willingness to encourage mortgage lending. Between 1947 and 1956, mortgage debt on one-to-four-family houses, as a percentage of gross national product, rose by twelve percentage points, and that on multifamily and commercial properties increased by slightly less than two percentage points. Though many factors influence the amount of mortgages outstanding, it seems reasonable to expect that the continued pressure for new construction will tend to make real estate values bear an increasingly higher ratio to the flow of economic activity.

The huge residential building program of the postwar period, however, has eliminated much of the great housing shortage that had developed during the war and depression years. It is therefore assumed that some moderation in the future rate of residential real estate growth will occur. The continued rise in the ratio of mortgage credit to the gross national product allows for the expected increases in the rate of family formation. The volume of outstanding mortgages in the commercial field has been considerably lower than in the residential area, but a narrowing in the differential is foreseen.

Based upon these assumptions, the nation's grand total of nonfarm mortgages outstanding in 1965, 1975, and 1985 on one-to-four-family houses will amount to 26, 28, and 30 per cent of the gross national product, respectively, compared with 24 per cent in 1956, and on multifamily and commercial properties will amount to 11, 13, and 15 per cent of the gross national product, compared with 9 per cent in 1956. According to these projections, the ratio of total nonfarm real estate mortgages to the gross national product will be about 45 per cent by 1985. Since 1929, this ratio has been exceeded only in the depths of the depression of the early 1930's. The high ratio projected for the future reflects our feeling of the importance of real estate in the economic scene.

In absolute amounts, the forecasts for the two categories of mortgage credit held in the nation—by banks and all others—are given in Table B-3.

Table B-3 Forecasts of Total United States Mortgage Credit

(in millions of 1955 dollars)

	One-to-four-family houses	Multifamily and commercial properties
1956	96,117	34,757
1965	155,900	65,958
1975	246,093	114,258
1985	387,922	193,961

In view of the apparent reluctance of the commercial banks to expand their direct holdings of real estate mortgages compared with their interest in short-term participations, it is believed that the percentages of the nonfarm mortgage debt held by the commercial banks in the future will remain at the levels prevailing in 1956, that is, at about 16 per cent for the mortgages on one-to-four-family properties and at 14 per cent for multifamily and commercial property loans. On this basis, the amounts of real estate mortgages held by the nation's commercial banks will be as shown in Table B-4.*

If these trends are achieved, the total mortgages of the country's banks will rise by 66 per cent by 1965, by another 62 per cent by 1975, and by another 61 per cent by 1985.

Securities Loans

In our analysis of historical movements, we indicated that variations in securities loans may be explained by the volume of new corporate and Government financing, the movements in securities

* The 1956 figures in Table B-4 will not add exactly to the mortgage loan figure in Table 4 in the text, mainly because mortgages on farm land are omitted here.

Table B-4 Forecasts of United States Banks' Mortgage Credit

(in millions of 1955 dollars)

	One-to-four-family houses	Multifamily and commercial properties
1956	15,632	5,005
1965	24,944	9,234
1975	39,375	15,996
1985	62,078	27,155

prices relative to other prices, stock trading, and changing margin requirements. These factors may be offsetting; thus, United States Government financing may be high when private financing is low or margin requirements may be increased when stock trading is high. For these reasons, it is difficult to isolate the effect of individual influences, and in the aggregate these loans show no clear-cut relation to the gross national product, ranging from less than one per cent to over 3 per cent since 1938.

Our underlying assumptions of an expanding economy and no major unsettling political conditions suggest that new corporate financing will be high, while increasing public participation in stock transactions may occur. Therefore, the commercial banks' loans on securities are expected to continue to grow. The question is: will they expand as rapidly as they did over the postwar years 1947–1956, when their constant dollar volume grew by 67 per cent? Our inclination is to feel that the restraints on securities loans will be sufficiently great to prevent a full duplication of this performance. We, therefore, selected an increase of 45 per cent for the nine-year period 1956–1965 and 50 per cent for the two following forecast decades. This projection roughly matches the rate of growth of the gross national product. Based on this assumption, our forecasts of securities loans on the books of commercial banks in 1965, 1975, and 1985 are presented in Table B-5.

This table gives a breakdown between loans to brokers and dealers

Table B-5 Forecasts of Securities Loans of United States Banks

(in millions of 1955 dollars)

	Total securities loans	Securities loans to brokers and dealers	Securities loans to others
1956	4,155	2,513	1,642
1965	6,025	3,615	2,410
1975	9,038	5,423	3,615
1985	13,557	8,134	5,423

and loans to others. Up to about 1947, these amounts were almost equal, with loans to "others" having a slight edge. Since 1947, however, loans to brokers and dealers have consistently exceeded those to others. We assume that loans to brokers and dealers will constitute about 60 per cent of the total.

"All Other Loans"

It will be recalled that one of our four indicators of banking output is the category of "all other loans"—that is, all besides consumer loans. The category consists principally of commercial, real estate, and securities loans, which have now been projected separately. But the nation's banks also make agricultural loans and loans to foreign governments, local governments, governmental agencies, other banks, and eleemosynary institutions. And in order to project the total amount of "all other loans," we must estimate what percentage of the whole category is made up of commercial, real estate, and securities loans, combined. In 1947, this figure came to about 86 per cent. Thereafter, it declined, then rose, and was about 85 per cent in 1956. For our projections, we assume that on a national basis, commercial, real estate, and securities loans will rise somewhat in importance relative to agricultural and miscellaneous loans, and that the ratio will be 87 per cent.

Therefore, in order to predict the total amount of "all other loans," we "blow up" the predictions for commercial, real estate, and securities loans by dividing their sum by 0.87. And this means that the "all other loans" total, in millions of 1955 dollars, is forecast as follows, compared with $75,061 in 1956:

1965	$102,037
1975	155,862
1985	238,539

Investments

Now that we have projected all kinds of loans, we are in a position to project investments. Previously we indicated the preference of commercial banks for lending and their tendency to buy securities with surplus funds. We expect that the ratio of loans to total loans and investments (that is, to earning assets) will continue to rise, but at a slower rate than has occurred since World War II. We assume that, compared with 55 per cent in 1956, total loans will constitute 58 per cent of earning assets in 1965, 61 per cent in 1975, and 64 per cent in 1985, with investments making up the rest. Accordingly, we arrive at the following forecasts of the investments of the nation's commercial banks, as compared with the actual 1956 figure of $72,-642 (all figures being in millions of 1955 dollars):

1965	$ 91,860
1975	126,787
1985	174,548

And we also arrive at the following forecasts of total earning assets (loans and investments combined), as compared with the actual 1956 figure of $161,829:

1965	$218,716
1975	325,096
1985	484,855

These projections imply a growth of investments of 26 per cent by 1965, 38 per cent by 1975, and 38 per cent by 1985. Total earning assets would rise by 35 per cent, 49 per cent, and 49 per cent, during these same periods.

Trust Income

It has been noted that all the major segments of the trust income of the nation's commercial banks have been growing, but at varying rates. On the basis of fragmentary evidence, we obtained indications that the rate of expansion has been slowest for personal trusts, faster for corporate trusts and agencies, and fastest for the pension funds.*

In 1956, private pension fund coverage of both insured and noninsured plans was estimated at 14 million persons, and contributions to the noninsured plans amounted to $2.3 billion. Assuming that the pension fund coverage in 1965 will be 20 million persons, representing 33 per cent of nonagricultural nongovernment employment, and that contributions to noninsured plans at that time will amount to $4.4 billion annually, it has been calculated that the assets of noninsured pension funds would be $51.7 billion at the end of 1965.** If these estimates are realized, the growth of these funds would be at about the same rate as that of the past half-dozen years.

We assume also that trust income will advance with the improvement in the general economy, but at a somewhat more rapid rate, because of the influence of pension funds and the likelihood of uncovering new sources of activity. Between 1946 and 1956, trust income, measured in constant dollars, increased by about 65 per cent, from $190 million in 1946 to $313 million in 1956. We assume a 65 per cent increase every ten years, which, with the 1955 base of $282 millions, gives us the following in millions of 1955 dollars:

1965	$ 465
1975	767
1985	1,266

* See Chapter 3, p. 68. Some of the reasons given to explain the surprisingly small growth in the actual volume of personal-trust business are the shrinkage in the wealth share of the high-income groups traditionally prominent in this field and the competitive disadvantage experienced in administering these funds compared with those handled by the investment counseling industry. See Raymond W. Goldsmith and Eli Shapiro, "An Estimate of Bank-Administered Personal Trust Funds," *Journal of Finance* (March 1959), p. 17.

** Vito Natrella, "Implications of Pension Fund Accumulations," *Annual Meeting of the American Statistical Association,* September 1957, p. 12.

On this basis, between 1956 and 1985, the trust income would rise from 0.078 to 0.098 per cent of the gross national product.

Deposit Requirements

Assuming that the banks will maintain the past ratio of earning assets to all assets and that no major change occurs in the capital-deposit ratio, a reasonably stable relation should exist between earning assets and deposits. For the purposes of our analysis, we have assumed that deposits would be 120 per cent of earning assets, which is approximately the level prevailing between 1947 and 1956. Consequently, our loans and investments figures imply the following total bank deposits, in 1955 millions, for the three target years, as compared with the 1956 figure of $191,762:

1965	$262,459
1975	390,115
1985	581,826

Employment

Having established the indicators of banking output for the forecast years, we convert them to employment by calculating the manpower related to $1 million of each component.* This conversion is made initially by means of the manpower relations for 1955.** The resulting estimates were then adjusted for expected changes in "productivity."

As described previously, the commercial banks have introduced a considerable amount of mechanization in order to reduce the unit costs of the large amount of clerical help they employ. Opportunities

* Except for trust department income, which covers insured commercial banks, our measures of banking output refer to all commercial banks. Because participation of noninsured banks in trust activities is small, we interpret all our measures to be applicable to all commercial banks.

** The 1955 relations were used because they seemed a little firmer statistically than those for 1956; however, the results based on 1956 relations would not be much different. For an explanation of statistical results see Appendix A.

for considerable further savings have been created by the electronic computer.

In 1958 and 1959, the banking industry took a grand step towards more effective mechanization when it began to introduce character sensing equipment which can inscribe a magnetic-ink language on checks, read the characters, and enter them into a processing system. It is probable that a number of years will elapse before fully integrated systems are generally used, while still more time will be required before the entire banking organization can be adapted to this "break-through" in mechanization. These prospective developments are taken into account by using as our function of productivity growth the rate of 3.0 per cent compounded annually. This is the rate that obtained in the period 1947–1956 but is higher than the rate of the 1950's.

The indicators of banking output do not cover all the activities of a commercial bank. Excluded are certain functions, such as those connected with the servicing of deposit accounts, collections, and safe deposits, which during the postwar period contributed, on the average, 12 per cent to operating earnings and 8 per cent to employment.* In order to account for these services, the next step in our procedure is to raise the basic forecast by 10 per cent.

Actual manpower in the nation's commercial banks was 536,000 in 1956. Based on 1955 manpower requirements, our forecasts for 1965, 1975, and 1985, would be 643,000, 1,039,000, and 1,678,000, respectively. And when these figures are adjusted for changes in productivity and for service coverage, as explained in the preceding paragraphs, they become 526,000, 633,000, and 760,000.**

* See Appendix A, Tables A-2 and A-4.

** At the initial stages of the break-through in mechanization, occurring probably in the late 1950's and early 1960's, the actual rate of "productivity" change may slightly exceed the long-term rate of 3 per cent which we have postulated. This factor by itself would have the effect of making our projections of banking employment in 1965 somewhat on the high side. On the other hand, the manpower coefficients which we used in translating the projected consumer loans into employment figures for 1965 were necessarily based on "other loans to individuals," which are not quite the same as consumer loans strictly defined. And the latter discrepancy, taken alone, has had

But this assumes that commercial banking functions will remain essentially unchanged. We must make one further adjustment, because the introduction of electronic equipment eventually will free much of the manpower resources of the commercial banks for other activities. If the banks do not move into these new areas, their future rate of growth will be relatively moderate. We are confident that the banks will invade the fields once dominated by the miscellaneous institutions. In making our forecasts, we have assumed that half of the growth of the miscellaneous financial institutions will be due to the expansion of existing lines and half will be due to innovation. We further assume that half of the rise ascribable to innovation will be taken over by the commercial banks.

On this basis we obtain the following figures for employment in the nation's commercial banks for our three target years:

1965	562,000
1975	729,000
1985	952,000

COMMERCIAL BANKING IN THE REGION

Our forecasts of banking functions on a national level have been a necessary preliminary for determining the share of the country's total that the banks of the New York Metropolitan Region may expect to obtain. Underlying this determination is the assumption that the large City institutions in the Region will continue to dominate the national money market in the performance of their banking functions, but that some weakening in their dominant position may occur. To traverse the gap between national and regional amounts, two approaches are used: one is an analysis of historical trends in the relation between the amounts of the various assets held by the banks of the country and of the Region; the other is an evaluation of economic conditions in the Region that may affect these relations. Each of the major banking functions is approached in this manner.

---

a depressing effect on our 1965 forecast of banking employment. In general we have estimated that these two factors tend to offset each other.

Consumer Credit

Since instalment loans are of a highly local nature, we assume that in the future the Region's share of these loans made by the banks in the nation will be the same as its share in personal income. In view of the relatively good performance of the Region's banks in the field of single-payment loans, it is expected that these banks will continue to hold about 18 per cent of the future single-payment loans.

In 1947, the Region's share of total personal income in the United States was 12.7 per cent and in 1956 it was 12.2 per cent. As indicated in Chapter 8, we have assumed here that this share will shrink somewhat to 11.8 per cent in 1965, 11.5 per cent in 1975, and 11.3 per cent in 1985.

According to these assumptions, our forecasts of consumer credit held by the Region's commercial banks, in millions of 1955 dollars, are as follows:

1965	$3,209
1975	5,351
1985	8,883

Commercial Loans

We have observed that the considerable volume of national lending undertaken by the Region's banks has enabled them to maintain a reasonably stable share of the commercial loans granted by all the banks of the country; during the postwar years, this ratio has varied between 29.6 per cent and 33.5 per cent. Because of the size advantage of the City's banks and their skills in this field, it is not expected that any serious inroads will occur. Accordingly, it is assumed that the Region's banks will hold at 31 per cent of the national total. Following, in 1955 millions, are the 1956 amount of the Region's commercial loans and our forecasts for the target years:

1956	$11,883
1965	15,056

1975	22,069
1985	32,469

Real Estate Loans

Since 1951, the relation between the growth of the amount of nonfarm real estate loans granted by the banks of the Region and country seems to have largely stabilized at about 10 per cent. We assume that the peak of the office expansion boom in New York City has passed and that the general pace of construction activity will slow down somewhat; as a result, the future rate of growth of real estate loans probably will be moderate, and will move more closely with the expansion of the Region's economic activity. As mentioned, the Region's economic growth is expected to lag somewhat behind that of the country. Accordingly, we forecast a slight decline in the amount of nonfarm real estate loans held by the Region's banks to 9.6 per cent in 1965, 9.3 per cent in 1975, and 9.1 per cent in 1985. Following, in millions of 1955 dollars, are the 1956 amount of the Region's total nonfarm real estate loans and our forecasts for the target years:

1956	$2,010
1965	3,281
1975	5,150
1985	8,119

Securities Loans

Our historical analysis has indicated that the Region's banks have been able to hold their share of the market for securities loans to "others" but their portion of the loans to brokers and dealers has been slipping. To a large extent, this shrinkage has been caused by the tendency of out-of-town brokers and dealers to finance locally. Because of the expected continuing strength of the New York money market, we do not foresee much of an extension of this decline. Therefore we assume that the ratio of loans to others held by the Region's banks compared with those of the country will remain unchanged at about 30 per cent, while their ratio of loans to brokers and dealers will decline from the average level of 73 per cent prevailing during the 1947–1956 decade to 68 per cent in 1965, 63 per cent in 1975, and 58 per cent in 1985. The forecasts of the securities loans of the Region's banks for the three target years appear in Table B-6. As usual we give the 1956 figure for comparison.

Table B-6 Forecasts of Region's Securities Loans

(in millions of 1955 dollars)

	Total securities loans	Securities loans to brokers and dealers	Securities loans to others
1956	1,917	1,491	426
1965	3,181	2,458	723
1975	4,500	3,416	1,084
1985	6,345	4,718	1,627

"All Other Loans"

The next step is to forecast, for the Region's commercial banks, the amount of "all other loans"—that is, other than consumer credit. When we went through this same procedure for the nation's banks, we made the assumption that 87 per cent of the category would consist of commercial, real estate, and securities loans, the remainder being agricultural and various other loans. For the Region's banks we assume that this ratio will be 95 per cent instead of 87. The Region's ratio has been somewhat higher than the nation's in past years. It is difficult to say how much higher because data are not available on a strictly comparable basis, but estimates indicate that the differential may have been about 5 or 6 percentage points—partly because the Region's agricultural loans are extremely small. We expect that the differential will widen somewhat in the future, because, as banks outside the Region grow, they may be able to obtain a larger share of the loans now made by New York City's banks to foreign governments, local governments, agencies of local governments, and eleemosynary institutions.

Therefore we arrive at the Region's "all other loans" category in the three target years by dividing the sum of the Region's projected commercial, real estate, and securities loans by 0.95. The results, in millions of 1955 dollars:

1965	$22,651
1975	33,388
1985	49,403

Investments

As long as other sections of the country grow more rapidly than the Region, funds will probably continue to move outward. Inasmuch as our projections assume that the Region will hold its share of national loans substantially intact, a further long-run decline in the Region's share of bank investments is likely to occur. Accordingly, we have assumed that the Region's share, which was 14.7 per cent in 1956, will drop to 14.0 per cent by 1965, to 13.0 per cent by 1975, and to 12.0 per cent by 1985, representing contractions somewhat milder than in the past. No more rapid shrinkage is foreseen because elimination of the differential reserve requirement for the big New York City banks probably will ease the pressure on them to sell securities to meet the demand for their services. Moreover, as investments become a smaller portion of the total assets of the Region's banks, they will become more reluctant to liquidate their holdings of securities.

Based on these assumptions, figures for 1956 and the forecasts of the Region's investments for the three target years are as follows (in 1955 millions):

1956	$10,655
1965	12,874
1975	16,482
1985	20,946

Trust Income

The nation's banks outside New York City will continue to obtain their share of the estate and personal trust business of the sort that requires intimate relationships; the growth of the Regional banks outside the City will help sustain the share of the Region in these trust areas; and the New York City institutions will retain their outstanding position in the more impersonal trust activities, although some loss may occur to other banks as the latter grow in absolute size. On those assumptions, it is estimated that by 1965, 1975, and 1985 the New York Metropolitan Region's share of trust income will drop very modestly from 34.8 per cent in 1956 to 33.0, 32.0, and 31.0 per cent of the national total, respectively. These ratios, applied to the national projections made previously, give the following trust income figures for the Region (in millions of 1955 dollars), as compared with the 1956 figure of $109:

1965	$153
1975	245
1985	392

Deposits

Pulling together our forecasts, we obtain the projections in Table B-7, which shows the Region's total earning assets, broken down into loans and investments. The 1956 figures are given for comparison.

For the Region, the ratio of deposits to earning assets has tended to be somewhat higher than for the country as a whole. We assume that the ratios for the different parts of the Region will be about the same as those for 1956, except in New York City. Here, we as-

Table B-7 Forecasts of Earning Assets of Region's Banks

(in millions of 1955 dollars)

	Total earning assets	Loans	Investments
1956	29,694	19,039	10,655
1965	38,734	25,860	12,874
1975	55,221	38,739	16,482
1985	79,232	58,286	20,946

sume that the ratio will drop to the national level because of the elimination of the differential reserve requirement for the large New York City banks which will result from 1959 legislation. Following, in millions of 1955 dollars, are the 1956 amount of deposits at the Region's banks and our deposit forecasts for the three target years:

1956	$37,130
1965	47,100
1975	67,249
1985	96,569

This would mean that the Region's share of the country's total deposits would be 17.9, 17.2, and 16.6 per cent in 1965, 1975, and 1985, compared with 19.4 per cent in 1956.

Thus, according to these estimates, the Region's share of national deposits will continue downward, though the rate of descent will be somewhat slower than in the postwar period. Because much of this relative contraction will undoubtedly be due to the more rapid economic expansion of other areas of the country, the Region's banks are likely to be faced with liquidity problems in meeting the demand for loans, a large proportion of which go to borrowers outside the Region.

Collectively, however, it seems probable that the banks of the Region will be able to resolve their liquidity needs without stripping their investment accounts. In view of the disparate economic character of the different geographic sections of the Region, though, it is entirely possible that the New York City banks may have a long-term stringency of funds while the suburban institutions are in a more comfortable position.

Employment

Our procedure for converting the activity forecasts to manpower needs in the Region is similar to that used for the nation. We project the Region's employment by multiplying the activity measure by the national 1955 unit manpower requirements; we adjust the result for the expected "productivity" improvement of 3 per cent per year (the same as for the nation); and then we raise the figure by 8 per cent (not 10 per cent as for the nation) to account for employment activities which are not included in our indicators of output.* Finally we make the same adjustment as we have done for the nation's banks to take into account their entry into new areas of activity. To do this we assume that one-fourth of the initially projected expansion of miscellaneous financial institutions will be taken up by commerical banks.

Our projections, adjusted for "productivity" and coverage of all present activities, but not for the banks' expansion into new fields, would be 83,800 for 1965, 96,900 for 1975, and 112,700 for 1985. (The actual employment in 1956 was 82,300.)

After the final adjustment is made, our projections of commercial banking manpower in the Region come to:

1965	87,500
1975	106,100
1985	130,100

Upon these assumptions, the Region's banks would have slightly greater employment in 1965 than they did in 1956. As in the case of the national picture, increase in service output would be largely balanced by enhanced productivity. Thereafter, as they extended their activities, employment would mount, but at a somewhat slower rate than for the country as a whole. As a result, their percentage of the national banking employment would decline somewhat, from 15.4 per cent in 1956 to 13.7 per cent in 1985.

* Application of our unit manpower coefficients to the activities covered by our analyses indicates that these activities may have accounted for approximately 92 per cent of employment of the banks in the Region, compared with about 90 per cent at the nation's banks. The higher coverage indicated in the Region, despite the large amount of international business done there, may be due to the fact that the unit manpower coefficients, which were calculated on a national basis, somewhat overstate manpower requirements in the Region. It is likely that the size of the Region's banks, which allows bigger transactions, permits certain economies that would justify somewhat lower unit manpower coefficients.

✓ Commercial banking—intraregion

Banking Activity

We now narrow our perspective further to consider the expected shifts in banking functions, manpower, and floor space within the 22-county Region. Our estimates are based on the following assumptions:

Consumer loans will be distributed among the different parts of the Region in the same proportions as jobs of all kinds.*

New York City will remain dominant in commercial loans of the Region. Projecting the historical rate of decline, the City will have 92, 90, and 88 per cent of the Region's commercial loans in 1965, 1975, and 1985, and the remainder will be distributed among the other parts of the Region in accordance with past patterns and trends.

Distribution of real estate loans is perhaps most difficult of all to forecasts. Like investments, mortgages seem a relatively passive component of bank holdings. Consequently, we assume the same distribution for all our target dates. The City's share will be 29 per cent (somewhat less than in 1956), Essex and Hudson banks will hold 14 per cent, other New Jersey counties 24, Nassau and Suffolk 15, and the remainder of the Region 18 per cent.

In each of the three target years, New York City will have 92 per cent of securities loans and the other four parts of the Region 2 per cent each.

The rest of the loans have been highly concentrated in the City. We expect them to remain so, with 92 per cent in the City and the remainder equally divided among other parts of the Region.

The past shifts in the relative distribution of investments are expected to continue, although at a somewhat more moderate rate. The past and projected distribution of investments is summarized in Table B-8.

* For the distribution of total employment in the Region we had to rely on preliminary forecasts which may differ from the final projections of the New York Metropolitan Region Study.

Table B-8 Actual and Projected Percentage Distribution of Commercial Bank Investments, by Parts of Region

	1947	1956	1965	1975	1985
Entire Region	100	100	100	100	100
New York City	83	73	67	62	58
Essex and Hudson Counties	6	8	9	9	9
Other New Jersey counties	6	9	12	14	16
Nassau and Suffolk Counties	2	4	6	8	10
Remainder of Region	3	5	6	7	7

We assume that the trust income will remain concentrated in New York City, with 92 per cent there. The remainder—for lack of data—is assumed to be distributed equally among the other parts of the Region.

Our forecast of banking output is summarized in Table B-9, along with figures for 1956.

Deposits

As mentioned previously, we assume that in each part of the Region except New York City, total deposits of commercial banks (the sum of demand deposits and time deposits) will remain in the same proportion to earning assets as in 1956; in New York City we assume that the proportion of total deposits to earning assets will drop somewhat to the national level because of the elimination of the differential applicable to the reserve requirements of the big New York City banks. Table B-10 shows the distribution of deposits within the Region based upon these assumptions.

Employment

Our employment picture, by parts of the Region, was derived in the same way as for the Region at large: first, by projecting on the basis of the 1955 unit manpower requirements; then, by adjusting for the expected "productivity" improvements, and next, by raising the result by 8 per cent to account for the activities not covered

Table B-9 Actual and Projected Indicators of Banking Output, by Parts of Region

(in millions of 1955 dollars)

		Consumer loans	All other loans	Investments	Trust income
Entire Region	1956	2,480	16,559	10,655	109
	1965	3,209	22,651	12,874	153
	1975	5,351	33,388	16,482	245
	1985	8,883	49,403	20,946	392
New York City	1956	1,593	14,263	7,805	102
	1965	1,785	18,772	8,626	141
	1975	2,729	27,032	10,219	225
	1985	4,174	39,036	12,149	360
Essex and Hudson Counties	1956	225	596	800	2
	1965	295	847	1,159	3
	1975	476	1,506	1,483	5
	1985	791	2,288	1,885	8
Other New Jersey counties	1956	256	670	1,000	2
	1965	497	1,174	1,545	3
	1975	985	2,022	2,307	5
	1985	1,812	3,099	3,351	8
Nassau and Suffolk Counties	1956	209	514	475	2
	1965	276	880	772	3
	1975	514	1,336	1,319	5
	1985	942	2,369	2,095	8
Remainder of Region	1956	197	516	575	2
	1965	356	978	772	3
	1975	647	1,492	1,154	5
	1985	1,164	2,611	1,466	8

before; and finally, by adding in one-fourth of the originally projected employment growth of the miscellaneous financial institutions. The employment forecast is shown in Table B-11, along with the figures for 1956.

Table B-10 Actual and Projected Commercial Bank Deposits, by Parts of Region

(in millions of 1955 dollars)

	1956	1965	1975	1985
Entire Region	37,130	47,100	67,249	96,569
New York City	29,501	35,020	47,976	66,431
Essex and Hudson Counties	2,023	2,876	4,331	6,205
Other New Jersey counties	2,549	4,245	7,014	10,906
Nassau and Suffolk Counties	1,357	2,179	3,581	6,109
Remainder of Region	1,700	2,780	4,347	6,918

Table B-11 Actual and Projected Commercial Bank Employment, by Parts of Region

	1956	1965	1975	1985
Entire Region	82,327	87,523	106,121	130,046
New York City	60,564	59,920	68,010	78,389
Essex and Hudson Counties	5,040	6,029	7,454	9,058
Other New Jersey counties	6,886	9,521	13,887	19,271
Nassau and Suffolk Counties	4,391	5,440	7,736	11,016
Remainder of Region	5,446	6,613	9,034	12,312

We have seen in Chapter 5 that the following distribution of banking employment, based on data of 13 reporting banks, existed in 1956 within New York City:

Below Chambers Street	74%
Chambers to 60th Street	13
Rest of New York City	13

However, we know that some redistribution is imminent. First National City Bank will soon move several thousand employees to the midtown area. Assuming some further moves along these lines, we allow for a transfer of 12,000 persons from downtown to midtown by 1965. This alters our proportions accordingly; and in the absence of any knowledge of events after 1965, we assume that that same proportionate distribution will prevail in 1975 and 1985 as in 1965. The forecast appears in Table B-12.

Table B-12 Actual and Projected Commercial Bank Employment, by Parts of New York City

	1956	1965	1975	1985
Below Chambers Street	44,817	32,340	36,726	42,330
Chambers to 60th Street	7,873	19,790	22,443	25,868
Rest of New York City	7,873	7,790	8,841	10,191
Total	60,563	59,920	68,010	78,389

Floor space

We have estimated, on the basis of a questionnaire survey, that in 1956 the average gross floor space per man in the Region's commercial banks has been 175 square feet. We assume that this ratio will increase somewhat in the future. The reasons for the expected rise are that more equipment will be used per man and that, as the skills of personnel increase, more space will be allotted per man, quite apart from equipment needs. We have found that over the period 1947–1956 the floor space-per-man ratios in New York City's banks have increased on the average by about 5 per cent. In the future we anticipate a somewhat greater gain in the floor space ratio, as major building programs are completed. By 1985, this increase should be 30 per cent over 1956. We interpolate the rise evenly for the intervening period, and obtain the following ratios of square feet per man:

1965	192
1975	210
1985	228

On the basis of our forecast of employment and the above ratios, we obtain the forecast of floor space occupied by commercial banks in the New York Metropolitan Region, as shown in Table B-13.

Table B-13 Actual and Projected Gross Floor-Space Use by Commercial Banks, by Parts of Region

(in thousands of square feet)

	1956	1965	1975	1985
Entire Region	14,407	16,805	22,285	29,651
New York City	10,599	11,505	14,282	17,873
Below Chambers Street	7,843	6,209	7,712	9,651
Chambers to 60th Street	1,378	3,800	4,713	5,898
Rest of New York City	1,378	1,496	1,857	2,324
Essex and Hudson Counties	882	1,158	1,565	2,065
Other New Jersey counties	1,205	1,828	2,916	4,394
Nassau and Suffolk Counties	768	1,044	1,625	2,512
Remainder of Region	953	1,270	1,897	2,807

II. LIFE AND HEALTH INSURANCE

We now shift our attention to the future of the life and health industry, starting with a forecast of the national picture and then moving to the Region.

LIFE AND HEALTH—THE NATION

Life Insurance Premiums

The amount of money that people devote to life insurance, it is assumed, is determined primarily by income. Premiums received by the life insurance carriers—other than accident and health premiums—constituted slightly over 4 per cent of disposable personal income in 1929 and slightly less than 4 per cent in the mid-1950's. During periods of depression and war, the ratio of life premiums to income varied considerably, but these were unusual times and are excluded from our projection base.

We assume that the factors (discussed in Chapter 6 in the text) that caused a relatively stable ratio between income and premiums will continue to govern in the future. We therefore estimate that in all our target years, the ratio of life and annuity premiums to disposable personal income will amount to 4 per cent, resulting in the following volume of premium payments (other than accident and health), expressed in millions of 1955 dollars. The figures may be compared with $10,959 million in 1956:

1965	$16,430
1975	24,083
1985	35,432

Accident and Health Insurance Premiums

Over the ten years 1946 to 1956, the volume of accident and health premiums grew by 377 per cent. Though there has been no evidence of a retardation in this rate of expansion as yet, we assume that a ceiling exists on the level that premium payments may be expected to attain, equivalent to the amount of private expenditure on medical care. We estimate that this ceiling will amount to 6.0 per cent of disposable personal income.* Applying this ratio to the future estimates of personal income, we obtain projected ceilings in 1955 dollars of $24,646 million in 1965, $36,125 million in 1975, and $53,148 million in 1985. By extrapolating the past rate of growth, we estimate the volume of accident and health premiums in 1965 at $18,302 million, which is still within the ceiling. For the two successive dates, however, the past rate cannot be extrapolated and the ceiling amounts apply, that is, $36,125 and $53,148 million.

Employment

We saw in Chapter 6 that the changing volume of life insurance premiums accounted for most of the changes in employment in this field. The ratio of premiums to personnel varied within fairly

* As we have seen in Chapter 6, from 1929 until about 1953, medical-care expenditure constituted an almost constant proportion of disposable personal income, which, except in war and depression, has varied between 3.5 and 4.1 per cent. Subsequently this ratio increased and reached 4.9 per cent in 1957. We have attributed this rise to the increased insurance coverage, to the changing age patterns of the population, and to higher income levels. Because these factors are expected to continue to operate in the future, we assume that medical-care expenditure will continue to grow faster than income and will reach 6.0 per cent of disposable personal income in our target dates.

narrow limits, in response to such factors as shifts in productivity, the relationship between new sales and insurance in force, and the relative importance of group and individual insurance.

We assume that in the future the ratio of premiums per man in life insurance will be increasing at a rate of 2 per cent a year, which amounts to about 22 per cent in ten years. The bulk of this increase will come from prospective improvements in productivity, but also from shifts in the relative importance of group insurance and in the ratio of new sales to insurance in force.

In 1955, $27,500 in life insurance premiums was paid per employee in the life field.* Assuming a 2 per cent increase per annum, the ratio will rise to $33,500 in 1965, $40,000 in 1975, and $49,800 in 1985.

In accident and health insurance, premiums per man have been rising very rapidly with the swift growth of the industry. Between 1946 and 1956, while the volume of premiums grew by 377 per cent, employment ** increased by only 88 per cent, because premiums per man increased by 155 per cent. We assume that between 1955 and 1965, premiums per man will rise by an additional 155 per cent, while the rapid growth of the industry continues. After 1965, when the industry probably will expand at a more moderate pace, this ratio is expected to grow at 3 per cent per year between 1965 and 1975, and at 2 per cent per year over the last decade. As a result, premiums per man are expected to rise to $92,100 in 1965, $123,800 in 1975, and $150,900 in 1985.

* In this context we select 1955 as our base year. As was pointed out in Chapter 6, employment in the life field equals employment by the life insurance carriers, excluding their employment in the accident and health business, but including 27 per cent of employment by the independent agents and brokers.

** As noted in the text, employment in the accident and health field consists of two parts: employment by the accident and health carriers and that associated with the accident and health activities of the life insurance companies. Employment in the accident and health business of life insurance companies was estimated from their accident and health premiums, by assuming that in each year premiums per man applicable to that business were the same as the comparable ratio for the accident and health carriers.

Employment in the life and accident and health industry was 504 thousand in 1956. Our estimates for the future, based upon the projections of premiums and premiums per man, are given in Table B-14.

Table B-14 Forecasts of United States Life and Accident and Health Insurance Employment

	Total	Life	Accident and health
1965	689,000	490,000	199,000
1975	881,000	589,000	292,000
1985	1,064,000	711,000	352,000

Employment by Type of Activity

We have seen in Chapter 6 that different locational forces have operated in the case of three major components of the life and health insurance industry: life insurance home offices, life insurance field activities, and accident and health carriers. In order to facilitate our forecast for the Region, we now translate our industry data into projections along these functional lines.

According to our estimates of the premium receipts generated by accident and health policies, the proportion going to life insurance carriers was 66 per cent in 1947, 61 per cent in 1950, and 61 per cent in 1956. We assume that the share of accident and health premiums collected by life carriers will remain stable, at 61 per cent.

In 1956, the home-office employment of life insurance carriers constituted 29.7 per cent of the entire life and health industry, excluding employees of the accident and health carriers. We foresee that the same ratio will apply in the future because of the expected offsetting forces that will be in operation. In the absence of more precise criteria, we assume that these forces will balance out.

We expect some centralization of routine functions in the home offices and a relatively slower growth of work in the field, as the ratios of sales to in-force business decline somewhat from their postwar highs. These two factors would contribute to a relatively slower expansion of the field force relative to home-office personnel. On the other hand, there probably will be some further delegation of responsibilities to the local field offices, and the productivity of field work, especially in selling, is expected to grow more slowly than in the centralized routine operations conducted at the home office.

Following these assumptions our forecasts of employment along functional lines develop as shown in Table B-15. The actual 1956 figures are given for comparison.

Table B-15 Forecasts of United States Life and Accident and Health Insurance Employment, by Functions

	Total	Life insurance, home offices	Life insurance, field activities	Accident and health carriers
1956	504,000	137,000	324,000	43,000
1965	689,000	181,000	430,000	78,000
1975	881,000	228,000	539,000	114,000
1985	1,064,000	275,000	651,000	137,000

Life and health—the region

We have seen that in the past the growth of the Region's home offices was slower than that of home offices in the nation at large. This lag was traced largely to the relatively sluggish expansion of the volume of business done by the Region's companies, and is expected to continue in the future. For the nation, as shown in the preceding section, we have projected a growth of home-office employment of 32, 26, and 21 per cent, respectively, during the 1956–1965, 1965–1975, and 1975–1985 periods. Allowing for the slower rise of the Region, increases of 16, 7, and 6 per cent are projected.

In the future, it is expected that the Region will have the same proportion of life insurance field employees and of accident and health carriers' employees as it will have of the personal income of the nation. This has been the case in the past, and we see no reason to expect a significant departure from the pattern in the future. Accordingly, the Region's share is expected to be 11.8, 11.5, and 11.3 per cent in 1965, 1975, and 1985.

Given these assumptions, we obtain the forecasts of the Region employment in life and accident and health insurance which appear in Table B-16.

Table B-16 Forecasts of Region's Life and Accident and Health Insurance Employment

	Total	Life insurance, home offices	Life insurance, field activities	Accident and health carriers
1956	83,200	42,900	35,000	5,300
1965	109,600	49,800	50,700	9,100
1975	128,400	53,300	62,000	13,100
1985	145,600	56,500	73,600	15,500

LIFE AND HEALTH—INTRAREGION

Our forecasts of employment by major parts of the New York Metropolitan Region are given in Table B-17 (along with our estimates for 1956), and are discussed briefly in the following paragraphs.

Home Offices

In Chapter 6, we have concluded that the big cities offer definite locational advantages for the large home offices. These advantages will continue to exert their influence, and there is little apparent reason to think that the large companies presently located in Manhattan and Newark will relocate within our forecast period. Smaller companies would find it easier to undertake a move to the suburbs, but even in the case of these organizations, there have been few signs of such a tendency. On the contrary, many of the Region's companies, both large and small, have indicated an intention to remain in their cities by acquisition or renovation of office space or by developing plans for such an investment.

Recognizing the possible margin of error contingent on the fu-

Table B-17 Actual and Projected Employment in Life and Accident and Health Insurance, by Parts of Region

	Total	Life insurance, home offices	Life insurance, field activities	Accident and health carriers
1956				
Entire Region	83,200	42,900	35,000	5,300
New York City	60,300	32,500	23,300	4,500
Essex and Hudson Counties	15,400	10,400	4,200	800
Other New Jersey counties	3,400	—	3,400	—
Nassau and Suffolk Counties	1,500	—	1,500	[a]
Remainder of Region	2,600	—	2,600	[a]
1965				
Entire Region	109,600	49,800	50,700	9,100
New York City	73,500	37,800	28,200	7,500
Essex and Hudson Counties	18,100	12,000	4,700	1,400
Other New Jersey counties	7,800	—	7,800	—
Nassau and Suffolk Counties	4,500	—	4,400	100
Remainder of Region	5,700	—	5,600	100
1975				
Entire Region	128,400	53,300	62,000	13,100
New York City	83,000	40,500	31,600	10,900
Essex and Hudson Counties	20,300	12,800	5,500	2,000
Other New Jersey counties	11,400	—	11,400	—
Nassau and Suffolk Counties	6,100	—	6,000	100
Remainder of Region	7,600	—	7,500	100
1985				
Entire Region	145,600	56,500	73,600	15,500
New York City	90,300	42,900	34,600	12,800
Essex and Hudson Counties	22,500	13,600	6,600	2,300
Other New Jersey counties	15,000	—	15,000	—
Nassau and Suffolk Counties	8,000	—	7,800	200
Remainder of Region	9,800	—	9,600	200

[a] Less than 50.

ture decisions of the smaller companies, we project the distribution of home-office employment within the Region in the same proportions as prevailed in 1956.

According to our estimates for 1956, New York City accounted for 76 per cent of the Region's home-office employment by the life insurance carriers, and Essex County for the remaining 24 per cent. It is believed that this pattern will continue in the future.

Field Activities

We expect that field employment will be distributed among the different parts of the Region in the same manner as the Region's total employment of all kinds. This amounts to assuming that field employment will follow the distribution of general economic activity. This forecast is in agreement with past experience; it takes into account the highly local nature of business performed in the field offices.

Accident and Health Carriers

We assume that the location of accident and health carriers will continue to be governed by proximity to businesses, which are their principal clients for insurance plans, and to a lesser degree by the availability of help and the need to be near hospitals. Because we foresee no significant departure from the present form of home-office operations, we expect that in the future the distribution of employment by the accident and health carriers within the Region will be the same as in 1956, that is, 83 per cent in New York City, 15 per cent in Essex and Hudson Counties, 1 per cent in Nassau and Suffolk Counties, 1 per cent in the remaining New York counties and Fairfield.

Floor Space Utilization

On the basis of a questionnaire survey, we have found that the ratio of gross floor space per man in the Region's home offices was about 188 square feet in 1956. In the field, the ratio has been only about 60 per cent of that prevailing in the home offices or 113 square feet, probably because of the large proportion of selling personnel who do not require much office space. Between 1947 and 1956, increases in the floor-space ratio averaged about 10 per cent.

Projecting the past experience, we assume that by 1985 the floor-space ratios will rise 30 per cent over 1956, and that this increase will be equally spaced over the intervening dates. This gives us the following forecasts of square feet of floor space per man in 1965, 1975, and 1985:

For life home offices and accident and health carriers, 207, 225, and 244.

For life insurance field activities, 124, 136, and 147.

Applying these ratios to the employment data, we obtain the floor-space forecasts which are shown in Table B-18, together with the estimates for 1956.

Table B-18 Actual and Projected Gross Floor-Space Use by Life and Accident and Health Insurance Industry, by Parts of Region

(in thousands of square feet)

	1956	1965	1975	1985
Entire Region	13,025	18,480	23,372	28,387
New York City	9,596	12,874	15,862	18,677
Essex and Hudson Counties	2,582	3,357	4,078	4,849
Other New Jersey counties	384	967	1,550	2,205
Nassau and Suffolk Counties	169	567	839	1,196
Remainder of Region	294	715	1,043	1,460

III. PROPERTY INSURANCE

THE NATION

We have observed in Chapter 7 that the volume of business done by the property insurance companies, as represented by the volume of premiums received, was related to the general level of economic activity. However, each of the main divisions of the line of business —automobile, fire and related lines, and miscellaneous insurance—

moves differently with the changes of the gross national product. Table B-19 summarizes these historical relations as well as our projections into the future.

We forecast further increases in the ratio of automobile premiums to gross national product, because we assume that ownership of automobiles will continue to rise faster than income, but at a slower rate than in the postwar years 1947 to 1956. Premiums in fire insurance and related lines make up a constant fraction of the gross national product, and this relation is expected to remain unchanged. Other insurance premiums increased slightly relative to the gross national product in the postwar period. We project a further increase in this ratio because this group will probably be affected by the innovations that will be developed in the property insurance field. By adding these ratios and applying them to the levels of the gross national product estimates for the target years, we developed our forecasts of the volume of business expected to be done by the property insurance companies. To this total, we then apply the premiums-per-employee ratios to obtain our employment projections.

Table B-19 Past and Projected U. S. Property Insurance Premiums as Percentage of Gross National Product

	All property insurance	Auto	Fire and related	Miscellaneous
1940	2.3	0.7	0.8	0.8
1947	2.3	0.7	0.8	0.8
1956	2.7	1.0	0.8	0.9
1965	2.9	1.1	0.8	1.0
1975	3.1	1.2	0.8	1.1
1985	3.3	1.3	0.8	1.2

Premiums per man in 1955 dollars increased from 16.6 thousand in 1940 to 17.5 thousand in 1947 and 21.1 thousand in 1955. Over the 1947–1955 period the increase in this ratio has been 21 per cent, or about 2.5 per cent a year. We assume that in the future, premiums per man will grow at 3 per cent a year. The acceleration in this rate of growth will come about as a result of increased utilization of technological innovations, mainly of electronic machines. The long-term rate of 3 per cent is higher than the rate projected for the life insurance industry, where premiums per man were expected to grow at 2 per cent. In the accident and health field, it will

Table B-20 Past and Projected U. S. Property Insurance Premiums and Employment

(premiums are in 1955 dollars)

	Total premiums (millions)	Premiums per man	Employment
1940	4,689	16,600	283,000
1947	6,280	17,500	358,000
1955	10,591	21,100	503,000
1956	10,801	20,700	523,000
1965	17,389	28,400	612,000
1975	27,246	38,200	713,000
1985	42,672	51,300	832,000

be remembered, a higher growth rate was projected until the industry reached maturity. The projected discrepancy in growth of premiums per man between property insurance and the life segment alone is consistent with experience.

The industrywide forecasts of premiums, premiums per man, and employment are shown in Table B-20, along with figures for 1940, 1947, 1955, and 1956.

THE REGION

The Region's share in the total employment of the property insurance industry has fallen from 17.0 per cent in 1947 to 13.9 per cent in 1956, probably in consequence of relative declines in both home-office and field-office activities. We expect that the same forces which occasioned this drop will continue in the future. It is unlikely, however, that the Region's share in property insurance employment will shrink below its share of the country's general economic activity, which has been projected at 11.8, 11.5, and 11.3 per cent, in 1965, 1975, and 1985, respectively. More likely it will remain above these minimum levels, and as the floor is approached, smaller relative declines are to be expected. Consequently, for the three forecast periods, we assume that the Region's share will recede by 0.6, 0.4, and 0.2 percentage points, and therefore will be 13.3 per cent in 1965, 12.9 in 1975, and 12.7 in 1985. This gives us the following property insurance employment picture for the Region in our three target years, as compared with 72,000 in 1956:

1965	81,400
1975	92,000
1985	105,700

Within the Region

We have seen that in the postwar years the suburban sections of the Region increased their shares of employment in property insurance at the expense of New York City. We assume that a further shift of employment toward the suburbs will occur. New York City is expected to retain most of its home-office employment, however, and the redistribution will affect mainly the field component of the industry. In Table B-21, we show the past and expected percentage distribution of employment in property insurance, by parts of the Region, based mainly on our projection of economic activity

Table B-21 Past and Projected Percentage Distribution of Property Insurance Employment, by Parts of Region

	1947	1956	1965	1975	1985
Entire Region	100.0	100.0	100.0	100.0	100.0
New York City	82.5	74.6	68.0	63.0	58.0
Essex and Hudson Counties	11.8	12.6	13.0	12.0	12.0
Other New Jersey counties	2.1	5.3	8.0	10.0	12.0
Nassau and Suffolk Counties	1.1	2.1	4.0	6.0	8.0
Remainder of Region	2.5	5.4	7.0	9.0	10.0

and on the assumption that the home-office employment will not relocate to any substantial degree.

This forecast of percentages applied to the projected totals for the Region yields the forecast of employment, by parts of the Region, as shown in Table B-22.

Table B-22 Past and Projected Property Insurance Employment, by Parts of Region

	1947	1956	1965	1975	1985
Entire Region	60,700	72,600	81,400	92,000	105,700
New York City	50,100	54,200	55,300	58,000	61,300
Essex and Hudson Counties	7,100	9,100	10,600	11,000	12,700
Other New Jersey counties	1,300	3,800	6,500	9,200	12,700
Nassau and Suffolk Counties	700	1,600	3,300	5,500	8,400
Remainder of Region	1,500	3,900	5,700	8,300	10,600

From information collected by questionnaire, we learned that in the New York Metropolitan Region, the ratio of gross floor space per man was about 140 square feet in the home offices and about 90 square feet in the field in 1956. Allowing for the fact that the home offices are concentrated in the central city areas, we concluded that, for property insurance in general, the floor space-per-man ratio was 120 square feet in New York City and in Essex and Hudson Counties, while it was 90 square feet per man in other parts of the Region. As in the case of the other industries, and for similar reasons, we expect that these ratios will rise in the future. We assume a 30 per cent increase by 1985, equally spaced over the intervening dates. This gives us the following floor space per employee, in square feet, for 1965, 1975, and 1985:

For New York City and Essex and Hudson Counties, 132, 144, and 156.

For other areas of the Region, 99, 108, and 117.

Applying these figures to our manpower projections, we obtained 1956 and expected future floor-space needs as shown in Table B-23.

Table B-23 Actual and Projected Gross Floor-Space Use by Property Insurance Industry, by Parts of Region

(in thousands of square feet)

	1956	1965	1975	1985
Entire Region	8,433	10,234	12,420	15,253
New York City	6,504	7,300	8,352	9,563
Essex and Hudson Counties	1,092	1,399	1,584	1,981
Other New Jersey counties	342	644	994	1,486
Nassau and Suffolk Counties	144	327	594	983
Remainder of Region	351	564	896	1,240

IV. THE SECURITIES INDUSTRY

THE NATION

From its peak level in 1929, employment in the securities industry declined by about two-thirds over the next 14 years. Despite a substantial increase thereafter, by 1956 it was still at about 60 per cent of its former high. Various factors accounted for these fluctuations, including the volume of securities outstanding and their rate of turnover. Over the same time, increases in productivity probably tended to diminish the number of persons required by the industry.

In the future, as the nation's economy expands, new securities will be offered and the growth in the volume outstanding will tend to increase activity and raise manpower requirements. Also, increases in incomes will stimulate demand for securities, thereby spreading purchases over wider segments of the population; and this again will have a positive effect on activity and employment.

As a result of these factors, we assume that employment in the securities industry will grow at a slightly more rapid rate than general economic activity. This relation could be upset seriously if massive development of the consumer or "retail" business occurred—something comparable to the recent entry of commercial banks into the consumer field. Although such a major entry seems unlikely, some further development of the "retail" market is probable. The rapid growth of branch offices is an indication of the industry's interest in broadening its market. It therefore seems reasonable to assume that a "diversification" of services will occur which will tend to raise the annual rate of employment growth above that of the economy. We assume that this increment will be 1.5 per cent annually.

Since the gross national product in the future is assessed to advance at a rate of about 4.0 per cent per year, the gross projected rate of growth of employment in the securities industry is placed at about 5.5 per cent. On the other hand, it is unlikely that the rate of securities turnover will increase; turnover is more likely to remain stable or even decline as the participation of investment-type buying increases. Thus, the effect of the turnover rate on employment will be either neutral or depressing. Productivity gains will also tend to lower the manpower required to handle a given volume of business.

To take these influences into account, we subtract an expected 3 per cent annual improvement in productivity from the 5.5 per cent rate indicated above, which leaves 2.5 per cent as the rate of employment growth adjusted for productivity. A slight modification is also made for a possible further decline in the turnover rate. This is done by assuming that the industry's employment will grow by 25 per cent in a ten-year period; that is, the procedure is a simple addition of the 2.5 per cent rate of improvement rather than a compounding effect, as was done in other instances. Here is the 1956 employment in the nation's securities industry, followed by our projections:

1956	119,800
1965	140,600
1975	175,800
1985	219,800

THE REGION

We have noted that despite a tendency for a relatively greater demand for securities to emanate from outside New York, reflected in a wider dispersal of branch offices, the Region's share of total employment has increased from 29.1 per cent in 1947 to 31.8 per cent in 1956. We ascribed this internal growth to the importance of headquarters activities, where New York's position has been unchallenged. In view of our general expectations that the New York money market will continue dominant in the face of more rapid economic expansion elsewhere, we foresee no essential change in the securities industry from the conditions that we have described. We assume, therefore, that in all our benchmark dates, the Region will absorb 31 per cent of the industry's national employment.* Here is the 1956 securities industry employment in the Region, followed by our three forecasts:

1956	38,100
1965	43,600
1975	54,500
1985	68,100

Within the region

We have seen that even though the securities firms established a large number of branches in the suburbs, the effect on the distribution of employment was minor, because of the small amount of manpower absorbed by sales compared with headquarters activities. For this reason, the relative position of New York City within the Region has remained unimpaired. Accordingly, we project only slight changes in the location of employment within the Region. Table B-24 shows the distribution of manpower in percentage terms, and Table B-25, the distribution of manpower in absolute amounts.

We do not have direct data on floor space per man utilized in the securities industry. We assume, however, that this ratio has been and will be the same as in the home offices of the property

* Productivity may be expected to increase faster in the home offices than in the branches, and the number of branches will grow faster than the number of home offices. This will be compensated by increased centralization of functions in the home offices, associated with technological change. There is no compelling need to assume a change in the Region's share in either direction.

Table B-24 Past and Projected Percentage Distribution of Securities Employment, by Parts of Region

	1947	1956	1965	1975	1985
Entire Region	100.0	100.0	100.0	100.0	100.0
New York City	98.6	97.8	97.2	96.6	95.9
Essex and Hudson Counties	0.8	1.3	1.5	1.7	2.0
Other New Jersey counties	0.2	0.3	0.5	0.7	0.9
Nassau and Suffolk Counties	—	0.2	0.3	0.4	0.5
Remainder of Region	0.4	0.4	0.5	0.6	0.7

Table B-25 Actual and Projected Securities Employment, by Parts of Region

	1956	1965	1975	1985
Entire Region	38,100	43,600	54,500	68,100
New York City	37,300	42,400	52,700	65,300
Essex and Hudson Counties	500	700	900	1,400
Other New Jersey counties	100	200	400	600
Nassau and Suffolk Counties	100	100	200	300
Remainder of Region	100	200	300	500

insurance companies. A spot check at some brokerage firms in lower Manhattan supports this conclusion. Consequently, on a gross basis, the floor space per man in the securities industry is estimated at 140 square feet in 1956. A projection is made in the same fashion as for other financial industries: a 30 per cent increase by 1985, spaced equally over the three projection periods. Here are the projections of floor space per man, in square feet:

1965	154
1975	168
1985	182

Applying these ratios to the employment data, we obtain floor-space use by the industry as shown in Table B-26.

Table B-26 Actual and Projected Gross Floor-Space Use by Securities Industry, by Parts of Region

(in thousands of square feet)

	1956	1965	1975	1985
Entire Region	5,334	6,715	9,156	12,394
New York City	5,222	6,530	8,854	11,884
Essex and Hudson Counties	70	108	151	255
Other New Jersey counties	14	31	67	109
Nassau and Suffolk Counties	14	15	34	55
Remainder of Region	14	31	50	91

V. MISCELLANEOUS FINANCIAL INSTITUTIONS

THE NATION

Between 1947 and 1956 the employment in the country's miscellaneous financial industries increased by 78 per cent. In the future we assume continued rapid growth of these institutions as the demand for their services mounts. This group of industries contains some types of institutions that have very rapid growth experience and potential. Moreover, new types of enterprises that may emerge in the future will, by definition, be placed in this group. However, we assume that the postwar rate of increase will not be duplicated, because there will be no backlog of demand such as existed after the war, and because we anticipate some acceleration of productivity advance.

In these circumstances, we would expect that miscellaneous employment would grow by 55 per cent over the nine-year period 1956–1965, and by 60 per cent in each of the two successive decades. As discussed previously, we also expect that a portion of the creation of new financial activities hitherto appearing in this category will be shared with commercial banks.

Before this last adjustment is made, our employment forecasts run as follows, compared with the actual 1956 figure of 258,000:

1965	400,000
1975	640,000
1985	1,024,000

But after transferring 25 per cent of the increase over 1956 to the commercial banks, we arrive at our final forecasts of national employment in the miscellaneous group:

1965	364,000
1975	544,000
1985	832,000

THE REGION

Before taking into account the increasing competition of commercial banks in areas of innovation, we assume that the Region's employment in the miscellaneous credit institutions will grow by 50 per cent in each of our projection periods while the Region's employment in the miscellaneous noncredit institutions will rise by 10 per cent in each period. The projected discrepancy in the rates of growth reflects the postwar growth difference. For both groups, however, these growth rates are somewhat lower than the expansion experienced for the postwar period 1947 to 1956. The reasons for projecting slower over-all expansion rates than in the past are the same as for the nation at large. On these assumptions, we forecast the Region's employment in the miscellaneous category as shown in Table B-27. The "unadjusted total" is the forecast without al-

Table B-27 Forecasts of Region's Miscellaneous Financial Employment

	Credit institutions	Noncredit institutions	Unadjusted total	Adjusted total
1965	42,400	7,900	50,300	46,600
1975	63,600	8,700	72,300	63,100
1985	95,400	9,600	105,000	87,625

lowance for the expected invasion by the commercial banks into new fields that would otherwise be classed as "miscellaneous." For comparison, the 1956 employment was 35,500, of which 28,300 was in credit institutions and 7,200 in noncredit institutions.

Within the Region

For the future, it is expected that employment in the noncredit institutions will remain concentrated in New York City. We assume that 94 per cent of it will be in New York City, 2 per cent in each of the New Jersey components of the Region and 1 per cent in each of the other two areas.

The employment by the credit institutions in the past grew faster in the suburbs than in central city areas; and with respect to the rate of growth, the suburban areas ranked in about the same order as they did in general economic gains, as was shown in Chapter 7. Because the suburbs are expected to continue to grow more rapidly than the central cities, we expect a further redistribution of employment by the credit institutions into the suburbs. Our forecast

Table B-28 Projected Percentage Distribution of Employment in Miscellaneous Credit Industries, by Parts of Region

	1965	1975	1985
Entire Region	100	100	100
New York City	66	60	55
Essex and Hudson Counties	9	9	8
Other New Jersey counties	10	13	16
Nassau and Suffolk Counties	6	8	10
Remainder of Region	9	10	11

of the intraregional distribution of employment by the credit institutions is related to our forecast of the redistribution of employment in general. The projected distribution is shown in Table B-28.

The employment picture based upon these calculations is shown in Table B-29. The adjustment made in the last column is the same as performed in making the Region forecasts.

Table B-29 Actual and Projected Employment in Miscellaneous Financial Industries, by Parts of Region

	Credit institutions	Noncredit institutions	Unadjusted total	Adjusted total
1956				
Entire Region	28,300	7,200	35,500	—
New York City	21,400	6,900	28,300	—
Essex and Hudson Counties	2,500	100	2,600	—
Other New Jersey counties	1,300	100	1,400	—
Nassau and Suffolk Counties	1,100	100	1,200	—
Remainder of Region	2,000	—	2,000	—
1965				
Entire Region	42,400	7,900	50,300	46,600
New York City	28,100	7,300	35,400	33,625
Essex and Hudson Counties	3,800	200	4,000	3,650
Other New Jersey counties	4,200	200	4,400	3,650
Nassau and Suffolk Counties	2,500	100	2,600	2,250
Remainder of Region	3,800	100	3,900	3,425
1975				
Entire Region	63,600	8,700	72,300	63,100
New York City	38,100	8,100	46,200	41,725
Essex and Hudson Counties	5,700	200	5,900	5,075
Other New Jersey counties	8,300	200	8,500	6,725
Nassau and Suffolk Counties	5,100	100	5,200	4,200
Remainder of Region	6,400	100	6,500	5,375
1985				
Entire Region	95,400	9,600	105,000	87,625
New York City	52,500	9,000	61,500	53,200
Essex and Hudson Counties	7,600	200	7,800	6,500
Other New Jersey counties	15,300	200	15,500	11,975
Nassau and Suffolk Counties	9,500	100	9,600	7,500
Remainder of Region	10,500	100	10,600	8,450

As for the use of floor space, we do not have information on the floor space-per-man requirements in the miscellaneous financial industries. In order to provide an estimate of floor-space requirements, we assume that the same utilization of space will prevail among the miscellaneous industries as in the commercial banks, which we projected from 175 square feet per man in 1956 to 192, 210, and 228 in 1965, 1975, and 1985, respectively. When we multiply our employment figures by these ratios we obtain the picture of gross floor-space utilization by the miscellaneous financial industries in the different parts of the New York Metropolitan Region shown in Table B-30.

Table B-30 Actual and Projected Gross Floor-Space Use by Miscellaneous Financial Institutions, by Parts of Region

(in thousands of square feet)

	1956	1965	1975	1985
Entire Region	6,212	8,948	13,251	19,979
New York City	4,952	6,456	8,762	12,130
Essex and Hudson Counties	455	701	1,066	1,482
Other New Jersey counties	245	701	1,412	2,730
Nassau and Suffolk Counties	210	432	882	1,710
Remainder of Region	350	658	1,129	1,927

Appendix C

Summary Tables

This appendix contains summary tables which pull together our projections of employment and floor space in the financial industries and which give more historical data than elsewhere in this book, and more detailed source notes. Employment data cover the United States, the New York Metropolitan Region, and the parts of the Region. Floor-space estimates have been made only for the Region and its parts. Because of rounding, breakdown figures may not add exactly to totals in each case. For the same reason, slight discrepancies may exist between data in this appendix and those in other parts of the book.

Table C-1 Past and Projected Employment in Financial Industries, United States, 1929–1956, 1965, 1975, 1985

(in thousands)

	Total financial employment	Commercial banks	Life and accident and health insurance	Property insurance	Securities industry	Miscellaneous finance
1929 ..	1,262	328	242	291	206	195
1930 ..	1,227	319	252	294	170	192
1931 ..	1,158	294	257	279	149	179
1932 ..	1,096	265	259	267	137	168
1933 ..	1,052	239	261	244	150	158
1934 ..	1,051	242	264	248	141	156
1935 ..	1,050	236	268	261	128	157
1936 ..	1,078	240	272	264	144	158
1937 ..	1,101	249	282	269	141	160
1938 ..	1,084	249	293	275	120	147
1939 ..	1,095	254	307	283	111	140
1940 ..	1,116	261	317	284	105	149
1941 ..	1,135	276	326	285	92	156
1942 ..	1,116	280	321	283	78	154
1943 ..	1,066	289	302	270	72	133
1944 ..	1,048	294	292	262	72	128
1945 ..	1,083	314	293	277	75	124
1946 ..	1,246	344	340	331	95	136
1947 ..	1,312	360	361	358	88	145
1948 ..	1,377	370	384	381	88	154
1949 ..	1,409	377	395	395	85	157
1950 ..	1,467	394	408	416	89	160
1951 ..	1,534	420	418	432	95	169
1952 ..	1,606	446	429	451	97	183
1953 ..	1,689	468	451	474	98	198
1954 ..	1,753	481	467	480	100	225
1955 ..	1,848	506	485	503	113	241
1956 ..	1,941	536	504	523	120	258
1965 ..	2,368	562	689	612	141	364
1975 ..	3,043	729	881	713	176	544
1985 ..	3,900	952	1,064	832	220	832

Sources on next two pages.

SOURCES FOR TABLE C-1

1. Total Financial Employment

This figure is the sum of the employment in the individual financial industries.

2. Commercial Banks

1929 to 1934. Employment in all banks, as reported in U.S. Department of Commerce, *National Income, 1954*, multiplied by 0.84812, which represents the 1935 ratio of commercial banking employment to all banking employment, obtained by dividing the 1935 commercial banking employment figure reported in the *1935 Census of Business* by all banking employment for 1935 as given in *National Income, 1954*.

1935. *1935 Census of Business.*

1936 to 1956. An annual index of commercial banking employment (1935 = 100) was constructed, for 1936, from employment data in Simon Kuznets, *National Income and Its Composition* (New York, 1941), p. 737, and for 1937 through 1956, from employment data for insured commercial banks published by the Federal Deposit Insurance Corporation. This index was multiplied by the 1935 figure from the *1935 Census of Business* to derive employment estimates for all commercial banks. We have satisfied ourselves that this method yields reasonable estimates for the recent years.

1965, 1975, and 1985. Appendix B, *passim*.

3. Life and Accident and Health Insurance

This series covers employment by life and accident and health carriers and that portion (27 per cent) of employment by independent agents and brokers which is attributed to life and accident and health activities. Figures for 1965, 1975, and 1985 are from Appendix B, *passim*.

Life insurance carriers:

1929 to 1941. An index (1935 = 100) was constructed—for 1929 to 1935, from employment data in Kuznets, just cited, p. 737, and for 1935 to 1941, from employment series for all insurance carriers. This index was multiplied by an employment estimate for 1935 of 222,000, which consists of the carrier employment figure of 183,000 reported in the *1935 Census of Business* plus 39,000 which is our estimate of additional personnel employment by the carriers in the field.

1942 to 1954. Theodore Bakerman, "New Totals List Insurance Job Trends," *The Spectator* (April 1956), p. 93.

1955 and 1956. The 1954 figure was extrapolated by an index of life insurance personnel obtained from Institute of Life Insurance data published in recent issues of *Life Insurance Fact Book*.

Accident and health insurance carriers:

1929 to 1935. Employment was assumed zero for this period.

1936 to 1941. A pattern of growth was assumed from 1,000 in 1936 to 12,000 in 1941.

1942 to 1954. Bakerman, just cited.

1955 and 1956. Figures for prior years were extrapolated, assuming the past rate of change in premiums-per-man ratios, on the basis of data on premiums paid, provided by the Institute of Health Insurance.

Agents and brokers:

This series includes 27 per cent of employment by insurance and combination agents and brokers, as reported in *National Income, 1954* and subsequent issues of the *Survey of Current Business.*

4. Property Insurance

1929 to 1956. This series consists of employment by all insurance carriers less employment by life and accident and health carriers, as estimated above, plus 65 per cent of employment by independent insurance and combination agents and brokers from *National Income, 1954* and the *Survey of Current Business* for subsequent years. Employment by all insurance carriers was estimated as follows: 1929 to 1941, data from *National Income, 1954* raised by 2.102 per cent to make the series consistent with data for later years; 1942 to 1954, Bakerman, just cited; 1955 and 1956, the figure for 1954 was extrapolated by employment data from the *Survey of Current Business.*

1965, 1975, and 1985. Appendix B.

5. Securities Industry

1929 to 1956. An index (1950 = 100) was constructed from data in *National Income, 1954* and the *Survey of Current Business* for subsequent years. The index was multiplied by the figure 89,458, which represents the industry's 1950 employment, as reported in U.S. *1950 Census of Population.*

1965, 1975, and 1985. Appendix B.

6. Miscellaneous Finance

1929 to 1956. This series includes employment in "Finance, n.e.c." as reported in *National Income, 1954* and the *Survey of Current Business* and employment in all banking from the same sources, less our estimates of employment by commercial banks.

1965, 1975, and 1985. Appendix B.

Table C-2 Past and Projected Employment in Financial Industries, New York Metropolitan Region, Selected Years, 1941–1985

(in thousands)

	Total financial employment	Commercial banks	Life and accident and health insurance	Property insurance	Securities industry	Miscellaneous finance
1941 . . .	n.a.	67.0	n.a.	n.a.	25.2	24.3
1945 . . .	n.a.	55.8	n.a.	n.a.	23.1	19.5
1947 . . .	244.1	65.5	68.1	60.7	25.6	24.2
1950 . . .	253.6	66.9	68.8	65.3	25.6	27.0
1954 . . .	n.a.	77.2	n.a.	n.a.	n.a.	n.a.
1956 . . .	311.7	82.3	83.2	72.6	38.1	35.5
1965 . . .	368.7	87.5	109.6	81.4	43.6	46.6
1975 . . .	444.0	106.1	128.4	92.0	54.5	63.1
1985 . . .	537.1	130.1	145.6	105.7	68.1	87.6

n.a. = not available.

Sources: Tables C-4 to C-8.

Table C-3 Past and Projected Total Financial Employment, by Parts of New York Metropolitan Region, Selected Years, 1947–1985

(in thousands)

	Entire Region	New York City	Essex and Hudson Counties	Other New Jersey counties	Nassau and Suffolk Counties	Remainder of Region
1947 . .	244.1	192.8	30.7	8.7	3.6	8.3
1950 . .	253.6	200.1	30.6	9.1	4.4	9.4
1956 . .	311.7	240.7	32.6	15.7	8.7	14.0
1965 . .	368.7	264.7	39.1	27.7	15.6	21.6
1975 . .	444.0	303.4	44.7	41.6	23.7	30.6
1985 . .	537.1	348.5	52.2	59.5	35.2	41.7

Sources: Tables C-4 to C-8.

Table C-4 Past and Projected Employment in Commercial Banking, by Parts of New York Metropolitan Region, Selected Years, 1941–1985

(in thousands)

	Entire Region	New York City	Essex and Hudson Counties	Other New Jersey counties	Nassau and Suffolk Counties	Remainder of Region
1941 ..	67.0	55.5	3.8	3.4	1.3	2.9
1945 ..	55.8	43.0	4.2	3.8	1.5	3.3
1947 ..	65.5	51.0	4.6	4.4	1.9	3.7
1950 ..	66.9	50.3	5.0	5.0	2.3	4.2
1954 ..	77.2	57.2	5.5	6.0	3.6	4.9
1956 ..	82.3	60.6	5.0	6.9	4.4	5.4
1965 ..	87.5	59.9	6.0	9.5	5.4	6.6
1975 ..	106.1	68.0	7.5	13.9	7.7	9.0
1985 ..	130.1	78.4	9.1	19.3	11.0	12.3

Sources: 1941 and 1945. New York State Department of Labor for New York counties; New Jersey Department of Labor data adjusted for under-reporting for New Jersey counties; and separate estimates for Fairfield County.

1947 to 1956. New York State Department of Labor for New York counties; New Jersey data are estimates based on all banking data from *County Business Patterns,* 1947, 1951, 1953, and 1956, and the relationship of commercial and noncommercial banking from New Jersey Department of Labor data; estimates for Fairfield County based on *County Business Patterns,* 1947, 1951, 1953, and 1956.

1965, 1975, and 1985. Appendix B.

Table C-5 Past and Projected Employment in Life and Accident and Health Insurance, by Parts of New York Metropolitan Region, Selected Years, 1947–1985

(in thousands)

	Entire Region	New York City	Essex and Hudson Counties	Other New Jersey counties	Nassau and Suffolk Counties	Remainder of Region
1947	68.1	45.9	17.3	2.5	0.7	1.7
1950	68.8	48.8	15.7	1.6	0.9	1.9
1956 ..	83.2	60.3	15.4	3.4	1.5	2.6
1965 ..	109.6	73.5	18.1	7.8	4.5	5.7
1975 ..	128.4	83.0	20.3	11.4	6.1	7.6
1985 ..	145.6	90.3	22.5	15.0	8.0	9.8

Sources: This table covers all employment by life and accident and health insurance carriers and 27 per cent of employment by independent insurance and combination agents and brokers.

1947 and 1950. Employment by insurance carriers in New Jersey and New York counties was obtained from data provided by New Jersey and New York State departments of labor; employment by agents and brokers and all employment in Fairfield County are from *County Business Patterns,* 1947 and 1951. *County Business Patterns* data for 1951 were reduced by 3 per cent to allow for the difference of one year.

1956. *County Business Patterns,* 1956.

1965, 1975, and 1985. Appendix B.

Table C-6 Past and Projected Employment in Property Insurance, by Parts of New York Metropolitan Region, Selected Years, 1947–1985

(in thousands)

	Entire Region	New York City	Essex and Hudson Counties	Other New Jersey counties	Nassau and Suffolk Counties	Remainder of Region
1947	60.7	50.1	7.1	1.3	0.7	1.5
1950 ..	65.3	53.4	7.9	1.6	0.8	1.6
1956 ..	72.6	54.2	9.1	3.8	1.6	3.9
1965 ..	81.4	55.3	10.6	6.5	3.3	5.7
1975	92.0	58.0	11.0	9.2	5.5	8.3
1985 ..	105.7	61.3	12.7	12.7	8.4	10.6

Sources: This table covers all employment by insurance carriers other than life and accident and health carriers and 65 per cent of employment by independent insurance and combination agents and brokers.

1947 to 1956. Employment by insurance carriers in New Jersey and New York counties was obtained from data provided by New Jersey and New York State departments of labor; employment by agents and brokers and all employment in Fairfield County are from *County Business Patterns,* 1947, 1951, and 1956. *County Business Patterns* data for 1951 were reduced by 3 per cent to allow for the difference of one year.

1965, 1975, and 1985. Appendix B.

Table C-7 Past and Projected Employment in Securities Industry, by Parts of New York Metropolitan Region, Selected Years, 1941–1985

(in thousands)

	Entire Region	New York City	Essex and Hudson Counties	Other New Jersey counties	Nassau and Suffolk Counties	Remainder of Region
1941	25.2	24.0	1.2	a	a	a
1945	23.1	23.0	0.1	a	a	0.1
1947	25.6	25.3	0.2	a	a	0.1
1950 ..	25.6	25.2	0.2	a	a	0.1
1956 ..	38.1	37.3	0.5	0.1	0.1	0.1
1965 ..	43.6	42.4	0.7	0.2	0.1	0.2
1975	54.5	52.7	0.9	0.4	0.2	0.3
1985 ..	68.1	65.3	1.4	0.6	0.3	0.5

[a] Less than 50 employees.

Sources:

1941 to 1956. Employment in New Jersey and New York counties was obtained from data provided by New Jersey and New York State departments of labor. Employment in Fairfield County was estimated independently for 1941 and 1945, and was based upon data in *County Business Patterns,* 1947, 1951, and 1956 for subsequent years. *County Business Patterns* data for 1951 were reduced by 3 per cent to allow for the difference of one year.

1965, 1975, and 1985. Appendix B.

Table C-8 Past and Projected Employment in Miscellaneous Financial Institutions, by Parts of New York Metropolitan Region, Selected Years, 1941–1985

(in thousands)

	Entire Region	New York City	Essex and Hudson Counties	Other New Jersey counties	Nassau and Suffolk Counties	Remainder of Region
1941	24.3	21.7	1.0	0.6	0.1	1.0
1945	19.5	16.9	1.2	0.3	0.2	1.0
1947	24.2	20.6	1.5	0.5	0.3	1.3
1950	27.0	22.5	1.8	0.8	0.4	1.6
1956	35.5	28.3	2.6	1.4	1.2	2.0
1965	46.6	33.6	3.6	3.6	2.2	3.4
1975	63.1	41.7	5.1	6.7	4.2	5.4
1985	87.6	53.2	6.5	12.0	7.5	8.4

Sources: See sources for Table C-7.

Table C-9 Actual and Projected Floor-Space Use by All Financial Institutions, by Parts of New York Metropolitan Region, 1956, 1965, 1975, 1985

(in millions of square feet of gross floor space)

	Entire Region	New York City	Essex and Hudson Counties	Other New Jersey counties	Nassau and Suffolk Counties	Remainder of Region
1956	47.5	36.9	5.1	2.2	1.3	2.0
1965	61.2	44.7	6.7	4.2	2.4	3.2
1975	80.4	56.1	8.4	6.9	4.0	5.0
1985	105.6	70.1	10.6	10.9	6.5	7.5

Source: Appendix B.

Notes

CHAPTER 1: THE RISE OF NEW YORK AS A MONEY MARKET

1. Raymond W. Goldsmith, *The Share of Financial Intermediaries in National Wealth and National Assets, 1900–1949,* Occasional Paper 42 of the National Bureau of Economic Research (New York, 1954), p. 19.

2. The percentages for 1870 and 1910 come from George J. Stigler, *Trends in Employment in the Service Industries,* National Bureau of Economic Research (New York, 1956), pp. 7, 140. The 1929 and subsequent ratios are based upon data of U.S. Department of Commerce, in supplements to *Survey of Current Business,* as follows: *National Income, 1954,* p. 198, and *U.S. Income and Output* (1958), p. 212. The ratios are based on the average number of part-time and full-time employees.

3. On the early period, see: Frederick L. Collins, *Money Town* (New York: G. P. Putnam's Sons, 1946), Chapter 10; Paul Studenski and Herman E. Krooss, *Financial History of the United States* (New York: McGraw-Hill, 1952); Joseph Edwards Hedges, *Commercial Banking and the Stock Market before 1863* (Baltimore: Johns Hopkins Press, 1938); Cleveland Rodgers and Rebecca B. Rankin, *New York: The World's Capital City* (New York: Harper & Brothers, 1948); Margaret G. Myers, *The New York Money Market,* Vol. I, *Origins and Development* (New York: Columbia University Press, 1931).

4. On New York in the eighteenth and early nineteenth centuries, see: *The Progress of the Empire State,* ed. Charles A. Conant (New York: Knickerbocker Press, 1913); Robert G. Albion, *The Rise of New York Port (1815–1860)* (New York: Charles Scribner's Sons, 1939); Margaret G. Myers, note 3, above; Hedges, note 3, above; Rodgers and Rankin, note 3, above; Davis Rich Dewey, *Financial History of the United States* (New York: Longmans, Green & Company, 1934); Davis Rich Dewey, *The Second United States Bank,* National Monetary Commission, U.S. Senate, 61st Cong., 2d sess., S. Doc. 571 (Washington: Government Printing Office, 1910), Vol. IV; William G. Sumner, *History of Banking in the United States* (New York, 1896).

5. On the securities markets, see Hedges, note 3, above; J. Edward Meeker, *The Work of the Stock Exchange* (New York: Ronald Press Company, 1930); Charles Amos Dice, *The Stock Market* (New York: A. W. Shaw Company, 1928); Vernon Louis Parrington, *Main Currents in American Thought* (New York: Harcourt Brace and Company, 1930), III, 31–43; Gustavus Myers, *History of the Great American Fortunes* (New York: Modern Library, 1937), pp. 568–581; Irwin Friend, *et al., The Over-the-Counter Securities Market* (New York: McGraw-Hill, 1958).

6. On the commercial paper market, see: Margaret G. Myers, note 3, above;

Albert O. Greef, *The Commercial Paper House in the United States* (Cambridge: Harvard University Press, 1938); Roy A. Foulke, *The Commercial Paper Market* (New York: The Bankers Publishing Co., 1931).

7. Data showing the amount of commercial paper sold are not available until after the Civil War, but Greef (note 6, above) documents New York's primacy in the field by a number of quotations from leading financial journals of the period. Greef, pp. 20–23.

8. The reasons for the concentration of factoring in New York City are described in Raymond J. Saulnier and Neil H. Jacoby, *Accounts Receivable Financing,* National Bureau of Economic Research (New York, 1943).

9. On the call money market, see: Marcus Nadler, Sipa Heller, Samuel S. Shipman, *The Money Market and Its Institutions* (New York: Ronald Press Company, 1955).

10. On the market for bankers' acceptances, see: American Acceptance Council, *Facts and Figures Relating to the American Money Market* (New York, 1931); B. H. Beckhart, *The New York Money Market,* Vol. III, *Uses of Funds* (New York: Columbia University Press, 1932); *Operation of the National and Federal Reserve Banking Systems,* Hearings before a Subcommittee of the Committee on Banking and Currency, U.S. Senate, 71st Cong., 3rd sess., Pursuant to S. Res. 71 (Washington: Government Printing Office, 1931), Part VI; Homer P. Balabanis, *The American Discount Market* (Chicago: University of Chicago Press, 1935).

11. Federal Reserve Bank of New York, mimeograph release, September 30, 1957.

12. On the Federal funds market, see: *The Federal Funds Market—A Study by a Federal Reserve System Committee,* Board of Governors of the Federal Reserve System (Washington, 1959); Parker B. Willis, *The Federal Funds Market—Its Origin and Development,* Federal Reserve Bank of Boston (Boston, 1957); Beatrice C. Turner, *The Federal Funds Market* (New York: Prentice-Hall, 1931).

13. On the Government securities market, see: *Treasury-Federal Reserve Study of the Government Securities Market,* Part I (Washington, July 1959), and the summary thereof in *Federal Reserve Bulletin,* August 1959; C. F. Childs, *Concerning U. S. Government Securities* (Chicago: Lakeside Press, 1947); E. A. Goldenweiser, *American Monetary Policy* (New York: McGraw-Hill, 1951); Robert V. Roosa, *Federal Reserve Operations in the Money and Government Securities Markets* (New York: Federal Reserve Bank of New York, 1956); Milton L. Stokes and Carl T. Arlt, *Money, Banking and the Financial System* (New York: Ronald Press Company, 1955).

14. Examples of investment accounts managed by the Treasury and serviced by the trading desk of the New York Federal Reserve Bank are the Federal Old-Age and Survivors Insurance Trust Fund, the Unemployment Trust Fund, the Civil Service Retirement and Disability Fund, and the National Service Life Insurance Fund.

CHAPTER 2: MONEY MARKET AND FINANCIAL COMMUNITY

1. The "export" estimate was derived as follows: At the close of 1956, the ratio of financial employment to total population in the United States was 1.2 per cent; in the Region, the ratio was 2.0 per cent. Presumably the 0.8 per cent differential reflects the manpower within the Region that is engaged in activities applicable to people and firms residing outside the Region. On this assumption, about three-fifths of total financial employment within the Region is engaged in local activities.

2. Our figure of 4.7 per cent for the New York Metropolitan Region is derived from our own estimates of financial and total employment, based on several sources including unpublished data from state governments. In order to compare the Region with other places in this respect, however, it is necessary to use federal statistics for Standard Metropolitan Areas, compiled under the Social Security program. (The New York-Northeastern New Jersey Standard Metropolitan Area contains five fewer counties than what we call the New York Metropolitan Region, the five being Fairfield, Orange, Dutchess, Putnam, and Monmouth.) Those statistics show the following ratios of financial employment (from which we excluded real estate jobs to conform with our practice throughout this book) to total employment in selected Standard Metropolitan Areas: Dallas 8.0 per cent; San Francisco 7.3; New York 6.4; Minneapolis 6.1; Atlanta 5.9; Philadelphia 4.7; Chicago 4.3.

3. Based on estimates of the Department of City Planning, New York City.

4. Bureau of Labor Statistics, "192 sector matrix" for 1947.

5. According to the *1950 Census of Population,* the managerial and professional categories accounted for only 20 per cent of total employment in "finance, insurance, and real estate."

6. Rates provided by the New York Telephone Company.

7. For a discussion of the changing policy of the Institutional Securities Corporation and its formation in 1933, see its *Twenty-fifth Annual Report to Stockholders* (New York, 1958), pp. 12, 13.

8. Other agencies include the Savings Bank Life Insurance System, the Savings Bank Employees Group Insurance Fund, the Savings Banks Retirement System, and the Savings Banks Association of the State of New York.

9. See our pages 86–88 for data illustrating this tendency.

10. *United States Monetary Policy: Recent Thinking and Experience,* Hearings Before the Subcommittee on Economic Stabilization of the Joint Committee on the Economic Report, 83rd Cong., 2d sess. (Washington: Government Printing Office, 1954), pp. 281–283, 286.

11. See our page 143.

CHAPTER 3: COMMERCIAL BANKING IN THE UNITED STATES—OUTPUT AND MANPOWER

1. Board of Governors of the Federal Reserve System, *Consumer Instalment Credit, Growth and Import,* Part I, Vol. I (Washington, 1957), p. 36.

2. Ogden Nash, "Anybody for Money? Or, Just Bring Your Own Basket," *The New Yorker,* Feb. 25, 1956. Copyright © 1956 by Ogden Nash.

3. For example, they have extended the features of revolving credit to the personal loan field. See "Expansion in Instalment Credit," *Federal Reserve Bulletin,* April 1959, p. 351.

4. Board of Governors of the Federal Reserve System, *Twenty-fifth Annual Report Covering Operations for the Year 1938* (Washington, 1939), pp. 7–8.

5. *Federal Reserve Bulletin,* June 1955, p. 623.

6. *Federal Reserve Bulletin,* December 1956, pp. 1279–1280.

7. J. E. Morton, *Urban Mortgage Lending: Comparative Markets and Experience,* National Bureau of Economic Research (Princeton University Press, 1956), p. 15; Saul B. Klaman, *The Volume of Mortgage Debt in the Postwar Decade,* Technical Paper 13, National Bureau of Economic Research (New York, 1958), p. 38. One problem in evaluating mortgage lending is that loans obtained on real estate collateral may be used for various purposes, while those intended to provide funds to purchase real estate may not be secured by the property. Moreover, the classification of corporate debt, as between a bond or mortgage, is not standardized but rather depends upon such factors as tradition, the terms of the indenture, and the number of holders.

8. Carl F. Behrens, *Commercial Bank Activities in Urban Mortgage Financing,* National Bureau of Economic Research (New York, 1952), p. 17.

9. *Ninety-fourth Annual Report of the Comptroller of the Currency, 1956* (Washington, 1957), p. 4. This is indicative rather than positive evidence, because the banks may not have been able to obtain suitable loans even if they were eager to make them.

10. Recently, some more concrete evidence on this subject has been made available. See Raymond W. Goldsmith and Eli Shapiro, "An Estimate of Bank Administered Personal Trust Funds," *Journal of Finance,* March 1959, pp. 11–17. The authors point out that, after deflating for the rise in common stock prices, total estimated assets of personal trust funds rose from $54.7 billion at the end of 1952 to $58.0 billion at the end of 1955.

11. See Securities and Exchange Commission, "Corporate Pension Funds, 1955," Statistical Series, Release Number 1426, Dec. 31, 1956.

12. *Ninety-third Annual Report of the Comptroller of the Currency, 1955* (Washington, 1956), p. 28.

13. Various commissions, charges, and fees—such as those for safe deposit and checking accounts—constitute the remainder of total operating earnings.

CHAPTER 4: THE REGION AS A COMMERCIAL BANKING CENTER

1. Board of Governors of the Federal Reserve System, *Fourteenth Annual Report Covering Operations for the Year 1927* (Washington, 1928), pp. 6–9.

2. Board of Governors of the Federal Reserve System, *Twenty-third Annual Report Covering Operations for the Year 1936* (Washington, 1937), pp. 28–29, and *Twenty-fifth Annual Report Covering Operations for the Year 1938* (Washington, 1939), pp. 7–13.

3. Board of Governors of the Federal Reserve System, *Twenty-ninth Annual Report Covering Operations for the Year 1942* (Washington, 1943), pp. 19–20; and Katherine Finney, *Interbank Deposits* (New York: Columbia University Press, 1958), p. 62.

4. Annual Reports of First National City Bank, 1956, p. 6; Guaranty Trust Company, 1956, p. 8; Irving Trust Company, 1953, p. 9; New York Trust Company, 1955, p. 3.

5. Irving Trust Company, *Annual Report,* 1956, p. 4.

6. The personal income data for the Region are estimates of the New York Metropolitan Region Study; those for the United States are from U.S. Department of Commerce, *Survey of Current Business.* Consumer loans data for the Region were furnished by the Federal Reserve Bank of New York, and those for the nation were obtained from the *Federal Reserve Bulletin.*

7. G. A. Mooney, *Pension and Other Employee Welfare Plans,* New York [State] Banking Department, 1955. The 60 per cent estimate comes from p. i; locations of head offices from Table 13.

8. This section is based primarily on Alan R. Holmes, "The New York Foreign Exchange Market," Federal Reserve Bank of New York, March 1959; and Frank M. Tamagna, "New York as an International Money Market," *Banca Nazionale del Lavoro Quarterly Review,* Rome, Italy, No. 49 (June 1959), pp. 201–234.

CHAPTER 5: COMMERCIAL BANKING INSIDE THE REGION

1. Chemical National Bank, *History of the Chemical Bank, 1823–1913* (Garden City, N.Y.: Country Life Press, 1913), p. 7.

2. Donald H. Davenport, Lawrence M. Orton, and Ralph W. Roby, "The Retail Shopping and Financial Districts," in *Regional Survey of New York and Its Environs,* Vol. 1B (New York, 1928), pp. 34, 39.

3. *Ibid,* p. 36.

4. *Ibid,* p. 36.

5. This paragraph based on *New York Times,* Sept. 21, 1958, Section 8, p. 1; Jan. 12, 1959, p. C121.

6. See, for example, the annual reports of Bankers Trust Company, 1958, p. 14; and 1957, pp. 20–22; Chemical Corn Exchange Bank, 1957, pp. 10–11; First National City Bank of New York, 1956, p. 13; Guaranty Trust Company, 1955, p. 13; Hanover Bank, 1954, p. 10; Irving Trust Company, 1957, p. 9;

Manufacturers Trust Company, 1954, p. 7; New York Trust Company, 1956, p. 4.

7. Chemical Corn Exchange Bank, *Annual Report, 1954,* pp. 8–9.

8. First National City Bank of New York, *Annual Report, 1956,* p. 16.

9. Edgar M. Hoover and Raymond Vernon, *Anatomy of a Metropolis* (Cambridge: Harvard University Press, 1959).

10. Regional Plan Association, Bulletin 91, *Hub-Bound Travel in the Tri-State Metropolitan Region: Persons and Vehicles Entering Manhattan South of 61st St., 1924–1956* (New York, 1959).

11. *New York Times,* Jan. 11, 1959, Section 3, p. 10F.

12. George Katona, *Business Looks at Banks* (Ann Arbor: University of Michigan Press, 1957), p. 46.

Chapter 6: life and health insurance

1. J. Owen Stalson, *Marketing Life Insurance, Its History in America* (Cambridge: Harvard University Press, 1942), p. 751.

2. Data furnished by the Institute of Life Insurance.

3. The asset figures in this paragraph do not include assets of fraternal societies, which were well under $100 million in 1900. Assets of United States and Canadian fraternal societies amounted to $973 million in 1930 and $2.8 billion in 1956 (see Institute of Life Insurance, *Life Insurance Fact Book, 1957,* p. 89).

4. *Life Insurance Fact Book, 1957,* pp. 8, 29.

5. J. L. Miner, *Life Insurance Ownership Among American Families, 1957* (Ann Arbor: University of Michigan), p. 9.

6. For medical-care expenditures, excluding death expense, see *National Income, 1954,* pp. 206–207, and *U. S. Income and Output* (1958), p. 150. Both of these are supplements to the U.S. Department of Commerce publication *Survey of Current Business.*

7. Employment in life and annuity insurance was estimated from employment of the life insurance carriers, by excluding their accident and health activities, and adding in 27 per cent of the employment of independent insurance and combination (insurance, real estate, etc.) brokers and agents. Accident and health employment by the life insurance carriers, in the absence of more direct information, was estimated on the basis of accident and health premiums of the life insurance companies; it was assumed that the ratio of premiums to manpower in these companies was the same as that reported by the accident and health carriers. The 27 per cent portion of employment by brokers and agents represents a rough estimate of the share which life and annuity insurance has in their activities. (It proved impracticable to estimate the accident and health employment of the brokers and agents, but in any case this is small.) Of the remaining employment of brokers and agents, 65 per cent represents those engaged in property insurance and 8 per cent in such non-insurance pursuits as selling real estate. This breakdown is considered reasonable by experts in the field and is similar to that made in the

course of inter-industry studies for 1947 by the U.S. Bureau of Labor Statistics. The following sources have served as the basis of employment estimates: *Survey of Current Business,* various issues; Theodore Bakerman, "New Totals List Insurance Job Trends," *The Spectator* (April 1956), p. 93; Institute of Life Insurance, *Life Insurance Fact Book,* recent issues.

8. We confine our analysis to the accident and health carriers because we have no independent employment figures for the accident and health insurance activities of life insurance carriers. See note 7, above.

9. See, for instance, Terence O'Donell, *History of Life Insurance in Its Formative Years* (Chicago, 1936), pp. 579–580. The writer states that late in the nineteenth century the life insurance companies used their connections with the banks to manipulate their funds so that the annual statements would meet legal requirements. Though not permitted to hold stocks, the companies still kept them as concealed assets by disguising the bookkeeping entries.

10. The New York law has since been modified to enable life insurance companies to invest a very small portion of their assets in common stocks that meet certain qualifications and to own real estate under certain limitations.

11. Between 1947 and 1956, the constant-dollar life insurance premiums (deflated by the gross national product deflators) received by the 21 life insurance companies domiciled in the Region and subject to New York State requirements increased by 26 per cent, while those received by 27 companies domiciled outside the Region but licensed to do business in New York State grew by 38 per cent. Over the same period, the increase for all the other companies in the nation was 85 per cent.

12. On the basis of data on ordinary life insurance premiums published by the Spectator Company, we find that between 1947 and 1956, for all states and the District of Columbia summed up together, premium payments to the domestic companies increased by 82 per cent, while those paid to the outside companies rose by 72 per cent. For states with a major life insurance industry (defined as Connecticut, Iowa, Massachusetts, New Jersey, New York, North Carolina, Texas, and Wisconsin), the domestic companies gained 72 per cent and the outside companies 67 per cent, while in all other states taken as a group, the increases were 102 and 74 per cent respectively.

13. The Prudential Insurance Company of America, *Annual Report, 1957,* p. 6.

14. This rough estimate was made by assuming that if that company had not chosen to decentralize, its home-office staff in 1956 would have borne about the same proportion to Metropolitan's home office as that existing between the resources of the two companies. To the extent that the number employed in Prudential's regional home offices may exceed this estimate, the differential probably represents the drawing in of manpower from the company's field offices into the regional home offices in the respective areas.

15. We hesitate to attach much significance to this increase, because of the margin of error present in the data. It may be that the relative changes in coverage and in the size of plans written were different in the Region and in

the rest of the nation and brought about the somewhat more rapid growth of employment in the Region.

16. See Raymond Vernon, *The Changing Economic Function of the Central City* (Committee for Economic Development, New York, 1959), pp. 57–59.

17. Donald H. Davenport, Lawrence M. Orton, and Ralph W. Robey, "The Retail Shopping and Financial Districts," in *Regional Survey of New York and Its Environs*, Vol. 1B (New York, 1928), p. 39.

18. *Ibid*, p. 39.

19. *Ibid*, p. 39.

20. Earl Chapin May and Will Oursler, *The Prudential: A Story of Human Security* (Garden City: Doubleday & Co., 1950), p. 35.

21. William Rankin Ward, *Down the Years: A History of the Mutual Benefit Life Insurance Company, 1845 to 1932* (Newark, 1932), pp. 23–28.

22. On a scatter diagram, the line below which the remaining 123 companies fell ran through the points of 1,000 home office workers for the cities of 100,000 population and 3,500 employees for the cities of 500,000.

23. It has been calculated that the average annual cost per employee to construct a large building in Westchester County would be about $1,240; this makes allowance for interest on money tied up in land and buildings as well as for maintenance, depreciation, and operating charges. The comparable cost to rent equivalent quarters in an air conditioned building in the central business district of Manhattan would amount to only $960 per year. See another volume in this series—Edgar M. Hoover and Raymond Vernon, *Anatomy of a Metropolis* (Cambridge: Harvard University Press, 1959), Appendix H.

24. See another volume in this series, Martin Segal, *Wages in the Metropolis* (Cambridge: Harvard University Press, 1960).

25. The 1910 data, covering all employees, were obtained from Edward Ewing Pratt, *Industrial Causes of Congestion of Population in New York City* (New York, 1911); the 1946 data, covering clerical, commissary, and building employees, were provided by the Metropolitan Life Insurance Company.

Chapter 7: The Rest of the Financial Community

1. In describing the development of the property and casualty insurance industry, we have drawn upon F. C. Oviatt, "History of Fire Insurance in the United States," in *Property Insurance*, ed. L. W. Zartnan (New Haven: Yale University Press, 1926); G. A. Maclean, *Insurance Up Through the Ages* (Louisville: Dunne Press, 1938); Henry R. Gall and William George Jordan, *One Hundred Years of Fire Insurance, Being A History of the Aetna Insurance Company, Hartford, Connecticut, 1819–1919* (Hartford: Aetna Insurance Company, 1919); Alwin E. Bulau, *Footprints of Assurance* (New York: Macmillan, 1953); E. R. Hardy, "History and Principles of Fire Insurance," in

Fire Insurance Lectures (Hartford: Insurance Institute of Hartford, 1914); Edward A. Ketcham and Murray Ketcham-Kirk, *Essentials of the Fire Insurance Business* (Springfield, S. D., 1922); J. W. Randall, "Failure to Carry Casualty Insurance Imperils Credit and Brings Bankruptcy," *Weekly Underwriter* (May 19, 1934); G. F. Michelbacher, *Multiple-Line Insurance* (New York: McGraw-Hill, 1957); Raymond W. Goldsmith, *Financial Intermediaries in the American Economy Since 1900* (Princeton University Press, 1958).

2. Article 46 of the New York State Insurance Law.

3. Roy J. Hensley, "Economies of Scale in Financial Enterprises," *Journal of Political Economy*, Vol. LXVI (October 1958), pp. 389–398.

4. *General Laws of Texas*, Article 4993; *Spectator Insurance Laws, Taxes, and Fees;* and *New York Insurance Law*, Section 311.

5. Association of Casualty and Surety Companies, *The Creation and Recording of Claims: Highlights of the Fourth Workshop on Cost Reduction and Control, October 21–22, 1953* (New York, 1954), pp. 72–75.

6. Based on a 1950 survey by the City Planning Commission of New York City.

7. George L. Leffler, *The Stock Market* (New York: Ronald Press, 1957), p. 468.

8. Irwin Friend, G. Wright Hoffman, Willis J. Winn, Morris Hamburg, and Stanley Schor, *The Over-the-Counter Securities Market* (New York: McGraw-Hill, 1958), Table 3–2, p. 116.

9. "386 Underwriters Have $921.6 Million Capital," *Finance*, Vol. 74 (March 15, 1958), pp. 27–29, 79–99.

10. Leffler, p. 468.

11. Letter to the Director, New York Metropolitan Region Study, from Ronnello B. Lewis, General Partner, E. F. Hutton & Company, April 29, 1959.

12. American Stock Exchange, *President's Report, 1956/1957*, p. 11, and *1957/1958*, p. 18; also New York Stock Exchange, *Annual Report, 1957*, p. 9, and *Annual Report, 1958*, p. 9; *New York Times*, June 11, 1956; and for a description of some Canadian experiments, *New York Times*, June 7, 1957.

13. See John Diebold, *Automation* (New York: Nostrand, 1952), pp. 46–50.

14. *New York Times*, April 29, 1957. This direct-wire system has been discontinued for technical reasons, but the pattern of the future is evident.

15. As we have seen, the securities industry is composed of many different kinds of firms. Because their practices vary, the influences affecting the distribution of their manpower are not necessarily the same. While these factors, therefore, may not apply to particular cases, in the aggregate they have been dominant.

16. *Wall Street Journal*, March 17, 1959.

17. *New York Times*, June 7, 1959, Section 3, p. 1.

CHAPTER 8: THE PROSPECTS

1. *Business Week*, April 11, 1959, p. 85.

2. On this last point see "Automation Trends in Banking Industry," *Finance*, April 15, 1959, pp. 59–60. From the very small to the giant banks, automation may occur in varying degrees. A complete system would provide for printing the required magnetic ink characters on documents as part of the normal proof and clearing operation; the sorting and reading of these documents for input into a data-processing system; the performance of the demand-deposit operations at electronic speed in the processing system; and the transmission of the resulting data to output units for preparation of various reports such as daily journals and monthly statements.

3. For further information on automation in banking, see *The American Banker*, Dec. 5, 1957; "Electronics in Banks," *The Banker*, January 1951, pp. 31–40; "Automation in Check Handling," *Burroughs Clearing House*, February 1958; *General Information Manual*, International Business Machines Corporation, 1959; *National's Automation Timetable*, National Cash Register Company, Dayton, Ohio; "The Electronic Abacus," *Business Review*, Federal Reserve Bank of Philadelphia, February 1958, pp. 3–11; also Bank Management Commission, American Bankers Association, "Magnetic Ink Character Recognition" (July 21, 1956), "Placement for the Common Language on Checks" (April 10, 1957), "Location and Arrangement of Magnetic Ink Characters for the Common Machine Language on Checks" (Jan. 9, 1958), and "A Progress Report, Mechanization of Check Handling" (July 7, 1958).

4. See Alvin H. Hansen, *Monetary Theory and Fiscal Policy* (New York: McGraw-Hill, 1949), pp. 1–8.

5. This issue is discussed in a forthcoming volume in this series by Benjamin Chinitz, *Freight and the Metropolis* (Cambridge: Harvard University Press, 1960).

6. For a discussion of this tendency, see Edgar M. Hoover and Raymond Vernon, *Anatomy of a Metropolis* (Cambridge: Harvard University Press, 1959).

7. Because of the varying nature of their operations, the different segments of the financial community do not require the same amount of floor space per man. Starting with the 1956 amounts, we assumed an increase per man of about 10 per cent a decade. This growth reflects the influences of mechanization, upgrading of skills, and the greater employee comforts incorporated into the new buildings. We then applied this higher ratio of floor space per employee to our projected employment data to obtain estimates of future space needs.

Index

N
W
E
S
NEW
YORK
DUTCHESS
ORANGE
PUTNAM
CO
FAIRFIELD
WESTCHESTER
ROCKLAND
Hudson River
Delaware River
PASSAIC
NEW
BERGEN
Long
MORRIS
BRONX
ESSEX
HUDSON
NEW YORK
NASSAU
QUEENS
JERSEY
UNION
KINGS
RICHMOND
SOMERSET
MIDDLESEX
Atlantic
Delaware River
MONMOUTH

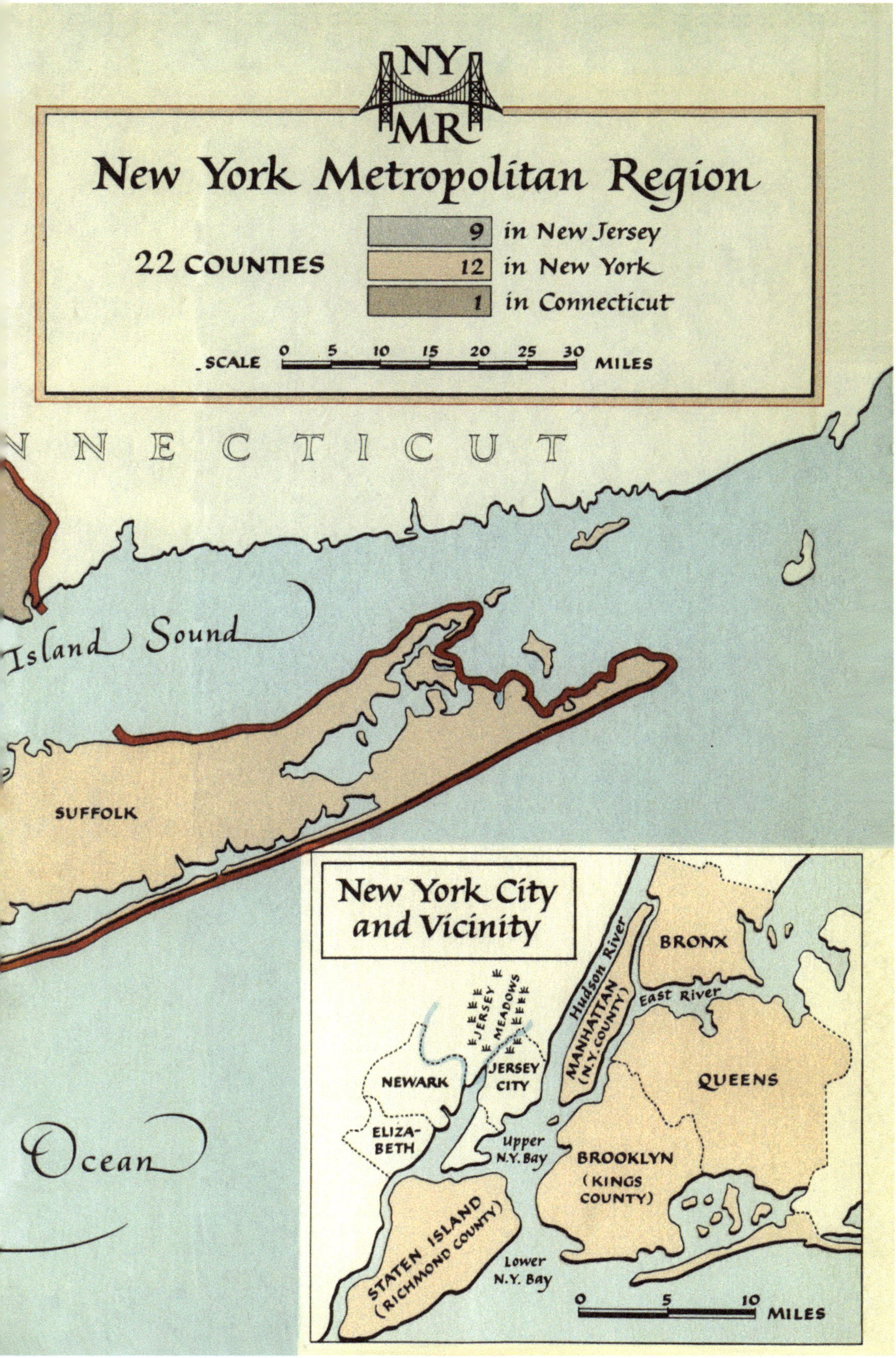
NY
MR
New York Metropolitan Region
22 COUNTIES
9 in New Jersey
12 in New York
1 in Connecticut
SCALE 0 5 10 15 20 25 30 MILES
NNECTICUT
Island Sound
SUFFOLK
Ocean
New York City and Vicinity
BRONX
Hudson River
East River
MANHATTAN (N.Y. COUNTY)
JERSEY MEADOWS
JERSEY CITY
NEWARK
QUEENS
ELIZA-BETH
Upper N.Y. Bay
BROOKLYN (KINGS COUNTY)
STATEN ISLAND (RICHMOND COUNTY)
Lower N.Y. Bay
0 5 10 MILES

Bei Fragen zur Produktsicherheit wenden Sie sich bitte an:
If you have any questions regarding product safety,
please contact:

Walter de Gruyter GmbH
Genthiner Straße 13
10785 Berlin
productsafety@degruyterbrill.com